BISMARCK, THE HOHENZOLLERN CANDIDACY, AND THE ORIGINS OF THE FRANCO-GERMAN WAR OF 1870

BISMARCK, THE HOHENZOLLERN CANDIDACY, AND THE ORIGINS OF THE FRANCO-GERMAN WAR OF 1870

by Lawrence D. Steefel

Professor of History, Emeritus · THE UNIVERSITY OF MINNESOTA

HARVARD UNIVERSITY PRESS

Cambridge, Massachusetts · 1962

Library of Congress Catalog Card Number 62–13271

Printed in the United States of America

To Genevieve Fallon Steefel

Preface

More than thirty-five years have gone by since Professor Robert Howard Lord published *The Origins of the War of 1870: New Documents from the German Archives* (Cambridge, Mass., 1924; Harvard Historical Studies XXVIII). "In the past year," he wrote in his preface, "I have had the privilege of using and transcribing in full the seven volumes of documents which contain the German official record of the diplomatic crisis leading up to the outbreak of the War of 1870. . . . In limiting the scope of this volume mainly to the weeks immediately preceding the war, I have been guided chiefly by the fact that not all of the German documents bearing upon the origins of that conflict are yet accessible. The papers relating to the early history of the Hohenzollern Candidacy to the throne of Spain — papers which must excite the liveliest curiosity of all who have delved into that fascinating mystery — down to the time when the question became public through the 'explosion' at Paris, are not yet open to investigators. I was told that these papers are reserved for a future official publication. But even apart from this, it is clear that the time has not yet come for an attempt at a complete and definitive study of the origins of the War of 1870. The great official publication of the French government is not yet half finished; and until its completion there will remain important gaps in our knowledge of French policy, not so much perhaps, with regard to the crisis immediately preceding the war as in respect to the earlier period. The British and Italian archives are not yet open at all. And any attempt to trace adequately the remoter causes of the conflict would involve a study of all the German but also of the Austrian records from 1866 onward — obviously a *travail de longue haleine*."

My own concern with this "fascinating mystery" began in my early years as a graduate student when I was in Professor Lord's seminar on Bismarck's foreign policy and his assistant in History 30a. For a number of years, I was occupied with other aspects of Bismarck's career but my interest in the origins of the War of 1870 was rekindled by the publication of Lord's book. During the years that followed, I watched with special attention the publications that filled many of the gaps he had noted in his preface. I hoped that he would take account of the revelations and would rewrite the story. As he did not — his interest and activity turned away when he left Harvard — I decided to undertake the task myself. I wanted to discuss the project with him but he died a few months before I could visit him in Boston on my way, in 1954, to a year of study in Europe. I never doubted, however, that I would have his blessing; he welcomed revision of his knowledge by the work of his students.

When I began this book, I thought that I could concentrate my attention on the earlier history of the Hohenzollern Candidacy and give it its place in the international situation of the time. Gradually I realized that this would not be enough; it was necessary to examine again the evidence for the whole course of the question. Given the materials at Lord's disposal, his study was thorough and penetrating. The new evidence, however, has upset some of his conjectures and conclusions.

Two groups of unpublished sources have been of outstanding importance for me: the Hohenzollern-Sigmaringen papers in the appendix of Jochen Dittrich's Freiburg thesis, omitted from his article in *Die Welt als Geschichte*, and the secret file found in the captured German archives and published eventually in English translation by Georges Bonnin. As my readings of the originals sometimes differ from those of Bonnin, I have continued to use my own translations but have added references to his. All other translations, except where the reference is to a work in English, are my own. In addition, I have examined a number of files of the German Foreign Office papers to supplement the material in *Die auswärtige Politik Preussens* (the last volume published ends with February 1869), Lord Augustus Loftus' reports from Berlin in the Public Record Office, London, and the George Bancroft papers in Washington, Boston, and New York. The printed sources are voluminous. I have studied all of the important books and articles about the problem and many that because of scanty evidence or distorted interpretation are no longer of any value. So much new material has become accessible since Lord wrote that it seemed clear that the time had come to re-examine the whole question in its light. It is now possible to show more completely and accurately than before how it really happened. That is the primary purpose of this book.

The interpretation of motives and policies has been hotly disputed ever since 1870. On the one hand, concealment of key evidence made it difficult to know what had happened and led to many conjectures, some of which were logical but many of which were without foundation; on the other, national feeling, self-defense, self-glorification, and sometimes the desire of a scholar to say something new, have contributed to keep the disputes alive. In dealing with this aspect of the problem, I have tried to look at the evidence from the point of view of 1866 to 1870 without benefit of hindsight.

Everyone who has worked with Bismarck's writings and statements knows that at many points the formal canons of historical criticism are of no avail in deciding what may be believed and what should be questioned. The decision is often subjective. In general, I have accepted statements made under circumstances where it would have been contrary to his own interest to deceive and those confirmed by action taken. Where my conclusions differ from those that have been long accepted by reputable scholars, it is because I have been led to them by the cumulative effect of new evidence or new combinations of evidence.

I owe much, of course, to earlier workers in the field who have gathered evidence and formulated questions that needed to be answered, especially to the works of Richard Fester, Robert Howard Lord, Jochen Dittrich, and Georges Bonnin. In addition, I have many kindnesses from many people and institutions to acknowledge.

I am indebted to the United States Department of State and the Educational Commission in the Federal Republic of Germany for a Fulbright research grant in 1954–1955 which made it possible for me to gather much of the new evidence on which this book is based and to the British Foreign Office Library for permission to study the documents I needed in the captured German archives and for aid in securing microfilm copy of the "secret file." An earlier fellowship from the John Simon Guggenheim Memorial Foundation was not directly concerned with my study of the Hohenzollern Candidacy but was of incalculable value for my understanding of Bismarck's diplomacy. A grant from the Graduate School of the University of Minnesota enabled me to examine the papers of Bismarck's friend and confidant, George Bancroft, in Boston, New York, and Washington. I am grateful to the University of Hamburg and to the Hamburg State Library for the facilities placed at my disposal. The staff of the Frank K. Walter Library of the University of Minnesota have been generous beyond measure in helping my study.

Preface

Many of my colleagues and friends have listened patiently as I talked about my work at all stages of its progress. For help in getting material or for criticism and comment, I want to name especially Dr. Robert Bahmer of the National Archives, Dr. Howard M. Smyth, Professors Joseph J. Kwiat, William L. Langer, Otto Pflanze, and John B. Wolf. Prince Otto von Bismarck received me at Friedrichsruh and generously answered my questions about his grandfather's papers. Professors Hans Rothfels of Tübingen and Alexander Scharff of Kiel let me test some of my conclusions before their seminars. Dr. Georges Bonnin freely and frankly gave me valuable information about the "secret file." Professors Rodolfo O. Floripe and Walter T. Pattison of the Romance Language Department of the University of Minnesota helped me make correct translations of Spanish sources.

I am deeply grateful to the editorial department of the Harvard University Press for patient, thorough, and intelligent aid in preparing the manuscript for printing. Finally, I thank my wife, Genevieve Fallon Steefel, for her steadfast encouragement, for critical reading of the manuscript at many stages of progress, and for sharing the drudgery of proofreading and indexing.

LAWRENCE D. STEEFEL

Minneapolis, Minnesota
December 1961

Contents

BISMARCK, THE HOHENZOLLERN CANDIDACY, AND THE ORIGINS OF THE FRANCO-GERMAN WAR OF 1870

Abbreviations Used in the Footnotes

A.P.P.   Reichsinstitut für Geschichte des neuen Deutschlands, *Die auswärtige Politik Preussens.*

Dittrich thesis.   Jochen Dittrich, "Bismarck, Frankreich und die Hohenzollern-kandidatur," dissertation, Freiburg, 1948.

G.W.   Bismarck, *Die gesammelten Werke.*

O.D.   [France, Ministère des Affaires Etrangères,] *Les Origines diplomatiques de la guerre de 1870–1871.*

Ollivier.   Emile Ollivier, *L'empire libéral.*

Secret file.   German archives, I. A. B. o. (Spanien) 32 secreta. Acta secreta betr. die Berufung eines Prinzen von Hohenzollern auf den Spanischen Thron.

Introduction

The Franco-German War of 1870 transferred the military and political hegemony of Europe from France to Germany. Hard-fought and bloody, it was, more than any that had preceded it, a national war. The passions it aroused made a political reconciliation of the belligerents impossible, and from 1870 to 1914, the hostility between France and Germany was a fixed point in the European system. Fear of a war of revenge by France on Germany was the most important cause of the alliances which divided Europe into two armed camps — "entangling alliances," which in 1914 made it impossible to isolate the Austro-Hungarian attack on Serbia and which turned it into a European and then a world war.

The war of 1870 was precipitated by an incident: the candidacy of a prince of the House of Hohenzollern for the throne of Spain. The basic causes reach back at least to 1866.[1] It has been said:

France could never forgive or forget the battle of Sadowa and the Treaty of Prague. She had expected to reap a golden harvest out of the collision between the Prussian and Austrian monarchies, arguing that the struggle would be long and exhausting, and that

[1] Antoine Agénor, Duc de Gramont, *La France et la Prusse avant la guerre*, p. 7; Robert Howard Lord, *The Origins of the War of 1870*, p. 10.

I

the moment would surely come when the Emperor would impose his mediation and claim his reward. But these plausible calculations were shattered by the swiftness of the Prussian triumph: the King of Prussia had made himself master of all Germany north of the Main, while the Emperor of France had gained nothing, not a Belgian fortress nor a German hamlet. A surprising and unpleasant series of contrasts became suddenly evident even to the most listless eye; the Head of the French State tranquilly composing a life of Julius Caesar while the Head of the Prussian State was forging the most powerful army in Europe; the prize of Venice shaken out into the weak arms of Italy from the superabundant cornucopia of Prussian victory; the prize of Mexico abandoned with every circumstance of humiliation at the imperious command of an Anglo-Saxon republic; on the French side a chain of diplomatic rebuffs in Poland, in Denmark, in Bohemia; on the Prussian side nothing attempted which the power of the State was not able to carry to a conclusion; on the one hand, evidence of intellectual design, on the other, of vague, ill-calculated and inconsistent policies.[2]

The victory of Prussia over Austria changed the relations of France and Prussia. Before and during the war of 1866, the attitude of Emperor Napoleon III was of fundamental importance for Otto von Bismarck's policy. If Napoleon had concentrated troops in eastern France, his armed neutrality would have hampered the Prussian campaign in Bohemia just as the Prussian mobilization of 1859 had checked Napoleon in Italy. It would probably have been necessary for the Prussian chief of staff, Helmuth von Moltke, to leave important forces to cover the western frontier, and they could hardly have been spared on the decisive day of Königgrätz. The emperor of the French, however, seems to have expected the two sides in the war to be evenly matched. He thought it possible that Austria might win and took care to insure, by formal treaty with that power, a settlement that would take account

[2] Herbert A. L. Fisher, "Ollivier's Memoirs," *Studies in History and Politics*, p. 62.

of French interests. He had failed to make a definite arrangement with Prussia and apparently counted on Bismarck's gratitude in case of Prussian victory. In this, he was mistaken. Before the war, Bismarck had been amiable and yielding. He had committed himself to nothing but had made Napoleon believe that he would make concessions to France. After the war, Bismarck no longer felt the same need of France, and he was unwilling to satisfy her demands in the way Napoleon had expected.

The dominant position that Prussia had acquired in Germany raised a question which divided French opinion. Should France accept frankly the unity of Germany under Prussian leadership and the prestige won by Prussia in Europe or should she prevent the completion of German unity and destroy the military preponderance of Prussia, if need be by war? The policy of peace and understanding with Germany was that of the emperor's cousin, Prince Napoleon, of Emile Ollivier, the rising politician in the imperialist party, and of Jules Simon and Jules Favre of the republican party. The policy of "revenge for Sadowa" was that of the generals, of the conservative party, and of many of the leaders of the opposition, including the Orleanist, Adolphe Thiers, and the republican, Leon Gambetta. Napoleon, himself, sick and discouraged, wavered between peace which he wanted and war which he was told was inevitable.[3]

The second of these policies was in accordance with tradition. For centuries it had been an axiom of French foreign policy that Germany should be kept divided and weak. At the same time, there was a strong current of French opinion that aimed to extend French territory to its traditional "natural limit," the Rhine. The importance of this desire for the left bank of the Rhine has sometimes been exaggerated, but there

[3] Pierre Lehautcourt, *Les Origines de la guerre de 1870: la candidature Hohenzollern 1868-1870*, pp. 3-4.

is ample evidence that it did much to produce the atmosphere of suspicion and fear that was poisoning the relations of Germans and French. Napoleon himself would probably have been satisfied with a slight rectification of frontier at the expense of Germany, the restoration to France of the districts that had been taken from her by the second Peace of Paris in 1815.[4] Beyond that he wanted Luxemburg, and if opportunity permitted, Belgium. The knowledge that many of his people wanted the Rhine frontier influenced his attempts to secure territorial compensation for the gains by which Prussia had disturbed the European balance of power.

The negotiations passed through a series of stages. At first, Napoleon agreed to approve the territorial gains of Prussia if France received the frontier of 1814 and in addition, the Grand Duchy of Luxemburg, for which the king of Holland should receive compensation. When informed of this by Count Vincent Benedetti, the French ambassador, Bismarck pretended to be astonished. He said that, personally, he had no objection to the restoration of the frontier of 1814 but that he did not see where compensation could be found for the king of Holland. He dropped a hint, however, that this might be sought in the Bavarian Palatinate. But he begged that the negotiations be kept unofficial so that he would not have to tell King William, who, flushed by victory, would have to be carefully prepared for the French demands.

In the meantime, the anti-Prussian party at the French court secured Napoleon's consent to more extreme demands. In accordance with new instructions, Benedetti asked for the territory ceded by France in 1815, certain Bavarian and Hessian lands on the left bank of the Rhine, including the fortress of Mainz. Limburg and Luxemburg were to be separated from Germany, and Prussia was to give up the right to garrison the

[4] Paul Bernstein, "The Economic Aspects of Napoleon III's Rhine Policy," *French Historical Studies*, vol. I, no. 3, pp. 335–347.

fortress of Luxemburg. These demands were refused. King William declared that he would not give up a single German village. Moltke prepared for war against France, and if necessary, Austria as well. To stir up German national feeling, Bismarck informed the correspondent of a French newspaper that Napoleon had made demands which could not be accepted. He also used the French actions to influence the south German states to accept offensive and defensive alliances with Prussia. Napoleon changed his minister for foreign affairs and withdrew the proposals. The negotiations were, however, not dropped. Benedetti received fresh orders to try to secure the Saar region, Luxemburg, and an offensive and defensive alliance between Prussia and France that would enable France to annex Belgium. If necessary, Napoleon would give up the German territory and, as a sop to England, agree that Antwerp should be a free city. In return, Prussia would have French consent to her conquests and a powerful ally. The demand for the Saar was dropped at once, and at Bismarck's suggestion a clause was added that France would not oppose a common parliament for the North German and South German Confederations. The changes were approved by the French government and Bismarck undertook "to prepare" King William. He then went on his vacation, having in his possession a draft treaty in the handwriting of the French ambassador on the stationery of the French embassy. It did not reappear until after the outbreak of war in 1870, when Bismarck published it in the London *Times* as evidence of the aggressive character of French policy.

Unable to make progress in the direct negotiations with Prussia, the French turned to the king of Holland and attempted to buy Luxemburg from him. That duchy had been included in the German Confederation in 1815 and the capital city had been made a federal fortress, garrisoned by Prussian troops. Luxemburg had joined the *Zollverein* in 1842. It was not included in the North German Confederation, but the Prussian troops stayed in the fortress. The king of Holland was willing to sell, but he did not want to run the risk of offending Prussia and refused to conclude the negotiations without the consent of that power. Bismarck, however, insisted that Prussia must have nothing to do with the matter. In the spring of 1867, news of the transaction began to leak out. Public opinion was aroused in France and Germany, and the two countries were on the verge of war. It was averted by a compromise. An international conference held at London arranged for the withdrawal of the Prussian garrison, the destruction of the fortress, and the neutralization of Luxemburg.

Foiled in his attempts to secure compensation and bitterly resentful of Bismarck's attitude, Napoleon turned in the autumn of 1867 to Austria.

In high circles in Austria there was great reluctance to accept the verdict of Königgrätz as final. A war of revenge against Prussia was obviously out of the question for some time, and Emperor Franz Joseph's first task was to recover Austria's position as a great European power. As a first step in that direction, it was necessary to have peace at home. The efforts to subject all parts of his state to a central parliament had been unsuccessful in every form in which it had been tried, and in the fall of 1865 the operation of the constitution had been suspended. Before the war with Prussia, the emperor had begun negotiating with Magyar leaders for a new settlement, and the defeat hastened the process. The dissatisfaction of the Magyars had contributed to the disastrous course of the war. The Hungarian regiments had been unreliable and if the war had continued, a revolt might have broken out in Hungary. The attempt of Franz Joseph to come to an agreement with Hungary was assisted by two capable men. As minister for foreign affairs and chief minister, he appointed Baron Friedrich Ferdinand Beust, formerly Saxon minister president. As such, Beust had not been involved in the earlier conflicts and was free from the passions and resentments that had made the solution of the Austrian problem so difficult. The claims of Hungary were presented firmly and temperately by Francis Déak, who favored a moderate liberal constitution. Even after Königgrätz, he told the emperor, Hungary asked no more than before. In the course of 1867 a compromise was reached — the *Ausgleich* — which established complete equality between the two parts of the monarchy dominated by the Germans and the Magyars respectively. Franz Joseph was now formally crowned king of Hungary. His dominions were divided into two parts, separated by the river Leitha, a branch of the Danube. Each had a government and administration of its own, the one with its center at Vienna, the other at Budapest, which handled all domestic affairs. In addition, there was a third government for affairs common to the monarchy as a whole, foreign affairs, war, and the common finance. This dualism produced temporary stability by satisfying the two most important national groups and made it possible for Austria to consider the overtures from France.

Beust wanted to hinder the union of the south German states with the North German Confederation by encouraging the formation of a South German Confederation. He hesitated, however, to join France in an alliance aimed directly at Prussia. He feared that the Germans of Austria and the Magyars of Hungary would not support such a policy. Instead, he suggested an alliance based on the interests of France and Austria in the Eastern Question, where both were opposed to Russia. If war should arise in the Balkans, from either the Rumanian or Serbian questions, the allies might even have the support of England. Moreover, such a war would present Prussia with the alternative of abandoning her ally, Russia, or of taking part in a war that did not affect German national sentiment. The negotiations, exact knowledge of which was confined to the monarchs and a few ministers in each country, were extended after 1868 to include Italy. No formal agreement, however, could be reached. The French were unwilling to accept the Austrian ideas for the Near East, the Austrians feared French plans against Germany, and Italy refused to conclude an agreement so long as French troops garrisoned Rome.

The last article of the constitution of the North German Confederation left the way open for the admission of the south German states. "The relations of the Confederation to the south German states shall be regulated by special treaties to be laid before the Reichstag for its approval as soon as the constitution is established. The entrance of the south German states or of any one of them into the Confederation follows the normal procedure of legislation on the motion of the President of the Confederation." Article 4 of the Treaty of Prague had provided that the emperor of Austria would recognize a union of the states lying south of the line of the Main, a union "whose national ties with the North German Confederation are reserved for future agreement, and which shall have an independent international existence." This clause meant that the South German Confederation should not be amalgamated with the North, but it was not clear how far it could go in forming "national ties." There was also no provision in the treaty for the situation that actually arose, the failure of the south German states to form a union. In that case, was it permissible for individual states to join the North by mutual agreement? Bismarck insisted that it was, but he had no intention of pressing them or even of permitting them to do so before the time was ripe. The consolidation of the North German Confederation and the all-important extension of the Prussian military system was task enough for the time. The military union of Germany had been established by the treaties of 1866 with the southern states, the economic union by the renewal of the Zollverein.

Bismarck knew that the political union of north and south might have serious international consequences. In France, it was generally believed that such a union, even with individual southern states, was contrary not only to French interests but also to the terms of the Treaty of Prague. The Austrian government was sympathetic to this view. In his memoirs as published, Bismarck said that he took it for granted that a war with France would have to be waged on the way to the further national development of Germany, whether intensively (by which he probably meant the modification of existing federal ties towards a more centralized political organization) or extensively (across the Main). In an earlier draft, however, the passage reads that it would be a war with France that would have to give Germany the impetus for further national development.[5]

There has been a sharp division of opinion among the students of this period as to whether or not Bismarck deliberately sought such a war. His own public and private utterances are almost uniformly against provoking it, and, at least before the crisis of 1870, he carefully avoided provocation. He did tell the British ambassador in Berlin in February 1890, "in 1870 I was obliged to have resort to a stratagem to force on war at that moment. It must have come later. It was everything to us to choose the time." [6] But it is well known that what Bismarck wrote or said in the 1890's was not necessarily true for the time to which he referred. As he wrote to a Prussian diplomat early in 1869: "That German unity would be furthered by measures of violence, I regard as probable. But whether we are called upon to bring about a violent catastro-

---

[5] *G.W.*, vol. XV, p. 282.
[6] Sir Edward Malet to the Marquis of Salisbury, Berlin, Feb. 12, 1890, *The Letters of Queen Victoria*, 3d ser., vol. I, p. 566.

9

phe and to take the responsibility for choosing the time for it is another question. An arbitrary interference . . . with historical development has usually resulted in knocking down unripe fruit; and that German unity at this time is not ripe fruit, seems to me obvious." [7]

On the other hand, he was not blind to the danger from the Austro-French negotiations. If war came, Bismarck felt reasonably certain of success. The German army organization was superior to the French, and the tsar of Russia had promised military support if Austria joined France. As Bismarck told the Russian minister at Berlin, he saw through Beust's policy of bringing about a state of affairs in which Prussia would be faced with the alternative of leaving Russia in the lurch in a conflict with France or of supporting Russia by an attack on France which would be unpopular in Germany. "We would," he said, "not fall into such a trap. We would, if such circumstances seemed imminent, have the means of giving events a different turn. We would try to create a situation which would force France to attack, or, at least, threaten Germany. Mobilization, national manifestations in Germany and Italy, our relations with Belgium or even with Spain, would give us the opportunity of a diversion which would bring us into the war without giving the appearance of an aggressive . . . war." [8]

[7] To Werthern at Munich, Feb. 26, 1869, *G.W.*, vol. VIb, no. 1327; see also Bismarck to Flemming, Feb. 28, 1868, *ibid.*, vol. VIa, no. 285.

[8] Bismarck to Reuss, Mar. 9, 1869, *G.W.*, vol. VIb, no. 1334; Oubril to Gorchakov, Berlin, Feb. 12/24, 1869, Chester W. Clark, "Bismarck, Russia, and the War of 1870," *Journal of Modern History*, vol. XIV, pp. 197–199. The reference to Spain was added by Bismarck when he revised the draft of the dispatch to Reuss.

-❧[I]❧-

Spain in Search of a King

In September 1868, a revolution had broken out in Spain which forced Queen Isabella II to flee across the border and take refuge in France. That this was to the disadvantage of France and to the advantage of Italy and of Prussia was at once taken for granted. The Prussian chargé d'affaires at Paris expressed a general opinion when he wrote:

It is easy to understand what colossal embarrassment the French government faces. If a widespread democratic movement develops in Spain with the republic as its goal, this can be of incalculable influence on the party of action in France as well as on the revolutionary factions in Italy. If Spain should join with Italy against Rome, the position of the emperor [Napoleon III] in maintaining the military occupation of that city would be awkward. If instead of the republic, a monarchy is re-established with an Orleans prince [1] at its head, the emperor's situation will be no better. . . . For us, the Spanish revolt has in the first instance this favorable effect, that the press has stopped shouting for war and no longer mentions the Rhine or Germany. If the revolution takes on greater dimensions, France's freedom of action toward the east will be crippled.[2]

[1] Antoine of Orleans, Duke of Montpensier, the youngest son of Louis Philippe, king of the French from 1830 to 1848, was married to Louise, the sister of Queen Isabella.

[2] Solms to Bismarck, Paris, Sept. 26, 1868, *A.P.P.*, vol. X, pp. 202–203; cf. Usedom to Bismarck, Florence, Sept. 29, 1868, *ibid.*, no. 158; Hoyos

This was all so obvious that it seemed equally obvious to many contemporaries that Bismarck must have had a hand in the events taking place in Spain. Emile Ollivier states that at the news of the revolution, there was in the chancelleries and political circles of Europe the single cry: "What a windfall for Prussia," followed by another: "It is she who prepared it." [3] More than two months earlier the story had appeared in the press and in diplomatic correspondence that the Duke of Montpensier, who was suspected of plotting to win the place of his sister-in-law on the Spanish throne, had sent an envoy to Berlin to get moral and financial support from King William and Bismarck. Eventually there was added the detail that when the success of the revolution was still in doubt and before the government of the queen had fled from Madrid, the Prussian minister in Spain received orders to assure the minister of foreign affairs, Señor Gonzalès Bravo, that Prussia had nothing to do with the affair, "although the Spanish minister had in his possession intercepted correspondence which proved the contrary." [4] Ollivier, who has every reason and inclination to be suspicious of Bismarck, admits, however, that the revolutionary movement in Spain was of long standing and needed no provocation from Berlin. His strongest proof of Bismarck's complicity is the familiar proverb "qui s'excuse, s'accuse." [5]

The reports that attribute the Spanish revolution and the

---

to Beust, Oct. 7, and Vitzthum to Beust, Oct. 13, 1868, H. Oncken, *Die Rheinpolitik Kaiser Napoleons III. von 1863 bis 1870 und der Ursprung des Krieges von 1870/71*, vol. III, nos. 635, 637. The situation is well presented by W. A. Smith in "The Diplomatic Background of the Spanish Revolution of 1868," *The Historian*, vol. XIII, pp. 130–153.

[3] Ollivier, vol. XI, p. 67.

[4] E. Tallichet, "La Guerre franco-prussienne, ses causes et ses consequences," *Bibliothèque universelle et revue suisse* (June 1871), p. 429. On the rumors and their rebuttal, cf. *A.P.P.*, vol. X, nos. 99, 156, 162, 163; *O.D.*, vol. XXII, no. 6295; Ollivier, vol. XI, pp. 67–70; W. A. Smith, "Napoleon III and the Spanish Revolution of 1868," *Journal of Modern History*, vol. XXV, p. 222.

[5] Ollivier, vol. XI, p. 70.

expulsion of Isabella II to the intrigues of Bismarck need not be taken seriously except, perhaps, as evidence of the readiness of people to believe anything and everything about him. There is, however, ample proof that he welcomed the change in the government of Spain. From his estate at Varzin, he wrote in a private letter to the minister of finance, Baron August von der Heydt, that regardless of the inclination of some factions, "especially the ultramontanes," for war, he had not considered it probable. The movement in Spain, if it developed some consistency, would be "an effective poultice in favor of peace." He added the expression of hope "that God will bless the love of peace which we demonstrated eighteen months ago [in the Luxemburg crisis] when we were obviously the stronger party; and if nevertheless they attack us, we are, with God's help, still superior to the French, and the Russians will hold Austria in check." [6] He instructed the Foreign Office that it was in Prussia's interest that the Spanish question remain open and that a solution of it satisfactory to Napoleon would hardly be useful for Prussia.[7] He urged the king to treat the new Spanish government in as friendly and courteous a way as possible. "Even if it should not last, it is decisive for us that the fallen régime was hostile to us, the present one friendly." [8]

In consideration of the question of war or peace, it was disadvantageous for Prussia to appear less friendly than France toward the Spanish government. In accordance with Bismarck's suggestions, the king's speech from the throne opening the Prussian parliament on November 4 emphasized the independence of the Spanish nation. "The events in the western

[6] Bismarck to von der Heydt, Varzin, Sept. 27, 1868, *G.W.*, vol. XIV(2), no. 1222.
[7] Varzin, Oct. 3, 1868, *G.W.*, vol. VIa, no. 1186.
[8] To the Foreign Office, Varzin, Oct. 15, 1868, *G.W.*, vol. VIa, no. 1189. Cf. Bismarck to Thile, Oct. 23, and the instructions to Saurma at Madrid, *G.W.*, vol. VIa, nos. 1200, 1202, Oct. 28; Reuss to Bismarck, St. Petersburg, Oct. 15, 1868, *A.P.P.*, vol. X, no. 182.

peninsula of Europe give rise in us to no other feelings than the wishes and the confidence that the Spanish nation will succeed in finding in the independent shaping of its institutions, security for its prosperity and its power." [9]

The gracious words about Spain, which some people were surprised to find in the speech, were attributed by the Paris *Journal des Débats* to the fact that the candidacy of Prince Leopold of Hohenzollern-Sigmaringen was more serious than had hitherto been realized in Paris.[10] A Madrid dispatch of the same date to the Vienna *Neue Freie Presse* stated that this candidacy was real and, unless blocked by France, would grow until it would be officially adopted: "proposed by Dom Fernando,[11] recommended by England, and — how shall I express it? — let us say 'spoken up for' by Prussia." The Prussian minister, Baron Julius von Canitz und Dallwitz, had suddenly returned to his post, although he had not been expected until the new Spanish government was firmly established.[12]

The suspicions were premature. Leopold of Hohenzollern-Sigmaringen had been mentioned in the press as a possible candidate from the moment that the provisional government was set up in Spain. He might be described as a serious candidate in the sense that his qualifications were better than those of many of the others who were talked about. He was of age, but not too old. He was a Catholic, but not ultramontane in his views, and would therefore probably be acceptable even to moderate anticlericals. His father had been president of

[9] L. K. Aegidi and A. Klauhold, *Das Staatsarchiv: Sammlung der officiellen Aktenstücke zur Geschichte der Gegenwart*, vol. XV, p. 133; cf. Perglas to King Ludwig of Bavaria, Berlin, Nov. 11, and Könneritz to Friesen, Berlin, Nov. 6, 1868, *A.P.P.*, vol. X, no. 223 and note 3.

[10] Article by P. David, Nov. 13, 1868, extract in R. Fester, *Briefe*, vol. I, no. 22.

[11] Ferdinand of Saxe-Coburg-Gotha married Queen Maria II of Portugal in 1836. After her death in 1853, he remained in Portugal. He was the father-in-law of Prince Leopold of Hohenzollern-Sigmaringen.

[12] *Neue Freie Presse* (Vienna), no. 1517, Nov. 19, 1868, dispatch dated Nov. 13 and signed by Michael Klapp; Fester, *Briefe*, vol. I, no. 23.

the Prussian council of ministers in the early days of the "new era," and his brother was head of a constitutional government in Rumania. He might, therefore, be taken as a moderate liberal suitable for the new order in Spain. Although officially a member of the Prussian royal family, he was related by blood more closely to Napoleon III than to William I. Above all, he was the husband of a Portuguese princess, which offered the possibility that some day his heir might succeed to both thrones, achieving the Iberian union of which many Spaniards dreamed. Yet it is improbable that at this time he had been proposed by "Dom Fernando," that at this or any other time he was recommended by England, or that Canitz would have been entrusted by Bismarck with the delicate task of "speaking up" for him. In Spain, the situation was too unsettled and the differences among the leaders too great to justify the assurance of the journalists.[13] Early in December 1868, the visit to Madrid of William, Prince of Putbus, accompanied by Colonel Karl von Strantz of the Prussian general staff, gave rise to additional rumors.[14]

When Bismarck first became interested in the Hohenzollern candidacy has from the beginning been a subject of controversy. That he was actively supporting it from the end of February 1870 is established beyond any doubt, but the evidence adduced to prove his activity before that date is not convincing.

Lord Acton, in an essay, "The Causes of the Franco-Prussian War," published in 1899, wrote:

Early in 1869 Bismarck learned from Florence that Napoleon was preparing a triple alliance against him. He sent Bernhardi to

[13] Cf. Saurma to Bismarck, Madrid, Oct. 20, 1868, *A.P.P.*, vol. X, no. 188, and W. A. Smith, "The Background of the Spanish Revolution of 1868," *American Historical Review*, vol. LV, pp. 806–807.

[14] M. Klapp, Madrid, Dec. 9, 1868, in *Neue Freie Presse*, Dec. 16, 1868, Fester, *Briefe*, vol. I, no. 25, and *Neue Freie Presse*, Feb. 28, 1869, *ibid.*, no. 32.

Spain to join the Prussian legation. Theodor von Bernhardi had been sent on a similar mission to Italy in 1866, and was certified by Moltke as the best military writer in Europe. He was eminent also as an economist, a historian, and a politician, and it would have been hard to discover his equal in any European cabinet. What he did in Spain has been committed to oblivion. Seven volumes of his diary have been published: the family assures me that the Spanish portion will never appear. The *Moniteur* of 7th June [*sic*] 1870 described him as the man who arranged the affair with Prim. The Austrian First Secretary said that he betrayed his secret one day at dinner. Somebody spoke indiscreetly on the subject, and Bernhardi aimed a kick at him under the table, which caught the shin of the Austrian instead. He was considered to have mismanaged things, and it was whispered that he had gone too far. I infer that he offered a heavy bribe to secure a majority in the Cortes. Fifty thousand pounds of Prussian bonds were sent to Spain at midsummer 1870. During the siege of Paris they came over here [to London] to be negotiated, and I know the banker through whose hands they passed. The money was thrown away, as the question never came to a vote. I associate this with the disgrace of the successful emissary.[15]

Although two more volumes of Bernhardi's diary were published after 1899,[16] including much about his stay in Spain and Portugal, the mystery was not entirely cleared up. The late Professor Alfred Stern of Zurich, author of the well known *Geschichte Europas*, asked the Bernhardi family for permission to see the unpublished parts of the manuscript and was refused.[17] The most conspicuous gaps are in the spring of

---

[15] *Historical Essays and Studies*, pp. 213-214. See H. Temperley, "Lord Acton on the Origins of the War of 1870, with Some Unpublished Letters from the British and Viennese Archives," *The Cambridge Historical Journal*, vol. II, pp. 68-73. "Acton's conversation with the banker . . . took place on 5th December, 1897, and the banker said 'at least £50,000 or £60,000 were sent from Berlin to Spain to secure the election of the Hohenzollern, and were cashed in Lombard Street.' Elsewhere he admits that they passed through his hands" (*ibid.*, p. 69). I have found no other reference to Bernhardi's "disgrace."

[16] Vol. VIII (1901), vol. IX (1906).

[17] Professor Stern told me this when I visited him in 1922.

1870.[18] At this time other secret missions were in Spain.[19] It may be that the missing passages refer to activity on behalf of the Hohenzollern candidacy, but apparently they were not in the copy submitted to the Foreign Office by Theodor von Bernhardi's son in 1903. Objection was raised by the Foreign Office to the publication of certain items which suggested that Bernhardi was in Spain on a mission, that he was receiving instructions from the General Staff through Moltke, that he was reporting regularly to Robert von Keudell and the Foreign Office, and that his reports had excited great interest in Berlin, an interest which was shared even by the king. Readers of the book, it was feared, might too easily draw the conclusion that his presence in Spain was connected with the question of the succession to the throne and had been a forerunner of the visits of Lothar Bucher and Maximilian von Versen in the spring of 1870.[20] Among the passages excluded by the Foreign Office were several which mentioned the Hohenzollern candidacy but neither they nor three letters from Bernhardi included in the secret file betray any confidential knowledge of it nor any interest in furthering it.[21]

---

[18] There are no entries published between March 18 and 28, April 3 and 8, 9 and 12, 14 and 29, April 29 and May 8.

[19] See below, pp. 68–74.

[20] See below, p. 67.

[21] See Bonnin, *Bismarck and the Hohenzollern Candidature*, pp. 19–20, and letters of March 11, 23, and June 8, 1870, secret file, translations in Bonnin, nos. 12, 43, 160. As the passages to be omitted from the published diary are not dated, it is difficult to fit them into the text of vol. IX. The most significant seem to be these:

"Bl. 45. Guerero wird mir einen Empfehlungsbrief an Prim mitgeben — ausserdem aber meinethalb direkt an Prim schreiben und ihn auf meine Ankunft vorbereiten. — Ob er schreiben soll, dass ich in bestimmter Mission nach Spanien gehe? — Nein! — Er soll nur sagen, dass ich längere Zeit preussischer Militärbevollmächtiger in Italien gewesen bin und in fortwährender Beziehungen zu Bismarck und dem General Moltke stehe."

"Bl. 50. Bülow sagt mir, dass von der Kandidatur eines Hohenzollern für den Spanischen Thron in den Zeitungen etwas verlautet. In welchen? Das erfuhr ich nicht und doch wäre es wichtig, dass zu wissen, um

And if, as Acton states, Bernhardi was entrusted with the money to secure a majority in the Cortes, it seems very strange that at the critical time he was sent from Spain to Portugal.[22] Bernhardi's account of his mission to Spain must be taken substantially at face value. The decision to send him there was made in December 1868, not, as Acton suggests, early in 1869. He was told about it on December 15 by Keudell, not by Bismarck, who was away from Berlin hunting with the king.[23] "At ten o'clock to Keudell. Learn from him that I am to be sent to Spain to observe the military events of which Spain may be the theater, but without being subordinated to the embassy." [24] From then until the middle of March he was at his estate in Silesia.

On March 29 Bernhardi records a visit with Moltke, who already knew that he was to go to Spain on a military mission. "In case of war," Moltke told him, "you will be very useful to us." For in such a case, France would have to maintain a strong army of observation along the Pyrenees. When Bernhardi answered that this would be the more certain because the way things were going, the only possible results would be

---

ermessen zu können, ob es Napoleon ist, ob Prim, der die Sache vorzeitig bekannt macht, um sie zu durchkreuzen — oder ob sie blos durch eine absichtlose Indiskretion bekannt geworden ist."

"Bl. 85. . . . . Meine Vorstellung bei Serrano muss ich später einmal bei Gelegenheit machen — in diesem Augenblick würde sie Aufsehen erregen, da sich kein bestimmter Grund dafür anführen liesse, und da man sie leicht mit der Kandidatur des Prinzen von Hohenzollern in Verbindung bringen konnte, von der jetzt gerade die Rede sei. . . ."

Other passages contained uncomplimentary expressions about Portugal, Italy, etc. *Aufzeichnung Klehmet*, Oct. 3, 1903, AS 1228, and A 4087, pr. March 9, 1904, in I.A. (Deutschland) 158g, Bd. 3 (microfilm copy).

[22] On May 30, 1870, Canitz telegraphed from Madrid: "Bernhardi in Süden Spaniens, von wo er demnächst zurückerwartet wird. Werde berichten, sobald er nach Portugal abgehen wird" (secret file; Bonnin, no. 138).

[23] H. Kohl, *Bismarck-Regesten*, vol. I, p. 357.

[24] Bernhardi, *Aus dem Leben Theodor von Bernhardis*, vol. VIII, p. 374.

equally unpleasant for Napoleon, Moltke commented: "Montpensier or Republic." [25] On April 5 he learned from Keudell that the time for his departure was approaching and that he was to stop en route at Paris to see what conditions there were. Keudell expressed the thought that it might be better if he stayed in Paris.[26] Before his departure he also talked about Spain with King William and said that he thought they must look forward to a long civil war in Spain. The king agreed with him.[27] Bernhardi left Berlin on April 10, spent the rest of the month in Paris, and arrived in Madrid on May 5. In a letter of May 11 he referred to the talk of the candidacy of the hereditary prince of Hohenzollern, "which was surely not taken seriously by anyone," and expressed his dissatisfaction that his presence should be linked to such feeble fancies.[28]

No Spanish civil war broke out while Bernhardi was in Spain. He did, however, pay special attention to the republicans. In Italy he had established contact with members of the international republican movement both in person and in correspondence. We who know the weakness of that movement in the 1860's and 1870's tend to underestimate the role it played in the political fears of that period. Although this

[25] Bernhardi, pp. 410–411. Moltke did not think war would come in 1869 because Austria was not yet ready. Two weeks earlier, however, Bernhardi learned from Major Brandt of the intelligence bureau that the situation had suddenly become threatening. Until recently they had been reassured about France so that it had been possible to employ his agents in other places; now he had had to recall them suddenly and send them to France. *Ibid.*, p. 397.
[26] Bernhardi, p. 424.
[27] Bernhardi, p. 428.
[28] A. Stern, *Geschichte Europas seit den Verträgen von 1815*, vol. X, pp. 297–298. The date is corrected by Thimme in *G.W.*, vol. VIb, p. 80. In his diary Bernhardi records under the date of April 24 a conversation with Guerero, a friend of Marshal Prim, who was reputed to be engaged in various secret missions. "Nun beschäftigen sich die Monarchisten mit einem neuen Candidaten, den sie auf den Thron berufen möchten, *und der ist ein Preussischer Prinz, de la branche catholique* de la maison royale — der Erbprinz Leopold von Hohenzollern-Sigmaringen, der mit einer portugiesischen Infantin vermählt ist" (Bernhardi, vol. IX, p. 27).

purpose is not specifically mentioned by Bernhardi as part of his mission, it is implied by the attention he actually gave to it, and, because of his experience in Italy, he was the obvious man to send to Spain to watch and report on its progress there.[29] Lord is more cautious than Acton in his conjectures:

Already in December, 1868, the visit to Madrid of the Prince of Putbus accompanied by Colonel Strantz of the Prussian General staff, seemed to indicate the Chancellor's interest in the Spanish situation. In the following May, Theodor Bernhardi, already used in Italy for diplomatic work of a somewhat ambiguous character, arrived in Spain, vested by Bismarck with some sort of secret mission, which kept him there till the outbreak of the war, and the true character of which has never been revealed.

He puts greater emphasis, however, on

an enigmatic notice, preserved by a sometimes very well informed Spanish historian of half a century ago which runs: "July 14, 1869. A banker of Berlin addressed a long letter to General [Francesco] Serrano, telling him that there was no candidate more suitable than the Prince of Hohenzollern. As a result of this, people in Spain began to consider him." Most recent writers have been tempted to see in this Bismarck's first effort to press the claims of his candidate, by roundabout channels, upon the attention of the Spanish government. Doubts have, indeed, been raised as to the credibility of this isolated statement, but it would seem to be confirmed by the fact . . . that a few weeks after the date in question the Austrian envoy, visiting Serrano at La Granja, heard the latter several times mention the Hohenzollern candidacy, "not as a probability but as a possibility," and Silvela, the Foreign Minister, told him directly that "overtures had been made from Berlin in favor of the Prince of Hohenzollern." The Austrian diplomat was led to infer that the Prussian government was behind these overtures, but had acted outside the official channels.[30]

[29] Bernhardi, vols. VIII, IX *passim.* Cf., *inter alia,* Moltke's concern about the victory of socialism, Bernhardi, vol. VIII, p. 425; King William's memorandum of a conversation with Gorchakov, Baden-Baden, Oct. 16, 1869, H. Oncken, *Rheinpolitik,* vol. III, p. 260.

[30] Robert Lord, *The Origins of the War of 1870,* pp. 17f.

The German archives do contain a copy of a letter dated July 6, 1869, from Leopold Katt, a German businessman, to Bismarck, which reports the suggestion to Serrano as his own original idea and which ends with an eloquent plea to the chancellor to adopt it.[31]

It is easy to understand how the visits of Prussian statesmen and officers to Spain, the mission of Bernhardi, the suggestions of Katt, the activity of the retired Prussian Consul-General Schramm,[32] and perhaps of others, gave rise to the plausible suspicion that Bismarck was back of it all. Bismarck knew that the candidacy had been talked about; he knew that the Sigmaringen family had rejected the idea in April 1869. It is also true that the candidacy had been mentioned frequently in the press and in diplomatic circles for some time and that he himself had thought of the use of the Spanish question to make France threaten Germany. It is hard to believe, however, that if Bismarck had wanted the candidacy, he would have done so little during 1869 to realize it. Some traces of his interest and activity would surely have survived in the Sigmaringen and Berlin archives. The argument from silence does

[31] "Hoheit! Aus dem Innern meines Herzens rufe ich Ihnen zu; Stellen Sie diesen Herrn und Prinzen als Kandidaten für die Krone Spaniens auf, und ohne ein persönliches Interesse meinerseits und ohne mich je tatsächlich mit hohen Politik beschäftigt zu haben, kann ich nicht unterlassen, freudigen Gefühles und dankbar gegen Gott, den Allmächtigen, mir als ein Resultat von Privatstudien zu gratulieren zu diesem Schritt, der mir die Feder in die Hand drückt" (*G.W.*, vol. VIb, p. 268).

[32] In October 1868 Schramm had suggested Prince Frederick Charles of Prussia as a possible king for Spain. *G.W.*, vol VIb, p. 79. Cf. draft dispatch to Brassier, no. 5, Jan. 5, 1870; memorandum to the same, Jan. 8, 1870, "Der Generalkonsul a. D. Schramm hat seine Thätigkeit in spanischen Angelegenheiten aus Liebhaberei, betrieb [*sic*]" (original *in actis* B.o. 31); Brassier's confidential dispatch, Jan. 9, 1870, enclosing a letter from Schramm dated Milan, Dec. 16, 1870 (all in I.A.B.e. [Italien] 51, vol. I; photostatic copies in Public Record Office, London, F.O. 520/ 319); and Schramm to Hohenlohe, Milan, Feb. 9, 1870, a copy of which was given to Werthern by Hohenlohe and sent by the former to Karl Anton of Hohenzollern; Sigmaringen archives, Dittrich thesis, appendix 5; cf. p. 49.

not offer absolute proof, but when we see the volume and variety of the evidence that exists for Bismarck's role in the first half of 1870, the lack of any convincing testimony for the preceding year is impressive.[33]

The earliest suggestion of Prince Leopold of Hohenzollern-Sigmaringen as an eventual candidate for the Spanish throne seems to have been made by Baron George von Werthern. He had been secretary of the legation in Madrid in 1850–1851, and returned there as minister in 1864. In the fall of 1866, while on leave at Biarritz, he attended a dinner party given by Mrs. O'Shea, widow of an English banker, whom he had known in Madrid in the early fifties. Among the guests were some members of the Spanish *Union liberal*, adherents and friends of Marshal O'Donnell, who had been forced out of office as head of the Spanish government in July and who hoped to turn the tables on his successor, Marshal Narvaez. The Spaniards talked of the impending overturn of the throne as self-evident, and the conversation turned to a discussion of the pros and cons of possible successors. To his neighbor at the table, Werthern remarked that they had overlooked the name of a candidate who was better suited to Spain than any other: the Hereditary Prince Leopold of Hohenzollern, the husband of a Portuguese princess, related both to the royal house of Prussia and to Napoleon III, and with several sons to carry on the line. Werthern did not recall the name of his table companion, but three years later he was reminded that it was Don Eusebio de Salazar y Mazarredo.[34]

[33] That Bismarck was not active in the candidacy before February 1870 is accepted by P. Renouvin, *Histoire des relations internationales*, vol. V. *Le XIXe siècle*, I. *De 1815 à 1871*, p. 380. Bonnin, p. 48, cites a Spanish document which he thinks may imply German initiative before February 17, 1870, but other documents, p. 283, show that this had nothing to do with the question of the throne.

[34] Werthern to Bismarck, Munich, July 25, 1870, Lord, no. 255, p. 267; Fester, *Neue Beiträge*, pp. 24–25. The date is uncertain. In his letter

Werthern was transferred from Madrid at the end of December 1866. On his return to Germany, he stopped at Düsseldorf to confer with his successor, Baron von Canitz, about taking over his furniture in Madrid. He then presented himself to Prince Karl Anton of Hohenzollern in the belief that it would be of interest to him to have the latest news from Spain and Portugal. Werthern claimed to have told the prince that the overthrow of Queen Isabella was just a question of time and that it would open up new and greater prospects for his sons Leopold or Frederick. He expressed his conviction that Leopold would be elevated to the Spanish throne after the expulsion of Isabella if he went now to Lisbon and from there paid a visit to Isabella in Madrid. His presence, as a representative of the victorious Prussian army, would be fixed in the memory of the Spanish army for the future. Karl Anton is said to have listened with interest, but the suggestion, if there really was one, seems to have made little impression on him.[35]

In a letter to Bismarck of July 25, 1870,[36] Werthern links this conversation with another episode. "On my return through Düsseldorf, on January 12, 1867," he wrote, "I mentioned this idea in conversation with the Prince of Hohenzollern . . . and at about the same time, I used it in a direct report to His Majesty the King and in one to Your Excellency as an argument for the expediency of conferring the order of the Black Eagle on Marshal Narvaez." Werthern's two reports, dated December 8, 1866, actually made no reference to an impending Spanish revolution, but they did recommend the Black

---

to Bismarck, Werthern recalls that it was early in November; Fester, who had information from Werthern's papers, says it was probably after October 19. Cf. Salazar to Werthern, Munich, Sept. 15, 1869, Fester, *Briefe*, vol. I, no. 78.

[35] Fester, *Neue Beiträge*, pp. 25–26, based on unpublished memoirs of Werthern.

[36] Lord, no. 255, p. 267.

Eagle for Narvaez because of his services to the Spanish monarchy and his influence in the army, which would enable him, in case of a conflict between Prussia and France, to bring Spain to the side of the former. "It should finally," Werthern wrote, "be taken into account, that if France should be forced by Catholic influence [eine Katholische Bewegung] to seek a diversion for its army on the side of the Rhine, Spain would be our natural ally and Marshal Narvaez, without doubt, would be the man on whom the attitude of the government here would depend." [37]

Werthern, who in 1870 was undoubtedly writing from memory, must have confused his reports with a letter he wrote a few weeks later, on February 4, 1867, to Princess Marie of Prussia.[38] In this, he said that all the indications were that it would soon be all up with the Bourbons in Spain. The time could not be determined, but it could be "as easily tomorrow as in ten years." He was convinced that the crisis could be accelerated if the antidynastic parties knew with whom they would replace the existing dynasty. "None of the candidates proposed so far had the necessary qualifications, neither King Luis of Portugal, nor the second son of the king of Italy, nor Don Carlos, son of the late Don Juan of Bourbon." If, nevertheless, Queen Isabella were forced to leave Spain, a civil war would be inevitable. It would be a short one, for material interests would be strong against it, and "great as is the antipathy of the Spaniards for a foreigner as sovereign, they would be forced by circumstances to seize on this as the only means of

[37] Thimme's note to no. 1389, *G.W.*, vol. VIb, pp. 78–79. Recommendations for the same purpose, in June and December 1867, by Canitz, who was more sympathetic to the existing regime in Spain than was Werthern, were referred to the chief of the military cabinet on March 18, 1868. Narvaez died on April 23, 1868, without the Black Eagle.

[38] Wife of Prince Frederick Charles, younger brother of William I. Her son, Prince Frederick Charles, was occasionally mentioned as a candidate for the vacant throne. Cf. *G.W.*, vol. VIb, p. 79; Fester, *Briefe*, index under Friedrich Karl.

salvation." They would then, he continued, have to choose between an archduke of Austria and a prince of the Catholic line of the Hohenzollerns. The army would have the final decision and on it the battle of Königgrätz would weigh heavily in the scales. "Who has eyes to see, can comprehend that the House of Hohenzollern is the successor to that of Habsburg. Just realize the great position in the world that would exist if His Majesty the King as emperor of Germany could extend his left hand to the east by means of Prince Charles of Rumania, and his right to Spain by means of another prince of his house." For this prospect, it would be worth the effort to keep alive the sympathy of a man who seemed likely to exercise for years an immense influence over the Spanish army. The combination was not, he urged, as chimerical as it might seem at first glance: "it would be only the revival of the position of Charles V, and what was then possible, is also possible today. How quickly and miraculously events move, was shown by the late war. But if there were even only a hundred chances to one, political good sense requires that we think of this one, and when luck is with us, play the number." [39] This letter was sent by the princess to King William and came to Bismarck's attention. It seems to have made no more impression on them than the reported conversation with Werthern had on the prince of Hohenzollern.[40]

In the two years between the flight of Isabella from Spain on September 30, 1868, and the election in November 1870 of Amadeus of Savoy to the vacant throne, the names of more than a score of candidates were mentioned in the press and

[39] *G.W.*, vol. VIb, p. 79. A memorandum of Geheimrat Sass, Oct. 15, 1930, states: "Die Hohenzollernkandidatur erwähnt Werthern erst später und zwar in einem schreiben an die Prinzessin Marie . . . vom 4/2/1867" (P.R.O., London, F.O. 520:216. Photocopies of German Foreign Office file on private use of archives).

[40] *G.W.*, vol. VIb, p. 78. I have found no hint of it in the confidential correspondence and memoranda for the following years which have been available to me.

public discussions.[41] The earliest reference to a Hohenzollern candidacy that has been found is in the morning edition of the Munich *Süddeutsche Presse* for October 9, 1868.[42] Under the date of London, October 5, it reports: "No one in England has any doubt that the first direct result of the Spanish revolution will be that France will make important concessions to Italy in the Roman question. What is most desired here would be that the Spanish nation choose a Prince of Hohenzollern-Sigmaringen as its king. In that way the prestige of Prussia, which people here want to see as powerful as possible, would be substantially increased. This election would be preferred even to that of Prince Alfred, who has also been talked about." [43] On the same date, October 9, the London *Times* carried a report from its correspondent in Madrid that there were numerous objections to the candidacy of Archduke Albrecht

[41] The list is given by Fester in *Neue Beiträge*, pp. 90–92.

[42] The earliest press clipping on the Hohenzollern candidacy in the Sigmaringen archives is from the *Uckermärkische Zeitung* of Oct. 13, 1868. Bonnin, p. 288.

[43] Fester, *Briefe*, vol. I, no. 6. There is no reference to this in the London *Times*. I have not examined other English newspapers. From the end of June 1868, Julius Fröbel, the publisher and editor of the *Süddeutsche Presse*, had been negotiating with the Prussian government for aid in carrying on the paper. Instructions from Under Secretary of State Thile, secret, dated October 6 but dispatched October 10, informed Werthern, Prussian minister at Munich, that Fröbel's proposals had been accepted and that a subsidy of 16,000 florins would be assured for the year 1869. (Cf. the correspondence in *A.P.P.* vol. X, pp. 94–96.) In his memoirs Fröbel states that he was in Vienna on December 4, 1868, that he traveled from there to Berlin, where he had his first interview with Bismarck on December 14, and that with this visit, his political and journalistic relations with Vienna came to an end. (Julius Fröbel, *Ein Lebenslauf*, vol. II, pp. 534, 539–541.) It is possible to conjecture that the article of October 9 was published to give evidence of the new pro-Prussian line — the London date-line is no proof that it originated in that city — or even that the article was inspired by Werthern, who in the past had shown so much interest in the matter, but I have found no specific evidence to support either hypothesis.

On Queen Victoria's attitude towards the candidacy of Prince Alfred, her fourth child and second son, see General Grey to Lord Stanley, private, Oct. 9, 1868, in Queen Victoria, *Letters*, 2d ser., vol. I, pp. 540–541.

of Austria, who had been mentioned by him in an article published the preceding day. Maximilian (late emperor of Mexico), if only he were still alive, would have been an excellent candidate, "and most of the objections that rise against his uncle might equally extend to the whole lot of Coburgs, Guelphs, Wittelsbachs, and Hohenzollern-Sigmaringens." [44] The Augsburg *Allgemeine Zeitung* on October 11 printed a Paris report dated October 9 that private letters from Madrid add a new name to the list of Spanish candidates, that of Prince Leopold.[45] On October 12 the London *Times* quoted from "an article from the clerical and Carlist point of view," published in *Le Monde* of Paris, that "Prussia, it is said, would furnish a Hohenzollern; but the race is turbulent, as is seen in Roumania, and many European powers are little anxious to make a second experiment." [46] The *Correspondance Havas* even reported from Lisbon on October 12 that Prince Leopold was leaving that city on the following day and traveling via Spain.[47] The newspaper stories continued,[48] yet, as Prince Karl Anton wrote early in December 1868: "The Spanish candidacy pops up so far only in the newspapers; we don't know a mortal thing about it, and if this idea were brought to us, I would never advise the acceptance of this dubious position, glittering with tinsel. Besides, because of our relation to Prussia, France could never permit the establishment of a

[44] *The Times*, Oct. 9, 1868, p. 7c. On the preceding day, Oct. 8, p. 8c, "The canvass for the Spanish throne of the Duke of Montpensier seems to have been abandoned by his partisans. The votes lately were divided between the Duke of Edinburgh and Prince Amadeus of Italy. More recently, however, the name of the Archduke Albrecht of Austria, the conqueror of Custozza, has been brought forward. This is only private talk, the subject of the succession to the throne being scrupulously and consistently avoided by the press."
[45] Fester, *Briefe*, vol. I, no. 8.
[46] *The Times*, Oct. 12, 1868, p. 10a.
[47] *Augsburg Allgemeine Zeitung*, Oct. 20, 1868, quoted in Fester, *Briefe*, vol. I, no. 9.
[48] Fester, *Briefe*, vol I *passim*.

Hohenzollern on the other side of the Pyrenees. She is already swollen with jealousy because one of the Hohenzollerns is master of the lower Danube." [49]

In Spain itself, the most serious public attention was given to candidates who could hope for support from at least one of the major revolutionary parties. The provisional government which had been established at the beginning of October 1868, with Marshals Francesco Serrano and Juan Prim as its leading figures, had come to power without agreement on a candidate for the throne. It had been easier for the coalition parties to overthrow the old dynasty, for which they had the support of the republicans as well, than to agree on a new one. The Liberal Union had the most definite policy. When that party broke with Isabella, its leaders seem to have joined the revolutionary conspiracy with the idea of substituting for the queen her sister Louise. In the spring of 1868 the princess refused to be a candidate, and the party decided to accept her husband, Antoine of Orleans, Duke of Montpensier. It was obvious, however, that this youngest son of Louis Philippe would be vigorously opposed by Napoleon III, and although, after the revolution, the duke worked hard for the throne, he was unable to secure the support he needed from the Progressists and Democrats. Marshal Prim, the strongest person in the government, remained absolutely opposed to Montpensier: he had made a revolution against the Bourbon queen, and he would not accept in her place the younger branch of the line and the husband of a Bourbon. By the beginning of 1869, the Progressist and Democratic leaders were ready to support Ferdinand, father of King Luis of Portugal, or in his place some other member of the House of Braganza. If necessary to avoid a vacant throne and the consequent danger of a republic, they seemed willing to accept a member of the House of Savoy.

[49] To Prince Charles of Rumania, before Dec. 9, 1868, Karl I, *Aus dem Leben König Karls von Rumänien*, vol. I, p. 311.

As an Italian prince would be unacceptable to many Spaniards because of the anticlerical and antipapal policies of Italy, it was felt that the Portuguese solution offered the most advantages and the fewest objections.[50]

While the names of suggested candidates made the rounds of the newspapers in a confusing medley of shrewd conjectures, farfetched guesses, and occasional *démentis*, the semiofficial soundings of the favored few by the leaders of the Spanish government were almost equally confusing. Here, as in the government itself, Prim seems to have been the recognized leader. In the middle of January 1869, he sent his representative, Angel Fernandez de los Rios, to Portugal to confer with the ex-king Ferdinand of Coburg, who was living in retirement at Cintra. The mission failed, and the envoy had to report that Ferdinand offered no hope that he would give up his peace and quiet to become a reigning king at Madrid.[51] Prim then accepted the suggestion of Francesco de Montemar, recently Spanish minister at Florence, and sent him back to that capital to try Amadeus of Savoy, Duke of Aosta and second son of King Victor Emanuel II.[52]

[50] "While excluding the Bourbons, the nation received with perceptible disdain the notion of a foreigner on the throne, unless it be someone whose ties with the peninsula were intimate and of long standing — a Braganza, perhaps" (W. A. Smith, *American Historical Review*, vol. LV, p. 809). Early in 1866, Prim had fled to Portugal and while there had issued a manifesto explaining the delay in executing his revolutionary plans and suggesting a closer union of Spain with Portugal. J. A. Brandt, *Toward the New Spain*, p. 85.

[51] Details of the discussion in A. Fernandez de los Rios, *Mi mision en Portugal*, pp. 241–249. Ferdinand spoke to the envoy in support of the Duke of Montpensier. Conde de Romanones says that Don Ferdinand, in his conversations with Fernandez de los Rios, advised that the crown be offered to his son-in-law, Leopold of Hohenzollern, who would gladly accept it. *Amadeo de Saboya*, p. 20. I have found no supporting evidence, and the statement, like many others by the same author, cannot be accepted, especially against the direct testimony of Fernandez de los Rios.

[52] J. A. Bermejo, *Historia de la interinidad y guerra civil de España desde 1868*, vol. I, pp. 551–552.

Before the public, the two leading candidates were still Ferdinand, whose election might pave the way for the Iberian union, and the Duke of Montpensier. Their adherents engaged in a steady controversy, each trying to denigrate their rival. The propaganda for the Portuguese candidate seems to have been the more successful, and the ablest presentation of his case was a pamphlet by Salazar, *La cuestion dinastica*, published at Madrid on February 1 as an open letter to the electors of Briviesca.

The result of the September revolution, he argued, must not be merely a change in the person of the head of the state. Political unity was the aim of all the peoples. The United States had demonstrated the power of federal organization. Germany, by methods that were perhaps to be censured, had extended its boundary to Jutland. In Scandinavia the memories of the Calmar union had produced a movement for the union of Denmark with Sweden-Norway. Italy had achieved its political unity under the most difficult circumstances. Only in Spain had there survived a remnant of foreign domination and the separateness of earlier centuries. The single aim of its policy must therefore be Gibraltar and Portugal. As England had ceded the Ionian Islands to Greece in 1864, it should be possible to win Gibraltar peacefully by purchase. The Iberian union of Spain and Portugal would not be hopeless if Spain could re-establish ordered conditions and if the union were prepared with greater skill than by the ministers of Philip IV. Every real political head in Portugal foresaw that this unification must come about sooner or later from the law of centripetal force. Apart, the two peoples were weak, together they would be strong.

But as the union must not be forced, Ferdinand, the father of King Luis, appeared as the obvious candidate for the Spanish throne. It was Ferdinand who during his regency really founded the system of representative government in Portugal.

His candidacy would not give offense to either nation. Ferdinand of Saxe-Coburg-Gotha was fifty-two years old, in good health, Catholic by birth and liberal by conviction, had political experience, loved the sciences and arts, and spoke Spanish like a Castilian. He had, to be sure, rejected the crown of Greece, but it would be hard to believe that if the constituent Cortes chose him by a large majority he would refuse to listen to the call of a great people with whom Greece could hardly be compared. Even the Spanish republicans, once the form of government was settled, would recognize this king in the interest of national unity as a famous Italian (Garibaldi) had recognized the House of Savoy. Under his rule, the customs barrier would fall; weights, measures, and coinage, river navigation, academic courses of instruction, and legislation would become common to both people; new market opportunities would be opened. Ferdinand would be equal to this lofty task. And at his death, who would inherit his throne? The eldest son of King Luis, but if this line should not be available, the male descendants of the two sisters of the reigning king of Portugal. Each had a five-year-old son, and the husband of Antonia was Leopold, a young man of thirty-five, well educated, a competent soldier, who belonged to the Catholic branch of the House of Hohenzollern. He was a brother of Queen Stephanie, who passed away just before the death of Pedro V (the eldest son of Ferdinand and Queen Maria de la Gloria). Then the Iberian banner would wave over the whole peninsula including Gibraltar, over Cuba, Porto Rico, the Azores and Canary Islands, Cape Verde, Guinea, Angola, Mozambique, and in India, China, and the Philippines. "Spain for Dom Fernando, Iberia for his descendants." [53]

This glowing description of the Iberian union met with more favor in Spain than in Portugal. In the former country

[53] Fester, *Briefe*, vol. I, no. 30.

the union continued to be a political factor of considerable strength, and the Spanish leaders kept the candidacy of Ferdinand as their most favored solution of the dynastic problem. But not until the middle of July 1870 were they able to shake his determination not even to consider the Spanish crown.[54]

The mission of Fernandez de los Rios to Lisbon in January had been backed only by the authority of Prim and three of his associates.[55] Early in April the report spread through the newspapers that the Spanish cabinet had agreed to offer the crown to Ferdinand, and that a formal mission would leave Madrid for that purpose on April 6. That very morning the Portuguese ambassador at Madrid informed the cabinet that he had received instructions to let them know that if Ferdinand were elected he would not accept and that he would not even receive the Spanish envoys. Even though Ferdinand tried to soften the crushing effect of the brusque telegram by a letter to Count d'Alte in which he courteously explained his motives, his answer could not be interpreted as anything but a categorical no.[56]

In the meantime, Montemar, the Spanish ambassador at Florence, was trying to persuade Amadeus of Savoy to be a candidate, but with no success. King Victor Emanuel suggested that the Spaniards consider his fifteen-year-old nephew, Thomas, Duke of Genoa.[57] It seems doubtful that Prim was

[54] At that time his morganatic wife, the Countess Edla, had some correspondence with Fernandez de los Rios which, for a short time, raised the Spanish hopes. Fernandez de los Rios, pp. 338–423.

[55] See p. 29 above.

[56] Tg., Marquis de Sa to Count d'Alte, Lisbon, April 6, 1869, Fernandez de los Rios, p. 339; tg., Bartholdi to La Valette, Madrid, April 6, 1869, 6:50 P.M., *O.D.*, vol. XXIV, no. 7374. Earlier that day, Bartholdi had been told that the Spanish ambassador to London would leave for Paris at the end of the week to inform Napoleon of the decision and to ask his support for the negotiations at Lisbon. Tg., Bartholdi to La Valette, Madrid, April 6, 1869, 3 P.M., received 9:10 P.M., *ibid.*, no. 7373. Cf. Fester, *Neue Beiträge*, p. 4.

[57] Son of Victor Emanuel's brother Ferdinand and his wife Elizabeth,

seriously interested in placing a minor on the throne, but he was apparently ready to accept the king's proposal. At any rate, Montemar and an official of the Italian foreign ministry are said to have traveled together to England at the end of May, interviewed the duke at Harrow, and were told that he would respect the will of his king and uncle.[58]

The name of Prince Leopold of Hohenzollern, which appeared only incidentally in Salazar's pamphlet, was also mentioned more and more frequently in the press and in behind-the-scenes discussions. The Marquis de Niza, Spanish minister at Lisbon,[59] wrote on March 7 to Fernandez de los Rios:

> A few days ago our minister to Belgium, Viscount de Seissal, a close friend of mine, arrived here [at Lisbon]. He is a perfect gentleman, loyal and frank. He is on confidential terms with Ferdinand, with the prince of Hohenzollern, and the Princess Antonia. We were talking about this and that when he suddenly put this question: "Why don't you take advantage of your relations with the influential men in Spain, especially Marshal Prim, to recommend to them the candidacy of the Prince of Hohenzollern? I know him well and he is an excellent person, thirty-four years old, well educated and very liberal. Prussia would be glad to see this, and also, I believe, Ferdinand, and only the emperor [Napoleon III] would have no taste for it but he would prefer it to Montpensier and he wouldn't dare to oppose it openly. Besides, this candidacy would be Iberian."

This question was repeated to Niza in almost the same words by the Marquis of Oldoini, the Italian representative in Lisbon in the middle of April, and was brought up several times during the second half of that month.[60]

---

daughter of King John of Saxony. Fester, *Briefe*, vol. I, no. 39; Bermejo, vol. I, p. 559; Fernandez de los Rios, p. 340.

[58] Fester, *Neue Beiträge*, pp. 130–131; Bermejo, vol. I, pp. 564–565.

[59] He had introduced Fernandez de los Rios to King Ferdinand in January and had been present at their conversation.

[60] The first letter incorrectly dated "Mayo." Fernandez de los Rios, pp. 338–343. Reprinted in Fester, *Briefe*, nos. 35, 40, 43, 51.

Shortly after the first conversation between Oldoini and Niza, Prince Karl Anton of Hohenzollern received a letter dated April 19 from his son-in-law, Philip of Flanders. Most of the letter dealt with the current controversy over the Belgian railroads, but at the end Philip wrote that the Belgian government had learned from Spain that if Leopold came forward as a candidate for the throne, his chances would be good. Karl Anton wrote at once to King William about this and expressed the hope that in case an offer did come from Spain the king would approve the decision of Leopold "to follow the example of his father-in-law King Ferdinand of Portugal." King William replied that he completely understood that Leopold would not accept the Spanish crown, and that neither Karl Anton nor the king himself would urge him to do so.[61]

The open rejection of the crown by Ferdinand left the Spanish cabinet in a difficult position. Some continued to hope for a Portuguese solution. If Ferdinand remained obstinate, perhaps the reigning King Luis could be induced to accept. Others favored an Italian prince. The Duke of Montpensier had lost ground for the moment. Many held him responsible for Ferdinand's refusal. Prim declared publicly that he would never accept a Bourbon, and was backed in this by the whole Progressist party. The French chargé d'affaires did not believe that the duke could be struck from the list of candidates, because "unfortunately I am not certain that some of the leaders of the Progressist party will never be influenced by the arguments that the duke knows so well how to use."[62] But even

---

[61] "On écrit d'Espagne au gouvernement Belge, que si Léopold se présentait comme candidat au trône il aurait des chances" (Philip to Karl Anton, Brussels, April 19, 1869). Karl Anton to King William, April 20; King William to Karl Anton, April 23. Cf. Stern, *Geschichte Europas*, vol. X, p. 297, and memorandum of Rottenburg on Sybel's manuscript, July 8, 1890, in secret file.

[62] An allusion to his great wealth which he was reputed to be ready to use to further his chances.

Marshal Serrano, his most influential supporter, had lost hope for the moment. The newspapers were still mentioning Leopold of Hohenzollern.[63]

At the moment, the Spanish provisional government had more pressing problems than the search for a candidate for the throne. With the Cortes in session, it was necessary to consolidate the regime by a monarchical constitution. The Liberal Unionists, the Progressists, and the Democrats put aside their differences to make common cause against the Republicans. An amendment that the chief of the state must be a Spaniard, born in Spain of Spanish parents, was voted down. As a matter of practical politics, this measure would have left no alternative but a republic. On May 21, by a vote of 214 to 71, the majority voted for a monarchy.

Late in the session, on June 12, Prim informed the assembly that the government had no candidate for the throne. If Ferdinand had not rejected the crown before it was formally offered to him, he would have contributed to the greatness of Spain and of Portugal. Prim tried to reassure the Portuguese that Spain had no intention of absorbing the Portuguese nation, but added that closer relations would be of mutual advantage. He went on to point out to his hearers:

That the government has still no candidate to present to the Cortes must be explained by the facts that Spain has only just completed its constitutional order, and that the disorders in Cadiz, Malaga, and Jerez, and the murder of the governor of Burgos in the cathedral, were of a nature to make any princes who might become candidates say: "Who would undertake to go to a country where such things happen?" The first task of the Regency is to establish order. After that, we can be sure that more than one candidate will be found.[64]

[63] See Bartholdi to La Valette, Madrid, April 9, 1869, *O.D.*, vol. XXIV, no. 7383; Mercier to Rouher, Madrid, May 24, 1869, *O.D.*, vol. XXIV, no. 7498; Fester, *Briefe*, vol. I, nos. 42, 44, 45–50, 52, 56–57, 59–60, 64–66, 68–69.

[64] Fester, *Briefe*, vol. I, no. 72.

On June 15 Serrano was made Regent, raising him above the political battlefield, and leaving Prim, as the strong man of the cabinet, in a better position to control the choice of sovereign.

The repeated mention of a Hohenzollern candidate for the throne of Spain could not, of course, escape the notice of the French. Count Vincent Benedetti, the ambassador at Berlin, informed his government on March 27, 1869, that Manuel Rancès y Villanueva, who had represented Spain at the Prussian capital from 1862 to January 1867, had returned to Berlin from Vienna, ostensibly to congratulate King William on his birthday and to express his gratitude for the kindness he had been shown during his mission. He had remained in Berlin for five days and had seen Bismarck twice. It was natural, therefore, to suspect that he might have had political reasons for the visit. Benedetti had obtained no information that permitted him to say whether there was any foundation for this conjecture, and he did not believe that Rancès had been charged to negotiate any agreement with Prussia.

Your Excellency knows, however, that the hereditary prince of Hohenzollern has been included among those members of sovereign families who might be raised to the throne of Spain. Given the difficulties that the choice of a new sovereign has created at Madrid, have they been thinking there of the prince of Hohenzollern,[65] and was M. Rancès ordered to confer with Bismarck about it, or did this idea perhaps come up at Berlin even or at Düsseldorf,[66] and did someone inform Rancès and did he decide to undertake the trip after receiving orders from his government? I have no knowledge of this; but it seemed proper, nevertheless, not to leave you unaware of these suppositions which will enable you to check any other information you may have which

[65] The original reads: "aurait-on songé au Prince"; the text published by Benedetti, *Ma Mission en Prusse*, pp. 302–304, and reproduced by Fester, *Briefe*, vol. I, pp. 14–15, has "aurait-on *de nouveau* songé au Prince" (my italics).

[66] The principal residence of Karl Anton.

would make you believe in the existence of negotiations on this subject." [67]

The French foreign minister had just learned from the chargé d'affaires at Madrid that the Spanish cabinet had reached an agreement to offer the crown to Ferdinand of Portugal and that a secret mission would leave for Lisbon early the next week.[68] Nevertheless, he instructed Benedetti by telegraph to try to find out if the candidacy of the prince of Hohenzollern was serious. "I do not need," he added, "to tell you that we would not favor it and I leave it to you to decide the extent to which we should let this be known [at Berlin]. The example of Rumania is there to enlighten us." [69]

Bismarck had already gone to his estate at Varzin, so Benedetti took up the question with the secretary of state, Karl Hermann von Thile, who gave the most formal assurance that he knew nothing that would justify the suspicion and that the Spanish minister had not even alluded to it during his stay at Berlin. According to Thile, Rancès had limited himself to telling Bismarck about what was going on in Spain in relation to the choice of a king. "The Cortes," he was reported to have said, "will elect King Ferdinand who will refuse to accept the crown. The majority will then be divided between the Duke of Montpensier and the Duke of Aosta but will probably decide in favor of the former of these two princes and he will accept." [70] Benedetti's comment that Thile was not always initiated into the personal views of Count Bismarck

[67] Benedetti to La Valette, Berlin, March 27, 1869 (Cabinet March 28; direction politique, March 31), *O.D.*, vol. XXIV, no. 7354. Also with slight textual variations in Benedetti and Fester as noted above.

[68] Tg., Bartholdi to La Valette, Madrid, March 27, 1869, 2:30 P.M., received 9:30 P.M., *O.D.*, vol. XXIV, no. 7357, and note 3, p. 108.

[69] Tg., La Valette to Benedetti, Paris, March 30, 1869, sent 7:15 P.M., *O.D.*, vol XXIV, no. 7360.

[70] Benedetti to La Valette, dispatch in cipher, Berlin, March 31, 1869, *O.D.*, vol. XXIV, no. 7363. Also in Benedetti, *Ma Mission en Prusse*, pp. 304–306; Gramont, *La France et la Prusse avant la guerre*, pp. 357–359; Fester, *Briefe*, vol. I, pp. 15–16.

was, in this case, not justified. At the end of about an hour of conversation with Rancès, Bismarck had spoken of his desire to see Spain established on firm foundations and to maintain with an independent Spain "our natural ally" the best possible relations. "We have," he said, "no business to meddle in the internal affairs of Spain, but if we were to recommend a candidate among those who have been mentioned for the vacant throne, we would choose the Duke of Montpensier, in my opinion the one who is the most seriously to be considered and the one who can assure the independence of Spain, which we want and which is in our own interest." [71]

While in Paris Benedetti had the opportunity of giving the emperor in full detail his personal impressions of the situation. In return, Napoleon summed up his own position that the candidacy of the Duke of Montpensier was antidynastic; it affected only himself, and he could put up with it. The candidacy of the prince of Hohenzollern was antinational; the country would not stand for it, and it must be averted. Eugene Rouher, acting foreign minister in the absence of La Valette, instructed Benedetti to talk to Bismarck about the candidacy but to use language which would avoid the appearance of seeking a cause for conflict. [72]

Soon after his return to Berlin, Benedetti reported that he had had no difficulty in turning his conversation with Bismarck

[71] Rancès y Villanueva to Sagasta, July 24, 1870, repeating what had been reported after his visit to Berlin in March 1869: "me dijo estas palabras textuales: 'En me resumant, je dis que nous avons le plus vif desir de voir l'Espagne se constituer et de maintenir avec l'État Espagnol, notre allié naturel, avec l'État faisant sa propre politique et non une politique de Cabinet, les meilleurs raports [*sic*]. Nous n'avions pas à nous mêler des affaires intérieures de l'Espagne, mais si nous avions à recommander une candidature parmi celles que l'on indique pour le trône vacant, nous choisirions celle du Duc de Montpensier, le plus sérieuse selon moi, et celle qui peut assurer l'independance de l'Espagne que nous désirons et qui est de notre intérêt'" (Conde de Romanones, *Amadeo de Saboya*, pp. 244–249).

[72] *O.D.*, vol. XXIV, p. 285, note 2.

to the subject of the present state of affairs in Spain and to ask him about the rumors that pointed to the prince of Hohenzollern as one of the candidates for the Spanish throne. Bismarck maintained that the sovereignty which could be offered to Prince Leopold could only be ephemeral and that it would expose him to dangers and not just disappointment. The king, convinced of this, would, if the case arose, certainly refrain from advising him to accept the vote of the Cortes. The father of the prince, Bismarck said, shared this opinion, and he had convinced himself, through the necessity of coming to the aid of his younger son, Prince Charles of Rumania, that sovereign power was a great burden on his personal fortune. He would not be disposed to compromise it further to help his eldest son ascend the throne of Spain. Bismarck did not cover up the fact that he had had occasion to confer with the king and Prince Karl Anton on this subject, but did not go into further detail. Benedetti drew the conclusion that if Bismarck's words were to be taken as sincere, it would be necessary to assume that "no proposal, or at least no formal proposal, had been received." He was, however, inclined to think that Bismarck had not been completely frank with him.

I remarked to him that Prince Leopold could not defer to the wish of the Cortes, if it should acclaim him, without the consent of the king, and that His Majesty would have to prescribe the decision which he would have to make in such a situation. Bismarck admitted it, but instead of assuring me that the king had irrevocably decided to recommend withdrawal, he returned to the perils which would surround the new sovereign of Spain from the moment of his accession. He went on to express the opinion that there probably would not be an election of any prince, that the personal ambitions of the men who had seized power in Spain — he named Prim particularly — would be a more formidable obstacle than was generally supposed. . . . Bismarck also told me that Prince Frederick Charles [a nephew of King William] might have been inclined to undertake "an adventure in Spain," but that he faced an insurmountable obstacle, his religion, which could not be overcome in the eyes of the Spanish people even by his conversion. This prince was a valiant and distinguished officer, but he had never given evidence of political aptitude and would hardly be able to deal with the complicated situation in Spain. He did not, however, say if that candidacy had been seriously posed or under what circumstances it might have been discussed and given up.

In summing up his impressions of the conversation and of the language, "so moderate and so little in accordance with his custom," Benedetti raised two questions: "Does he think that Prince Leopold could be elected by the Cortes and has he been careful to express himself in such a way as not to limit the king's freedom of choice in such a case? Or has he set out only to let us suspect that it would be easy for him in case of need to have a member of the House of Hohenzollern chosen in Spain?" These hypotheses were, in Benedetti's judgment, equally probable.[73] The reasoning was shrewd but the Hohenzollern candidacy was still only a future possibility, not yet a fact.

Not until August did Prim begin again to search for a king. Fernandez de los Rios was sent as ambassador to Portugal. His general instructions were to consolidate and improve the relations of the two countries and especially to convince the Portuguese that closer relations did not threaten their national independence.[74] At the same time, Prim told him not to take any steps toward a candidacy without special instructions, but to study the situation and to prepare the ground if one should arise spontaneously.[75] At the end of August Prim went to Paris and to Vichy. He won the support of the influential Duke of Saldanha, at that time Portuguese ambassador to France, and

[73] Benedetti to Rouher, May 11, 1869, *O.D.*, vol. XXIV, no. 7466; Bismarck to Solms, May 11, 1869, *G.W.*, vol. VIb, no. 1389.

[74] Silvela to Fernandez de los Rios, Aug. 9, 1869, Fernandez de los Rios, *Mi mision en Portugal*, pp. 249–251.

[75] Fernandez de los Rios, p. 350.

persuaded him to urge Ferdinand to accept the Spanish proposal.[76] Montemar traveled to Florence, whence he brought word that the Duke of Genoa would certainly accept an offer.[77] At about the same time, Prim authorized Salazar to get in touch with the prince of Hohenzollern.

In his pamphlet of February 1,[78] Salazar had mentioned Prince Leopold, not as a candidate for the Spanish throne, but only as an eventual heir of King Ferdinand. During the summer, however, he seems to have come to the conclusion that the hereditary prince himself would be the most suitable candidate and, at Vichy, he had presented his views to Prim.[79]

Salazar arrived in Munich on Wednesday, September 15, and called at the Prussian Legation to find Werthern. The latter was absent at Augsburg, where he had gone to meet his brother, but on his return he found Salazar's card, asking for an interview, and a letter which Salazar had written some time later, on the stationery of the Prussian Legation, to explain the object of his journey. He had, he wrote, left a note on a visiting card to ask for a few moments "on a subject of which you were the first to talk to me three years ago when dining at Mrs. O'Shea's at Biarritz." He had come to Munich to try to bring the matter to a favorable conclusion, and asked Werthern to introduce him at the Hohenzollern castle at Weinburg with a letter that would give him the opportunity to meet Prince Leopold in person. Finally, Salazar added, he had just learned that Leopold's brother, Prince Charles of Rumania, was in town, and he asked Werthern to receive him before the departure of that prince, "for the affair that

---

[76] Fester, *Briefe*, vol. I, nos. 74, 75; Saldanha to King Ferdinand, Paris, Sept. 12, 1869. Carnota, *Memoirs of the Field Marshal the Duke of Saldanha*, vol. II, pp. 377–378.
[77] Fester, *Briefe*, vol. I, no. 75. Bermejo, vol. I, p. 586.
[78] See pp. 30–31 above.
[79] Fester, *Neue Beiträge*, p. 27.

has made me undertake this journey is of the highest importance." [80]

Prince Charles of Rumania received Werthern and his secretary of legation, Joseph Maria von Radowitz, at the Hotel Vier Jahreszeiten that evening, but left for Weinburg early the next morning on the six o'clock train for Lindau without meeting Salazar and apparently without learning of his mission. [81]

After his call on Prince Charles, [82] Werthern went to the Hotel Maximilian on the Promenadenplatz, and had Salazar, who was already in bed, awakened. Salazar explained his purpose at greater length than in the letter, and added that he had come to Werthern rather than to the Prussian minister at Madrid, Canitz, "who was neither initiated in nor interested in the matter." [83]

Werthern and Salazar left Munich on Friday, September 17, by the early morning train and reached Weinburg early in the afternoon. [84] While Salazar remained unobserved in the background, Werthern wrote a note to Karl Anton requesting a few minutes alone with him. After some delay — the castle was filled with guests — he was received cordially by Karl Anton and explained briefly to him why Salazar had come.

[80] The letter, written in French, was published by Fester, *Neue Beiträge*, p. 26, and reprinted in Fester, *Briefe*, vol. I, no. 78.

[81] Karl I, *Aus dem Leben König Karls von Rumänien*, vol. II, p. 5; Hajo Holborn, *Aufzeichnungen und Erinnerungen aus dem Leben des Botschafters Joseph Maria von Radowitz*, vol. I, p. 187; and *Augsburger Allgemeine Zeitung*, Beilage, no. 260, Friday, Sept. 17, 1869, p. 402.

[82] The order of the visits is not established by the sources — Werthern says nothing about meeting Prince Charles — but it is a reasonable inference that protocol would give priority to the call on a prince. After Werthern and Radowitz left, Prince Charles received a visit from Isabella II's husband, Francis. Werthern's call on Salazar was late in the evening. It is impossible to know if Werthern had read Salazar's letter before he saw Prince Charles.

[83] Werthern's memorandum, Fester, *Neue Beiträge*, p. 27.

[84] My account of Salazar's mission to Weinburg is based on Fester, *Neue Beiträge*, pp. 26–32. The dating is corrected by Karl Anton's notes, Dittrich thesis, appendices 1, 2.

Karl Anton seemed to be pleased that Prim himself was interested in the candidacy. He talked it over with his two sons, Charles and Leopold, and agreed to receive Salazar, who was then sent for. In an interview on the castle terrace, lasting about two hours, Salazar presented his case "clearly and convincingly." He succeeded in meeting the objections and in resolving some of the doubts of Karl Anton, who, in Werthern's words, "with intelligence and dignity accepted the affair as a sacrifice demanded by its historical importance." Finally, Salazar was introduced to Prince Leopold, and then withdrew to the hotel at nearby Rheineck "so as not to be exposed to the inquisitive eyes of the Rumanian retinue and the associates of Duke Charles of Parma." Werthern remained as a guest at the castle. At dinner that evening he sat next to Princess Antonia and tried to rouse her interest in the prospect, but found her as little eager as her husband to wear the Spanish crown.

Salazar did not visit the castle on Saturday, and Werthern left that evening to return to his post at Munich. Karl Anton had made an appointment to meet Salazar Sunday morning on the Rhine promenade. He took with him not Leopold but Charles. Either from Castilian politeness or as another string to his bow, Salazar tried to persuade Prince Charles to become a candidate: the eyes of the Spanish people were turned on him, for he had already had the courage to undertake a similar and difficult mission. Charles courteously but definitely refused to do so; his sense of duty made it impossible for him to exchange the modest hat of a Rumanian prince even for the proud crown of Spain.[85]

In the afternoon, Salazar at last was allowed to have a conference with Prince Leopold and Princess Antonia. The prince showed little inclination to take up the offer, but he did not reject it absolutely. He insisted, however, on a number of

[85] Karl I, *Aus dem Leben König Karls von Rumänien*, vol. II, p. 6.

conditions, above all that he must be chosen unanimously without having to contest with other candidates, and that he must not be drawn into any political combination which could turn to the disadvantage of Portugal because of his wife's relation to that country.

In a letter to Bismarck on the occasion of Salazar's second mission in the following February, Karl Anton wrote that he and his son had refused to commit themselves but had discussed the chances of success in finding a suitable person for the candidacy. He dismissed "the not uninterested" Don Salazar, he claimed, with these words: "If you can persuade the Emperor Napoleon to approach my king and to point out to him that the founding of a Spanish Hohenzollern dynasty is a security for the peace and quiet of Europe, and if then my king speaks favorably of such a solution of the problem, — then the first moment would have come for us to consider whether our family interests permit acceptance or make rejection a duty." [86]

Salazar left Weinburg "fairly satisfied" with the results of his visit. He had made no formal offer — he was not authorized to do that — and no formal consent was received. He had found the princess charming and the prince, too, had pleased him, but he still had some doubts about Leopold's energy and firmness of character for the difficult task of ruling Spain. He noted Leopold's concern about the attitude of King William and his wish not to appear ambitious, to have his hand forced rather than to show what he wanted. How that could be managed, Salazar did not know. The Spaniards would try to secure Napoleon's approval for the candidacy and perhaps Werthern could go to meet King William at Baden and "feel the doctor's pulse." With his letter to Werthern Salazar en-

[86] Karl Anton to Bismarck, Düsseldorf, Feb. 25, 1870, secret file; Bonnin, no. 5.

closed the summary of the points to be made in a pamphlet which was published on October 23 to present Leopold's candidacy to the Spanish public.[87]

The content of Werthern's answering letter of September 29 is unknown. He did go to Baden and tried to persuade Prince Charles of Rumania, whom he met there, that the House of Hohenzollern ought not to reject the Spanish crown off-hand.[88] His memorandum of 1869 notes an audience with King William at which they discussed the first performance of Wagner's opera *Das Rheingold*, but there is no evidence that he informed the king of what had been going on at Weinburg.[89]

Prim and his associates did not follow up Salazar's mission to the Hohenzollern princes. Instead, they decided to proceed with the candidacy of the Duke of Genoa. A commission, composed of delegates of the monarchist parties was established at the beginning of October and after a month of deliberation, it voted, 128 to 52, in favor of the choice. The opposition in political circles to the selection of the fifteen-year-old boy was so intense, however, that several members of the cabinet resigned, to the great embarrassment of the leaders of the government. Prim retained, or pretended to retain, a measure of optimism as the negotiations dragged on. A circular dispatch of December 17, 1869, instructed the Spanish representatives at the principal capitals to prepare public opinion for the accession of the young Italian. The pressures and counterpressures at Florence matched those at Madrid and at the end of December, King Victor Emanuel informed the Spanish ambassador that he had been unable to overcome

---

[87] Cf. Fester, *Neue Beiträge*, pp. 28–33; Werthern to Karl Anton, Nov. 19, 1869, Dittrich thesis, appendix 4; Leopold to Karl Anton, Feb. 27, 1870, *ibid.*, appendix 13.

[88] Karl I, *Aus dem Leben König Karls von Rumänien*, vol. II, p. 10.

[89] Fester, *Neue Beiträge*, pp. 32–33.

the opposition of the duke's mother and that he must withdraw the assurances he had given.[90] Fifteen months had gone by since the revolution, and Spain was still without a king.

[90] Cf. Fester, *Neue Beiträge*, pp. 139–143; W. A. Smith, *Journal of Modern History*, vol. XXV, pp. 231–232; *O.D.*, vol. XXV, nos. 7691, 7710, 7737; vol. XXVI, nos. 7797, 7847, 7852; Bonnin, pp. 45–46.

-[II]-

The Candidate is Found

The news that the Duke of Genoa would not accept the Spanish crown reached Madrid on January 2, 1870. It produced another cabinet crisis. The council of ministers resigned in a body and Prim was charged to form a new one. It was said that his program was to bring into the government the most reputable leaders of the monarchist parties, to postpone the solution of the dynastic problem, and to devote the energies of the government to domestic difficulties, especially the struggle against republican and "anarchical" elements. There was talk of extending the regency of Marshal Serrano and of giving him all the attributes of a constitutional monarch. The cabinet was completed at the end of the week. A circular dispatch of January 13 to the Spanish representatives abroad revoked that of the preceding month which had instructed them to prepare for the accession of an Italian prince. The missions were informed that one of the first things agreed upon by the new government of the Regent had been to defer the attempt to find a king and that they should abstain from all action in connection with the choice of a monarch.[1]

It proved easier to defer the decision than to escape the

---

[1] See Fester, *Neue Beiträge*, pp. 144–146; W. A. Smith, *Journal of Modern History*, vol. XXV, pp. 223–224, 232; Bonnin, *Bismarck and the Hohenzollern Candidature*, pp. 46–47.

problem. The range of possible choices had been narrowed by the positive refusal of the Portuguese and Italian candidates. The Duke of Montpensier continued his efforts; Prince Alfonso, the son of Isabella II, seemed to be gaining support in Paris; Archduke Karl Salvator of Austria, the Princes Albert and Otto of Bavaria, the Duke of Alençon, and others were mentioned in conversation and in the press.[2] The Duke of Montpensier and Prince Alfonso, as Bourbons, faced the absolute opposition of Prim, and none of the others named seemed better than a last resort. Under the circumstances, then, it was only natural to think again of Leopold of Hohenzollern.

Early in February 1870, Salazar undertook to sound the dispositions of the Sigmaringen princes. In a letter to Werthern on the sixth, he painted a rosy picture of their chances. The candidacy of the Duke of Genoa, he said, had been only a maneuver whose failure had been foreseen. The Carlists and the republicans were steadily losing ground. The Duke of Montpensier had lost in two by-elections, and if he could not be elected deputy he could hardly succeed in becoming king. In a few weeks the members of the monarchical parties in the Cortes planned a caucus, not to discuss a specific candidate, but to show their confidence in the government and to bind themselves to vote for whomever the government should present to them, provided he fulfilled three conditions: he must be of a royal family, of age, and Catholic.[3] The num-

---

[2] See, *e.g.*, Mercier to Daru, Madrid, Feb. 4, 1870, *O.D.*, vol. XXVI, no. 7915.

[3] According to information reported by the French ambassador, Manuel Ruiz Zorrilla, president of the Cortes, made a deal with the Liberal Unionists to table anticlerical legislation if they would accept a candidate chosen by the government who fulfilled these conditions, excluding the Duke of Montpensier and the Spanish Bourbons (*i.e.*, Prince Alfonso and the Carlist candidates). Mercier to Daru, Feb. 4, 1870, *O.D.*, vol. XXVI, no. 7915. A different version was reported in his dispatch of Feb. 6, *ibid.*, no. 7919.

ber of possible choices had, however, become very limited. The chances for a Hohenzollern were very good and were improving day by day. The pamphlet which Salazar had published in October [4] was in great demand, and Hereditary Prince Leopold as first choice or his youngest brother, Frederick, as second would be very popular. In a supplementary note, Salazar added that everything in his letter, "which you can send where you like," was the exact truth. In case, however, it proved impossible to secure one of the Hohenzollerns, he asked for Werthern's opinion of the Bavarian princes: Louis Leopold, Leopold Maximilian, and Charles Theodore.[5] Werthern received the letter on February 11, and on the following day forwarded a copy to Karl Anton at Düsseldorf.[6]

Werthern also enclosed a copy of a letter from Milan which Prince Chlodwig Hohenlohe-Schillingfürst, the president of the Bavarian council of ministers, had given him the evening before. The writer was the former Prussian consul general Schramm, "now a speculator and well known in Spain," who from time to time supplied Hohenlohe with news from Italy "which is always reliable." Schramm's letter, dated February 9, reported that letters sent him from Madrid on February 5 described the changes in the situation produced by the failure of the Duke of Montpensier to win election to

[4] See p. 45.
[5] Salazar to Werthern, Madrid, Feb. 6, 1870, Fester, *Neue Beiträge*, pp. 37–40; *Briefe*, vol. I, no. 98. As the letter begins: "Je suppose que vous aurez reçu à temps la lettre que je vous envoyai aussitôt après mon retour à Madrid," it shows that Werthern had not answered Salazar's letter of October 7, 1869. See Fester, *Briefe*, vol. I, no. 88.
[6] Werthern to Karl Anton, Munich, Feb. 12, 1870, Dittrich thesis, appendix 5. Fester, *Neue Beiträge*, p. 40, quotes a marginal note of Werthern on the original: "Am 20. März habe ich Salazar unterrichtet, dass der Fürst H. *sogleich* nach Empfang dieses Briefes (10 February) vom Inhalt desselben in Kenntnis gesetzt worden ist." The letter cited above says the letter was received "gestern"; *i.e.*, February 11. In his letter of February 12 Werthern told Karl Anton that he had communicated to Salazar "eine Physiologie" of the Bavarian candidates that would be enough to eliminate them once and for all.

the Cortes. He concluded that the moment had come for a serious candidacy and that a Catholic Hohenzollern would have good prospects.[7]

In the meantime, between February 6 and 17, Prim decided to let Salazar go to Berlin with letters to Prince Leopold, Bismarck, and King William.[8] To the king, Prim wrote that Prince Karl Anton of Hohenzollern and Count Bismarck would have informed him of the confidential mission, which in his capacity as president of the council of ministers of the Regent of the Kingdom of Spain, he had entrusted to M. de Salazar y Mazarredo, deputy to the constituent Cortes and councillor of state. If the king desired to have fuller and more direct details before reaching a definite decision in this important matter, Salazar was instructed to present this letter to His Majesty and to express to him the sincere good wishes

---

[7] Werthern assured Karl Anton that he had given Hohenlohe no inkling of his letter from Salazar or of the subject there treated.

[8] Bonnin, p. 47, concludes from the cryptic language of a dispatch of January 31, 1870, from Olózaga, the Spanish ambassador to France, "that the actual decision to turn to Leopold of Hohenzollern was taken in January, for Olózaga had been called to Madrid to attend conferences to which he refers in a mysteriously allusive way, adding that for reasons he does not need to quote, prudence requires that the question of the candidates for the throne should not be mentioned at all." He adds in a footnote: "If during these conversations of Olózaga in Madrid the Hohenzollern candidature was actually debated, the Marquès de Lema must be considered as ill-informed when he attributes Olózaga's attitude in July 1870 to his previous ignorance of the Hohenzollern candidature (*De la Revolucion a la Restauracion*, Vol. I, p. 340, Madrid, 1927)." I see no reason to suppose that the decision to turn to Leopold was debated at these conferences or that Olózaga knew of it before July 1870. He had arrived in Madrid at the end of December 1869 for consultation on the general political situation. On the eve of his return to Paris (on or about January 15), he told Mercier, the French ambassador, that he feared that Prim might go over to a republican solution. Mercier to Daru, Jan. 15, 1870, *O.D.*, vol. XXVI, no. 7869. See also Mercier's reports of Dec. 31, 1869, and Jan. 4, 1870, *ibid.*, nos. 7844, 7850; Bermejo, *Historia de la interinidad y guerra civil*, vol. I, pp. 848–850; Bernhardi, *Aus dem Leben Theodor von Bernhardis*, vol. IX, pp. 236, 238, 243, 245; and Olózaga to Sagasta, July 1, 1870, in Conde de Romanones, *Amadeo de Saboya*, pp. 176–177.

of the government of the Regent for his personal welfare and for the prosperity of Prussia.[9]

The letter to Bismarck also begins with the statement that Prim, in his capacity as president of the council, had charged Salazar with a confidential mission to Prince Leopold of Hohenzollern. The minister of foreign affairs of the Regent, the letter continues, could have opened direct and official negotiations with the government of His Majesty, the king of Prussia, but had judged it more suitable and more useful, at the beginning, to use completely confidential channels in order not to stir up apprehensions which could have harmed the success of the projects, "the exclusive aim of which is to serve the interests of Spain without infringing on the rights of the other nations." Europe could never misapprehend the loyalty of the intentions of the Spanish government, yet it was necessary to take account of the hostile designs of political partisanship.

Spain wanted, Prim continued, to have a liberal monarchical government; she was eager for freedom from disturbance and for progress. The House of Bourbon had failed to achieve this, and if there was a fact in the long history of Spain worthy of the meditation of deep thinkers, it was the example of a dynasty which, in its blindness, had spared nothing to alienate the affection of one of the most generous peoples of the entire world. The reactionary party might conspire, but the Bourbon cause was destined to have in Spain the same fate which had befallen the Stuarts in England and the descendants of Louis XIV in France. The republican cause had suffered severe setbacks, and those districts of Cadiz and Jeres, which had begun by sending republican representatives to the Cortes, had just given large majorities to monarchists. To complete the task to which the Spanish government in concert with the people had set their hands, it was necessary to elect a sincerely

[9] Prim to King William, secret file; translation in Bonnin, no. 1.

constitutional king who could represent "tradition in so far as it is respectable, and progress in so far as it is legitimate." Salazar had been informed in detail of the plans and feelings of his government, and Bismarck could place full credence in all that he had to say about his mission.[10]

Prim's letter to Leopold [11] begins with a reference to Salazar's visit at Weinburg in the preceding September, and suggests that the delay in following up the subject had been caused by the internal situation, especially the need to meet the republican menace. Since that time, the government had gained strength and had been able to devote calm study to its problems. It had put into force a constitution which had been accepted by most of the great parties of the country. A king was needed to crown the edifice.

You, Sir, unite all of the qualities that we wish for, and I am proposing to your Royal Highness, in my capacity of President of the Council of Ministers of His Highness the Regent, the request that you deign to give a favorable reply to the confidential overtures that M. Salazar and Mazarredo will make to you.

A glorious era is open to Your Highness. It is not free from difficulties, but a prince of the Royal House of Prussia can easily surmount all the obstacles, sure in the support of a people illustrious for centuries of loyalty, greatness, and devotion.[12]

Salazar arrived at Düsseldorf on February 24 only to find

[10] The letter ends with a paragraph of platitudes about the cordial relations between Spain and Prussia, and a request that Bismarck present Salazar to the king in case the latter wanted to hear details from him. Prim to Bismarck, Madrid, Feb. 17, 1870, original and copy in secret file; copy, with a few mistaken readings, in Dittrich thesis, appendix 9; translation in Bonnin, no. 2.

[11] The Spanish draft of a letter from Prim to Leopold dated February 17, which Lord published from the Archives of the Ministry of Foreign Affairs at Madrid (*The Origins of the War of 1870*, appendix III), differs from versions actually sent; part of it is included in the letter to Bismarck.

[12] Prim to Leopold, Madrid, Feb. 17, 1870, copy in secret file and Dittrich thesis, appendix 8; translation in Bonnin, no. 3.

that Leopold had gone to Berlin a fortnight before.[13] He was, however, received by Karl Anton. This time, he explained, he had come not merely to sound out the feelings of the Hohenzollerns but with full powers from the Spanish government to negotiate. On the following day he traveled on to Berlin, where he arrived in time for an interview with Leopold that evening.

Karl Anton seems to have been impressed by Salazar's arguments and by the vision of a glorious destiny opened up to the House of Hohenzollern. His personal feelings, he said, were as in April and September 1869, against accepting the proposal. The affair was not, however, merely private business and as reasons of state might be on the other side, he must appeal to the king to decide whether the best interests of Prussia would be served by acceptance or rejection.[14] To his son Leopold, Karl Anton wrote that he thought it was his duty to place the decision in the hands of the king. "If he wants it for reasons of high politics and of state, it will be for us to make world history with him — if he does not want it, it would be folly for us to enter a situation in which we would have to dispense with Prussia's support and good will." He warned Leopold, above all, to keep cool and calm, to avoid haste and agitation, for the question would have to be considered objectively before proceeding to a subjective decision. "Inform me at once," he continued, "of the king's impressions. . . . The king will follow his first inspiration and reject it emphatically,[15] but with that nothing will really

[13] "Mittwoch, kamen die Erb-Hohenzollern. . . ." King William to his sister, Dowager Grandduchess Alexandrine of Mecklenburg, Berlin, Feb. 12, 1870 (the preceding Wednesday was Feb. 9), in *Kaiser Wilhelms I. Briefe an seine Schwester Alexandrine.* Fester, *Briefe,* vol. I, no. 108, says that according to Zingeler, "Leopold was in Berlin as early as Feb. 19" — perhaps a misreading of 9.

[14] Karl Anton to King William, Karl Anton to Bismarck, Feb. 25, 1870, secret file; Bonnin, nos. 4, 5.

[15] "verwerfen — und weit wegwerfen."

be accomplished — the decision must be based on rational and mature consideration, not on emotion." The affair must not appear to be in any way one of Leopold's ambitions. "If the king rejects it for reasons of state — good — you will refuse categorically, but if he wants to give it further consideration, then he should summon me to Berlin. The crown prince must have his opinion listened to, for the future belongs to him. A 'family' decision must be reached.[16] Bismarck, too, must be consulted." [17]

When Salazar arrived in Berlin on the evening of February 25, he was received by Leopold and, in the prince's words: "calmly and objectively, we, or rather he, discussed the whole question." Leopold again disclaimed any personal ambition and made it clear that his own inclination was against accepting the Spanish crown. He could, however, appreciate reasons which would subordinate his personal wishes to considerations of high policy and he would submit to the will of the king as head of the family.[18]

The next morning at about 11:30 Leopold went to see Keudell to ask him to arrange an appointment for Salazar with Bismarck. Keudell also agreed either to have Bismarck come to visit Leopold or to let him know his opinion of the problem.[19] On that day there was neither visit nor word from Bismarck, but on the next afternoon a letter of excuse came from Keudell. The chancellor had been unable to come on account of illness, a severe cold and threat of erysipelas. His

---

[16] "Es sollte ein sogenannter Familiebeschluss darüber gefasst werden."

[17] Karl Anton to Leopold, copy, no date but marked "präs. Berlin, 26 Februar 1870," Dittrich thesis, appendix 10. In his reply on February 26, Leopold expresses thanks for the letter "aus dem ich mit Beruhigung sehe, dass ich mit Deiner Gefühlsanschauung mich nicht im Widerspruch befinde. . . . In diesem Sinne habe ich dem Herrn Salazar auch gestern abend geantwortet" (*ibid.*, appendix 11).

[18] Leopold to Karl Anton, Berlin, Feb. 26, 1870, Dittrich thesis, appendix 11.

[19] Dittrich thesis, appendix 11.

health had improved enough overnight so that he had received Salazar that noon (February 27) and hoped to make a short report to the king.[20]

On March 1 Leopold reported to his father that the affair was not making as rapid progress as Salazar wished.

The king has reached no decision and has had no extensive conversation with me about it. Bismarck has made a report to him, but apparently only in general terms as you will see from Keudell's letter to me. The Reichstag and South German conditions seem to be seriously preoccupying the government at the moment. I had a conversation with Count Bismarck yesterday evening during the ball given by Loftus.[21] On his part it was largely a resumé of the points of view contained in your letters to His Majesty and to the count and the reasons for acceptance derived from his conversation with Don Salazar. I did not find any new aspects in it. The count emphasized how important it was for the development of European political relations that a monarchy should be founded in Spain and not a republic; that it would add to the luster of the whole house if a Hohenzollern reigned in Spain. He added that I was at the best and most robust age to undertake such a fine task; that if I refused, a Bavarian prince might be elected who, then, influenced by Rome, would play into the hands of the ultramontanes, something to be seriously regretted. Of possible dangers, he would not speak to a member of the Hohenzollern family. . . . The king would be reluctant to put any pressure on me and therefore he [Bismarck] wishes that you would come here as soon as possible. He will remind the king of it again today, even though the latter is unusually occupied with important and serious business.[22]

[20] Keudell to Leopold, Berlin, Feb. 27, 1870, Dittrich thesis, appendix 16. Horst Kohl, *Bismarck-Regesten*, does not list "Vortrag beim Könige" for February 27, a Sunday, but does for February 26 and 28. I have found no other evidence that Bismarck actually reported to the king on February 27; it may have been an informal meeting or it may not have occurred until the 28th.

[21] Kohl, *Bismarck-Regesten*, does not mention Bismarck's presence at the ball given by the British ambassador on the 28th; it is established by Leopold to Karl Anton, March 1, 1870, Dittrich thesis, appendix 14.

[22] Leopold to Karl Anton, March 1, 1870, Dittrich thesis, appendix 14. A note from Salazar to Bismarck dated March 2 includes the state-

As Karl Anton anticipated, King William was unpleasantly surprised by the news. It was, as he wrote Bismarck in a well-known letter, like a bolt of lightning from a clear sky.[23] He had suspected nothing and had recently joked with Leopold about the earlier mention of his name for the Spanish crown, and both of them had rejected the idea in the same spirit. As Bismarck had received additional details from Karl Anton, they must confer about it, although he was dead against the affair.

He invited Leopold to tea "en famille" on the 26th. The latter did not venture to take any initiative, but as he was leaving, King William said that he had received Karl Anton's letter, "clasped his hands together," and asked if he had known about it long. Leopold answered that except for a short interview with Salazar in the fall, he had not known a single word about it and that he himself had a strong aversion to it.[24]

Salazar presented Prim's letter to Bismarck at noon on February 27, but no record of their conversation has come to light.[25] If we may trust his recollections, Keudell happened to come in soon afterwards to make a report. When he had finished, Bismarck asked him to see to it that no one else

ment that Leopold had told him "yesterday" that his father was expected in Berlin "tomorrow, Friday." According to Fester, *Briefe*, vol. I, no. 108, Karl Anton arrived in Berlin on March 5 and Bismarck was among those who received him at the station. An undated note from Salazar to Bismarck says that Leopold has just informed him that his father has not yet arrived. This is placed in the secret file between items dated March 9 and 10. It must be of earlier date, because on March 6 Salazar wrote to Bismarck that he had come to take leave of him at quarter to five, "after a long conference with the two Hohenzollern Princes." The undated note probably should be dated March 3, the day on which Leopold had told Salazar his father was expected.

[23] King William to Bismarck, Feb. 26, 1870, *Anhang zu den Gedanken und Erinnerungen*, vol. I, p. 207; Fester, *Briefe*, vol. I, no. 106.

[24] Leopold to Karl Anton, Feb. 26, Feb. 27, 1870, Dittrich thesis, appendices 11, 13.

[25] Keudell to Leopold (Sunday), Feb. 27, 1870, Dittrich thesis, appendix 16. The date usually given, February 26, cannot stand against Keudell's specific statement.

was admitted; he had just received a letter from Marshal Prim about the election of a king for Spain, and he needed quiet to think the matter through.[26] The fruits of Bismarck's meditations were the memorandum which he dictated to Keudell as the basis for an "unofficial" report to the king.[27]

As might be expected in a memorandum intended to persuade the king, Bismarck found nothing but advantage in accepting the Spanish offer and nothing but disadvantage in rejecting it.[28]

The first of the advantages that he stressed was the improvement of relations with Spain. The acceptance of the Spanish crown by a prince of His Majesty's exalted house would strengthen the sympathy that already existed between the two nations, "which have no conflicting interests because they are not contiguous." For Germany, it was desirable to

[26] Robert von Keudell, *Fürst und Fürstin Bismarck. Erinnerungen aus den Jahren 1846 bis 1872*, p. 430. Keudell gives the date as before the end of February. He gives no hint that he had arranged the meeting and leaves the impression that neither he nor Bismarck had any earlier knowledge of Salazar's mission. Actually, Leopold had told Keudell something about it (see Leopold to Karl Anton, Feb. 26, 1870, Dittrich thesis, appendix 11), and it must be presumed that Bismarck had already received Karl Anton's letter of February 25 (Fester, *Briefe*, vol. I, no. 104; original in secret file) and King William's of February 26 (see p. 56 above).

[27] Keudell, p. 430. His words, "ausser amtlichen Berichte," reflect Bismarck's insistence that the Prussian government was not involved.

[28] The substance of most of this memorandum was first published by Keudell in *Fürst und Fürstin Bismarck*, pp. 430–433. This may be the first draft as dictated by Bismarck but it is not certain. A draft, closer to the final version, with Bismarck's autograph corrections is in the secret file but not in Bonnin. The full text of the final version was published from the crown prince's copy by Eduard von Wertheimer in "Kronprinz Friedrich Wilhelm und die spanische Hohenzollern Thronkandidatur," *Preussische Jahrbücher*, vol. CCV, pp. 273ff., and reprinted in *G.W.*, vol. VIb, no. 1521. Friedrich Thimme, in his introductory note to the document, infers that the crown prince loaned it to Prince Leopold before March 12. This seems impossible, for it was on March 14 that Frederick William asked for a copy (to Bismarck, March 14, 1870, secret file; Bonnin, no. 13), and Bismarck, with the king's permission, instructed Keudell to make the copy. The secret file contains a fair copy of the memorandum with King William's marginal comments; translation in Bonnin, no. 9.

have on the other side of France a country on whose sympathies she could depend and with whose feelings France would have to reckon. In a war between France and Germany, if conditions should prevail as they had been under Queen Isabella, "when an alliance of the Latin-Catholic Powers was in prospect," France could dispose of from one to two army corps which could not be used if Spain had a government friendly to Germany. In the former situation, additional French troops could be freed for service in the war by Spanish replacements at Rome; in the latter, France would have to maintain at least one army corps on the Spanish border.[29] The acceptance of the Spanish crown, Bismarck went on to argue, would therefore diminish rather than increase the danger of war, for the love of peace in France would always wax or wane in proportion to her estimate of the hazards involved in war with Germany. "In the long run, we must expect the preservation of peace, not from the good will of France, but from her impression of the strength of our position." In addition — though this can hardly have been a major factor in Bismarck's calculations — the national welfare of Spain would thrive under Hohenzollern rule and the commerce of Germany with Spain increase.

The second advantage of acceptance would be the effect on Germany of the increased prestige of the dynasty. It was in the political interest of Germany to have the House of Hohenzollern win the prestige and the position in the world for which the only precedents were those of the House of Habsburg at the time of Charles V.

Refusal of the proffered crown would, it might be anticipated, have unwelcome consequences. It would, in the first place, outrage the feelings of the Spaniards if a crown which

---

[29] Moltke's estimate of the numbers that would be held back is lower. See his reckoning in *Moltkes militärische Korrepondenz. Aus den Dienstschriften des Krieges 1870/71*, Erste Abtheilung, p. 120.

had always enjoyed a high rank in history should be rejected and if that nation of sixteen million people, which asked to be rescued from anarchy, were left to sink into it by the refusal to give them the king of their choice. In the next place, in case of rejection, the Spaniards would probably turn first of all to Bavaria. If the line of Prince Adalbert or the ducal line accepted the offer, the new dynasty in Spain would seek its support in France and in Rome. It would maintain contact with the antinational elements in Germany and would offer them a point of support, distant, perhaps, but sure. Under Carlist rule, Spain would move in the same direction of dependence on Rome, France, and Austria, while favoring ultramontane reaction at home. She would, then, be found regularly in the ranks of the opponents of Germany. If neither the Bavarian nor the Carlist candidates succeeded in winning the throne, Spain would probably fall to the republicans. The effects of this would be felt in Italy and France. The increased danger from the republican movement might even push the Emperor Napoleon to break the peace.

For all this: the ill-humor in Spain and the dangers with which a Spanish republic would menace Europe, public opinion in Germany — for the present transactions could hardly remain secret forever — would hold responsible those from whom the rejection of the Spanish crown came. Acceptance, on the other hand, would initiate an evolution of the Spanish problem that would be free from risk. It would be of great value to France to know that the Orleanist candidacy and the republic in Spain were definitely averted. The election of the hereditary prince of Hohenzollern by the Cortes was certain; according to information received, it would be by a majority of more than three fourths of all the votes. There would be no infringement of the legitimate rights of other claimants: the Bourbon dynasty had been imposed on Spain at the beginning of the eighteenth century by foreign arms, and since 1808, a

series of revolutions and acts of violence had cast doubt on
every claim to the throne. Yet in all these revolutions, the
idea of any outrage against the person of the rulers had never
appeared nor any threats against them been uttered. Any danger to the person of the king was inconceivable. The troops
of the present Spanish army had shown extraordinary devotion to the principle of monarchy and had been valiant in com-
batting republican risings in the cities. They would provide
reliable support for the future monarch "whose happy task it
will be to develop the rich resources of the country by his
benevolent regime."

For all these reasons, positive and negative, Bismarck urged
the king not to let the Spanish crown be refused, unless the
repugnance of Prince Leopold was insuperable. He himself,
he concluded, was not willing to accept before history and
public opinion the responsibility for that refusal.

What mental reservations Bismarck may have had when he
drew up this memorandum for the king can never be surely
known. His policy in adopting the Hohenzollern candidacy
has been interpreted over a wide range from an innocent attempt to supply Spain with a king who would be more acceptable to Napoleon III than the Duke of Montpensier or a republic, an attempt from which Bismarck could not have anticipated danger of war, to the deliberate intention to provoke
a declaration of war from France. The former position is
clearly untenable. The latter in its extreme form seems improbable; it was not characteristic of Bismarck to tie his hands
by adopting a policy that could have only one outcome. That
there were risks in letting a prince of the Hohenzollern family
accept the crown of Spain could not have escaped his attention: Benedetti had made it sufficiently clear that France did
not like it and Bismarck himself had thought of the Spanish
problem as a means by which France could be brought to
threaten or even attack Germany. That France would work

against the candidacy was an ever-present fear of Prim, Salazar, and other Spanish leaders and of Karl Anton and other Germans who were in the secret. The extent of this opposition was the uncertain factor and in the memorandum as well as in oral discussion, Bismarck played down the danger of war.

King William's doubts about the acceptance of the Spanish crown by Prince Leopold were not removed by Bismarck's memorandum of March 9.[30] He persisted in his resolution to give his approval only if the prince on his own volition asked for it. He did, however, accede to Bismarck's proposal that a few others be initiated into the secret and that His Majesty, in the presence of Crown Prince Frederick William and Karl Anton, prince of Hohenzollern, listen to the counsel of "these judicious and faithful servants." Albrecht von Roon, Helmuth von Moltke, Rudolf Delbrück, and at the king's suggestion, Werner Schleinitz and Karl Hermann von Thile, were invited to a small stag dinner [31] given in the apartment of the prince of Hohenzollern in the royal palace so that after the dinner they would discuss the question that had come up: "the acceptance of the Spanish crown by the hereditary prince of Hohenzollern." [32]

[30] See his marginal notes, secret file; Bonnin, no. 9.

[31] The invitation, dated March 15, was published by Gustav von Diest, *Aus dem Leben eines Glücklichen*, pp. 546–547; reprinted in Fester, *Briefe*, vol. I, no. 110. See also King William to Bismarck, March 15, 1870, secret file; Bonnin, no. 15. The invitation included the information: "Dass Fürst und Erbprinz grosse Abneigung zeigen, diese Krone anzunehmen, der Ministerpräsident aber in einem Memoir sich für Annahme ausgesprochen hat, ich aber bei meiner Abneigung auch gegen die Annahme [mich] aussprach, so will ich nicht in einer so wichtigen Frage entscheiden, ehe ich die Ansicht der zum Diner eingeladenen Staatsmänner gehört habe."

[32] In the first of a series of cryptic messages, Bismarck informed Salazar: "Les banquiers intéressés vont se réunir ce soir pour discuter l'emprunt en ma présence. Je vous informerai du résultat. Erquelines." The text is in Fester, *Briefe*, vol. I, no. 111, with incorrect citation, from H. Hesselbarth, *Drei psychologische Fragen zur Spanischen Thronkandidatur Leopolds von Hohenzollern*, p. 28. The draft in the secret file is in pencil, in Bismarck's hand. It was addressed to Canitz with in-

The party moved after dinner into one of the other rooms. The king reminded the guests that he had called them together for a confidential discussion but that no decision was to be adopted until later. He was, he said, fully convinced of the importance and bearing of the matter before them but, at the same time, he could not overlook the great doubts which stood in the way of accepting the offered crown. Conditions in Spain were still too unsettled and too little was known about the attitudes of the foreign powers to justify exposing a member of his dynasty to such an uncertain future. He appreciated completely the political arguments in favor of acceptance, but these alone did not outweigh the other serious considerations. He was opening the discussion and wished to hear the views of the men whom he had called together for this conference and who enjoyed his full confidence. He then directed Bismarck to report on the way in which the problem had arisen and to read to the company the relevant documents.

After a few introductory remarks Bismarck read the letters from Prim to King William, Prince Leopold, and himself; those from Karl Anton to King William and himself; Leopold's memorandum dated March 2, and his own dated March 9.

After Bismarck's brief conclusion, the crown prince took up the word. He too, according to Karl Anton's notes, expressed his complete appreciation of the chancellor's political analysis, but he found other and very substantial grounds for not accepting, such as the existence of opposing and in their way, justified claims on the part of legitimate pretenders to the throne, the uncertainty about the balance of votes in the Cortes, and the uncertainty about the sentiments and attitudes of the Great Powers. The fact that the Spanish proposal

---

structions: "Theilen Sie Folgendes an Anastasio Alonzo, 34 Hortaleza in unauffälliger Weise mit:"; at the end Bucher noted in ink, "chiffriert mit chiff. no. 265 and 1189. Zur Station 15 März 12:45 Mittags." Text from secret file; Bonnin, no. 18.

put so much emphasis on the choice of a Catholic Hohenzollern was itself such adequate satisfaction to Prussian pride that
acceptance was not an imperious necessity. The separation of
a flourishing branch of the royal house for the sake of an
uncertain future was a serious act to be decided not alone by
the light of the reason but also of the heart. The former might
be in favor of acceptance, the latter was struggling against it.
According to his own memorandum, the crown prince pointed
out that the strengthening of the ties between Prussia and
Spain, which Bismarck had emphasized, would depend on the
success to be achieved by the new king and on the influences
which Prussia would have to be in position to exercise in
Spain, and he was skeptical about the suggested advantages for
Prussian commerce. For the interests of Prussia, he admitted
only two solid benefits from the acceptance of the crown: the
advantage in case of a war between Prussia and France, and
the elimination of Bavarian and Carlist candidates. These benefits, however, depended on the assumption that the ground was
prepared for the establishment of a firm monarchical regime
in Spain. From the standpoint of Prussian interests, he concluded, it might be desirable to accept the candidacy if Prince
Leopold had the assurance to face the difficulties and sacri-
fices of the position.

Schleinitz, as a former minister of foreign affairs, was reluctant to express an opinion about the political issues involved. As minister of the royal household, called upon to
safeguard the dynastic interests of the crown, he could see
that the adoption of the project would give, on the one hand,
satisfaction to Prussian and to German sentiments, but, on the
other, possible dangerous eventualities. He wanted more certainty that the prince could count on a reliable and firm party
for his election and the assurance that the Spanish constitution
would make it possible for him to carry out under it a "sen-
sible and humane" reign. He was not against the acceptance of

a "great and glorious" mission, but he insisted that Prince Leopold must be left to make his own decision.

The other guests were unanimous in favor of acceptance, although each supported his conclusions in accordance with his background and special interests. Roon, the minister of war, urged that acceptance would provide a guarantee that the conservative interest would be secured and that "the European danger" of a Spanish republic would be averted. A Hohenzollern on the Spanish throne would, to be sure, have to feel and act as a Spaniard, yet he could throw his Prussian-Hohenzollern sympathies into the balance. The army would welcome him, for it yearned for a virile king; if up to this time it had been tossed in the maelstrom of revolution, it was because it had lacked direction, and deprived of the directives of the monarch, had been given into the hands of the generals.

Moltke, chief of the general staff, agreed. He too stressed the special characteristics of the army and the preference for a German dynasty in Spain. The German name was of good repute among this proud people, and the greatest period of Spanish power and glory was when the Habsburg dynasty reigned in its prime. The Spanish crown was a worthy object of ambition, and he was wholeheartedly in favor of acceptance in the interest of the country, of the monarchical principle, and of the dynasty.

Delbrück, who had traveled much in Spain, was optimistic about the future. He saw in the establishment of a Hohenzollern dynasty in Spain the guarantee of significant developments in trade and commerce with auspicious repercussions on Germany as a whole. Since the problem had now been illuminated from the standpoints of dynastic, political, military, and commercial interests, Thile stressed the national. From his knowledge of the Spanish language, literature, and national psychology, he contrasted the Spaniard's hatred for France with his affection for Germans. The contrast between

Bourbon and Habsburg rule was vivid in Spanish minds, and Charles V lived in their fancy in an aureole of almost poetic glory.[33]

The unanimous opinions of the "most experienced and weightiest" advisers of the crown in favor of accepting the Spanish throne, and even more the shift in the attitude of the crown prince,[34] made a deep impression on the two Hohenzollern princes. It became difficult for Leopold to oppose to the important reasons they brought forward, those emotional ones which had hitherto been decisive for him. On the evening of the sixteenth, father and son visited the king. Leopold was ready to make "the sacrifice," but he remained firm in his determination not to do so except at William's express command. This the king refused, and continued to refuse.[35]

In order to demonstrate, however, that there was no objection in Berlin to the election of a Hohenzollern prince, Karl Anton proposed to the king that they adopt Bismarck's suggestion that Prince Frederick, the youngest son, be put forward in place of his older brother. King William agreed to this but added that it could not, of course, be done without the knowledge and consent of the candidate. As he was expected in Berlin in a fortnight, they should await his arrival.

Bismarck learned of the king's decision on the next morning, March 17. He wrote at once to Karl Anton, enclosing the king's letter for his information, and urging that Fred-

[33] Cf. Karl Anton's notes, Dittrich thesis, appendix 22; translation in Bonnin, pp. 291–294; Wertheimer, *Preussische Jahrbücher*, vol. CCV, pp. 273–307.

[34] "Wir suchten seit gestern einen gewichtigen Grund mehr, nicht abzulehnen," the crown prince wrote in his diary for March 16, 1870. Wertheimer, *Preussische Jahrbücher*, vol. CCV, p. 286.

[35] Leopold's memorandum, March 17, 1870, Dittrich thesis, appendix 24 (translation in Bonnin, p. 294); King William to Bismarck, March 17, 1870, secret file, Bonnin, no. 26; Bismarck to Karl Anton, March 17, 1870, Dittrich thesis, appendix 25, secret file, and Bonnin, no. 27. In King William's letter, paragraph 2, Bonnin has read "castles" (Burgen) for "eyes" (Augen).

erick be recalled from his travels. "If as I venture to hope, Your Royal Highness is disposed to advance the affair in the interests of the country and of our dynasty, it is urgently necessary that the prince be summoned. I fear that the secret and with it the prevention of foreign intrigues cannot be maintained much longer." [36] He also telegraphed to Salazar in the arranged code that at the conference of the bankers, the two great houses maintained their opposition, but had consented that the loan would be made tomorrow if their associate, who was abroad, would accept the share allotted to him.[37]

Karl Anton's memorandum pointed out that Prince Frederick was not seeking the crown and did not feel that his personal inclinations and training made him equal to the demands of this great task. He would, however, yield to the clearly expressed will of the king and was not hindered by any ties of family relationship [38] or descent from subordinating his personal convenience to such a great historic mission. Karl Anton's language suggests that he was beginning to find the opportunity more tempting for his family. He agreed with Bismarck that it was time to reach a definite decision, and he proposed an interview with the king in which he should participate both as representative of his son and for himself.[39] In a letter to the crown prince he shifts his ground a little

[36] Bismarck to Karl Anton, March 17, 1870, secret file.

[37] In an attempt to avoid the risk of garbling in France, the message was telegraphed to Bernstorff, the ambassador in London, to be transmitted as directly as possible to Canitz in Madrid. Bernstorff acknowledged receipt on March 18 and added that the direct line did not go to Madrid. The body of the message was written by Bismarck in pencil: "1189. Remettez ce qui suit à Anastasio Alonzo, 34 Hortaleza. A la conference des banquiers les deux grandes maisons ont maintenu leur opposition, mais en consentant que l'emprunt se fasse demain, si leur compagnon en voyage accepte la part pour laquelle il est coté. [Sgd.] Erquelines. Chiff. u — zur Station 17 März, Uhr." Secret file; Bonnin, no. 21.

[38] A reference to the fact that one of the reasons given by Leopold for not accepting the offer was his marriage to a Portuguese princess. See Leopold's memorandum of March 2, 1870, secret file; Bonnin, pp. 66–67.

[39] Karl Anton to Bismarck, April 1, 1870, original in secret file; Bon-

more when he writes that it would be enough if the king would say that acceptance of the throne was in the interest of the Prussian state; [40] it would make it possible for Karl Anton to exert his paternal authority.[41] Even this was more than the king would do.[42]

Just before his departure from Berlin, on April 4, Karl Anton had a conference with King William and Bismarck. The latter repeated with emphasis that acceptance was a political necessity, but the king could not be induced to change his opinion to the contrary. Karl Anton, on the other hand, was now willing to put off the final decision. Before coming to a conclusion, he wanted assurance about three points: that there would be a majority of from two thirds to three quarters of the votes in the Cortes; that there was no danger of state bankruptcy; and that the projected anticlerical laws would be passed in time so that the Catholic prince of Hohenzollern would not have to share the odium for them or run the risk of excommunication. It was agreed that Councillor of Legation Lothar Bucher should go to Madrid with Bismarck's answer to Marshal Prim's letter of February 17, and to seek a clear answer to the three questions. An experienced general staff officer, to be selected by Moltke, would go to study the condition of the Spanish army. The question was thus adjourned but not abandoned.[43]

---

nin, no. 64; copy from Sigmaringen archives in Dittrich thesis, appendix 28. Cf. Karl Anton to Princess Marie of Flanders, March 30, 1870, Fester, *Briefe*, vol. I, no. 130.

[40] Wertheimer is mistaken in interpreting Karl Anton's letter as a request to the crown prince that he persuade the king to command the acceptance. *Preussische Jahrbücher*, vol. CCV, p. 286.

[41] Karl Anton to Crown Prince Frederick William, April 2, 1870, Dittrich thesis, appendix 29.

[42] Karl Anton to Bismarck, April 4, 1870, secret file; Bonnin, no. 68; undated copy from Sigmaringen archives in Dittrich thesis, appendix 30; memorandum of Karl Anton, Dessau, April 5, 1870, Dittrich thesis, appendix 31.

[43] King William to Bismarck, April 3, 1870; Crown Prince Frederick William to Bismarck, April 3, April 4; Karl Anton to Bismarck, April 4; Bismarck to Frederick William, April 4; secret file; Bonnin, nos. 66, 67,

On the following day, April 5, a telegram was sent to Salazar to let him know that an envoy bringing the answer would arrive in Madrid early the following week.[44] Bucher left Berlin (before Bismarck's letter was ready) on the evening of April 9 and stopped at Düsseldorf for a conference with Karl Anton on the following day. They talked over the three points about which Bucher was to seek information.[45] Bucher gained the impression that Karl Anton had been won over and already in his mind saw his son as king of Spain. "In accordance with Your Excellency's instructions," he would exploit the result of this conference at Madrid.[46]

As soon as Bucher arrived at Madrid, on April 13, he went to see Salazar and although he "had not taken off his clothes for five days and four nights and was feverish," they conferred until midnight.[47]

Early the next morning Bucher was introduced by Salazar to Prim, who received him graciously in spite of his disappointment that Bismarck's answer to his letter of February 17 had not yet arrived. Prim had evidently been briefed by Salazar on his talk with Bucher. He did not refer specifically to the three points, but his comments, though less detailed than those of Salazar, were essentially the same and completely reassuring. Both of the Spaniards insisted on the importance of a quick decision. As Salazar wrote to Bismarck, the marshal was under pressure from every side. "They accuse him of

---

69, 68, 70. The last letter is also in *G.W.*, vol. VIb, no. 1548. Memorandum of Karl Anton, Dessau, April 5, Dittrich thesis, appendix 31.

[44] The message — "Une entrevue avec M. Gama aura lieu un des premiers jours de la semaine prochaine" — has given rise to much conjecture. See Fester, *Neue Beiträge*, pp. 155–156. Its meaning is established from the letter of Salazar to Keudell, March 26, 1870: "c'est-à-dire que l'emissaire porteur des réponses arrivera à Madrid tel jour à peu près" (secret file; Bonnin, no. 54).

[45] See p. 67 above.

[46] Bucher to Bismarck, April 10, 1870, secret file; Bonnin, no. 78.

[47] Bucher to Bismarck, April 14, April 20, 1870, secret file; Bonnin, no. 82.

having no plan and no policy, of keeping the country in a provisional state of affairs which is paralyzing commerce and industry, of doing nothing to crown the constitutional structure. As he cannot tell anyone what is actually going on, his position and that of the Regent [Serrano] are becoming untenable and they are suspected of intentionally prolonging the interim. If those who accuse them only knew the secret anguish that I have witnessed!!!" Since the Cortes was due to meet again on April 19, they must receive a telegram of acceptance on that day or the next. The two marshals, Serrano and Prim, had instructed Salazar to let Bismarck know that the new dynasty would be established on a firmer foundation by Leopold than by his brother. The question of the latter's marriage would create embarrassing difficulties. Leopold would provide the solution for a crowd of very important problems: carrying on the dynasty, family respectability and age, the good will of the Portuguese, and so on. Delay in a definite decision could compromise everything. The French ambassador, Mercier, had begun to suspect something, and although Serrano had indignantly declared that the open opposition of Napoleon would be much more helpful than harmful to the enterprise, "it would be more prudent to have the candidate elected by the majority of the Cortes in secret session without advance warning." Once the vote had been won, it would be possible to give a satisfactory explanation to France, for there were at stake the interests of Spain and not those of Prussia. The Spaniards could not be reproached for risking the displeasure of France after they had tried in vain to find a king in Lisbon and Florence.[48]

Major von Versen, carrying Bismarck's letter, arrived in Madrid on April 18 and was introduced to Prim by Salazar

---

[48] Bucher to Bismarck, April 14, April 20, 1870; Salazar to Karl Anton, April 14, 1870; Salazar to Bismarck, April 14, 1870; secret file; Bonnin, nos. 82, 83 (with incorrect date "17 April"), 84.

and Bucher on the following day. The letter was a long apology for the delays. Prim, Bismarck wrote, had no doubt already learned from Salazar that he had received the overtures with sympathetic attention, resulting from the harmony of his personal convictions with the attitude of public opinion in Germany. He had associated himself with Prim's plans loyally and without hesitation, but he had found the terrain untilled.[49] Prince Frederick was traveling incognito in Italy, and it was not until he arrived in Paris that he could be recalled to Berlin.

In reigning families, decisions of great importance are not made more easily than by us ordinary mortals. We must expect to meet delays and doubts, especially when it is a question of bringing a young prince to accept the responsibility of an historic mission which up to now has been foreign to his thoughts, and whose difficulties are perhaps exaggerated by the anxiety inspired in his parents' minds by the perspective of separation from him for life and of an uncertain future. The prince is, it is true, of age, but morally he is bound to respect the decision of his parents, in whom up to now I have been unable to allay all the apprehensions and to remove all the scruples which arise from a mother's heart rather than from political reasoning.

He would have liked to answer Prim's letter with the announcement that the success of their plan was assured. He was convinced, he went on, that with a little patience they would see the moment arrive. It was necessary to let Prim know the state of affairs and, especially, the more important questions in the minds of the persons concerned. He had instructed Bucher, who was thoroughly acquainted with his thoughts, to explain all this with the utmost frankness, but he had been unable to complete the letter in time for Bucher to deliver it because of a violent attack of rheumatism which made writing at first impossible and even now difficult.[50]

[49] If Bismarck had been active in bringing up the candidacy in 1869, could he have written this to Prim?

[50] Bismarck to Prim, draft, Berlin, April 11, 1870, secret file; Bonnin, no. 79. See Appendix B below.

In a second long conversation with Bucher on April 20, Prim renewed in detail his assurances about the situation in Spain and again stressed the importance of a quick decision. "We are sure of a majority of 2/3, but every additional day threatens some loss. Many deputies are going home to take care of their own business. By May 20 the heat will be great, and everything must be completed by that time, the official acceptance received, and the constitutional provisions for founding the new dynasty passed." It was urgent, out of consideration for Prim's friends in the Cortes and to avoid foreign interference. "Our press," Prim said, "is to some extent susceptible to influences even from outside; there are some papers which love gold even if it comes from France." [51]

Karl Anton was disturbed by the references in Salazar's letter and in other messages from Madrid which implied that Leopold might yet accept the offer. "He has definitely refused," he wrote to Bismarck, "because of his dislike of the Iberian union and his concern for the succession of Hohenzollern-Sigmaringen. The only possibility is Frederick." He warned against precipitate action, but said that he would come to Berlin if needed for further discussion.[52] In general, however, the reports from Spain in answer to the three questions about the Cortes majority, the finances, and especially the church, satisfied him.[53]

On April 21 Karl Anton arrived again in Berlin. He told

[51] Bucher to Bismarck, April 20, 1870, secret file; Bonnin, no. 99.

[52] To Bismarck, Düsseldorf, April 17, 1870, Dittrich thesis, appendix 34; original, with date April 17, in secret file; Bonnin, no. 91. The two marshals had asked for photographs of Prince and Princess Leopold. Salazar to Karl Anton, April 14, 1870, postscript, copy in secret file; Bonnin, no. 83, with incorrect date. Karl Anton did not comment in his letter to Bismarck on the preceding lines of the postscript, but they can hardly have been reassuring: "Le bombe qui va éclater ici quand on saura le résultat, aura une grande influence pour déterminer le nombre de voix du plébiscite français." Salazar's letter of the same date to Bismarck, which was enclosed with the one to Karl Anton, gave detailed reasons for preferring Leopold over Frederick. Secret file; Bonin, no. 84.

[53] Karl Anton to Bismarck, April 17, 1870, Dittrich thesis, appendix 34; secret file; Bonnin, no. 91.

the king "frankly and emphatically" that Frederick was averse to accepting the Spanish crown, and later in the day the prince confirmed this in person. William, too, maintained his position. He refused to issue an order or even to express a wish. After a final meeting with the king on the afternoon of April 22, in which they recapitulated the negotiations, Karl Anton noted that the affair must be considered closed and, that evening, he started on the return journey to Düsseldorf.[54]

Bismarck was no longer in Berlin. He had been since April 14 at Varzin, where he had gone to spend the Easter holidays. He had intended to remain about five days but had suffered an attack of jaundice, and it was not until early in the second week of May that he began to think of returning to the capital and not until May 21 that he actually did so.[55]

In Bismarck's absence, Thile carried on the secret correspondence with Madrid. Canitz, on April 19, had transmitted the message from Salazar for Bismarck that Prim had received his letter and had renewed the statements made to Bucher on the present state of affairs and the need to avoid foreign complications and to hold the needed votes.[56] Thile answered on the following day that Bismarck was seriously ill at Varzin and unable to deal with business. "The fourth article of the loan [Leopold] cannot, unfortunately be accepted. The sixth [Frederick] will be discussed today. Everything will be done to speed up a final decision." [57] This was followed on April 22 by the message that the fourth article of the loan contract had been definitely eliminated and that equally insurmountable obstacles stood in the way of the sixth. "Unfortunately, therefore, the loan is completely impossible. This result of such a

[54] Karl Anton's memoranda, April 21, 22, 1870, Dittrich thesis, appendices 35, 36.
[55] See tg., Bismarck to Thile, Varzin, April 18, 1870, secret file; Bonnin, no. 88; and p. 80 below.
[56] Secret file; Bonnin, no. 94.
[57] Secret file; Bonnin, no. 98.

long negotiation is deeply regretted. Tell Bucher to return to Berlin." [58] In his conference with Thile, Karl Anton had insisted on the necessity of quick action, because France seemed to have gotten wind of the affair and it was important to document the fact that the rejection was not on the ground of any regard for French antipathy to it but purely from personal reasons of the eventual candidate for the throne.[59]

When the telegram of rejection was received at Madrid, Salazar in great disappointment asked Bucher if he could see any way out. "I answered," Bucher reported to Bismarck, "that if, for the time being, the telegram was regarded as *non avenu*, and if Marshal Prim would expedite his letter to Your Excellency, Your Excellency might find it possible to secure reconsideration of the project." Salazar eagerly grasped at the straw and accepted the responsibility for withholding the telegram. If it should turn out that there was no further hope, he asked to be informed by a telegram: "On regrette infiniment que l'emprunt ne puisse se faire." [60]

Prim's letter, dated April 24, 1870,[61] was handed to Bucher on the morning of that day. It expressed his understanding of the reasons Bismarck had given for the delay, but continued to urge that the situation in Spain did not permit him to wait very much longer. "I have expressed in it," he told Bucher,

my wish to have Count Bismarck's answer in the first fortnight of May. In the letter I felt that I must use this indefinite phrase;

[58] Thile to Canitz, April 20, 1870, secret file; Bonnin, no. 100.

[59] Karl Anton's memoranda, April 21, 22, 1870, Dittrich thesis, appendices 35, 36.

[60] Bucher did not believe that Salazar kept Prim from *actual* knowledge of the message. Bucher told Salazar that if on April 13 and 14 the Spaniards had shown the patience that was now necessary, the matter would have taken a calmer and more promising course. Bucher to Bismarck, April 24, 1870, secret file; Bonnin, no. 103.

[61] Prim to Bismarck, autograph, April 24, 1870, original in secret file; Bonnin, no. 102; copy from Sigmaringen archives in Dittrich thesis, appendix 40.

verbally I add that I can wait for an answer only ten or twelve days reckoned from the day of your arrival, that is, only until the seventh or ninth; after that my position will be untenable. Tell them in Berlin that if one wants to found a dynasty, one must run a little risk.[62] Anyway, you can bear witness to the fact that the country is quiet. A few shots are fired here and there in the mountains, but even that would come to an end as soon as we had a king. He will find here people who know how to maintain order.[63]

Bucher presented an account of his mission to King William on April 30, and Abeken took up the "Spanish affair" with him on May 3. Again the answer was a firm "no." Salazar was informed that the loan could not be made. The young man had conscientiously considered his qualifications for the "noble and arduous" task and did not feel that he could undertake the responsibility which it would impose.[64]

When the discouraging message was received from Berlin, Fernandez de los Rios and Salustiana de Olózaga, the Spanish ambassadors at Lisbon and Paris, were called to Madrid. The former was instructed to return to his post and to try again to win the consent of Ferdinand; the latter, to secure the support of Napoleon for the Portuguese candidacy. Ferdinand received Fernandez de los Rios on May 13, listened to his presentation of Spain's urgent need for a king, and with reluctance agreed to think it over. Two days later, he wrote to the Spanish envoy that he was unwilling to reverse his earlier decision to refuse. Adolph Ollivier, brother of the head of the French cabinet, arrived in Lisbon on May 19 with a letter from Napoleon to King Luis. It was the very day on which Marshal Saldanha seized power at Lisbon, an event which at

---

[62] "un peu courir d'aventure."

[63] Bucher to Bismarck, Madrid, April 24, 1870, received April 27.

[64] Bucher to Bismarck, May 2, 1870, secret file; Bonnin, no. 115. Abeken's diary cited by Fester, *Briefe*, no. 153. Thile to Canitz for Salazar, May 4, 1870, secret file; Bonnin, no. 116. A copy was sent to Karl Anton by Bucher on May 4 and received by him on May 5, secret file; Bonnin, no. 119.

first impression seemed encouraging. Saldanha was reputed to favor a closer Iberian union and in the preceding September he had urged Ferdinand to accept the Spanish offer. Ferdinand, however, remained firm, and King Luis had to write to Napoleon that his father, having refused once, found it out of character to change his reply.[65]

Prim also wrote to Marshal Baldomero Espartero, Duke of Vitoria, probably the one Spaniard who could be thought of as a candidate, to ask if he would accept an eventual election. He, too, refused, giving his advanced age and feeble health as excuse.[66]

On May 12, even before any replies had been received to his *démarches* elsewhere, Prim sent a telegram to Bismarck saying that he had received the message of May 4 with great regret and inquiring if the state of Bismarck's health would permit him to reply in ten days or a fortnight to his letter of April 24.[67] This did little, however, to relieve Bismarck's anxiety. "The Spanish affair," he wrote to Rudolph Delbrück on May 13, "has taken a miserable turn. Unquestionable *raison d'état* has been subordinated to the private inclinations of

[65] Fernandez de los Rios, *Mi mision en Portugal*, pp. 351–357; Ollivier, vol. XIII, pp. 421–429; cf. Fester, *Briefe*, vol. I, nos. 161, 182; Mercier to Ollivier, May 6, May 17, 1870, *O.D.*, vol. XXVII, nos. 8139, 8156. Fernandez de los Rios had a long conference with Prim on May 7. *Mi mision en Portugal*, pp. 351–353 (misprinted 335).

[66] Bermejo, *Historia de la interinidad y de la guerra civil*, vol. I, p. 944; extracts in Fester, *Briefe*, vol. I, nos. 165, 172; Mercier to Ollivier, May 11, 4:10 P.M., May 17, 1870, *O.D.*, vol. XXVII, nos. 8146, 8156.

[67] The version published by Hesselbarth, *Drei psychologische Fragen*, p. 30, is correct in substance. The copy in the secret file is a deciphered telegram from Canitz to Bismarck, Madrid, May 12, 1870: "Télégramme d'Alonso: Maréchal Prim reçut avec grand regret dépêche télégraphique du 4. Il désire savoir si état santé M. de le Comte Bismarck lui permetta répondre dans dix ou quinze jours à sa derniere lettre. Réponse pourrait venir sûrement par estafette Legation prussienne." It was probably in transmitting this to Bismarck at Varzin that Thile added a note of regret for having to send so many Spanish telegrams. "Eine grosse Freude wärs mir wenn Sie mir befehlen sollten nach Madrid zu telegraphieren, man sollte den Don Leopoldo proclamiren. Dann wäre der Zahn heraus." Thile to Bismarck, Berlin, May 12, 1870, secret file; Bonnin, no. 125.

the princes and to the influence of ultramontane females. Depression caused by it has weighed heavily on my nerves for weeks." [68]

While Bismarck was fretting at Varzin, the Hohenzollern candidacy was gradually coming back to life. Bucher and Versen had apparently been successful in convincing Salazar and Prim that the case was not as hopeless as it seemed, that Bismarck, when restored to health and energy, might yet be able to supply them with a Prussian king. They were even more successful in reviving the interest of the Hohenzollerns by their reports on conditions in Spain and their enthusiasm for the political values at stake.

Karl Anton, who had shown more understanding of the political factors than had his sons or even King William, was the first to waver. He wrote to his son, Prince Charles of Rumania, that there was great anxiety about what would become of Spain "which we have spurned." There was fear that it would become a republic, which would be a great danger for Italy where "the secret societies have already prepared the ground." It could also affect Rumania, "because such political revolutions are doubly contagious among peoples of the Latin races." [69]

King William, who had received written and verbal reports from Bucher on April 30,[70] did not receive Versen's until May 11. He wrote at once to Karl Anton that he found them interesting but somewhat rose-colored and now that his orientation was completed, he saw no reason to change his view of the whole affair. "That your youngest son has declined is

---

[68] *G.W.*, vol. XIV (2), p. 776

[69] Karl Anton to Charles of Rumania, *Aus dem Leben König Karls*, vol. II, p. 85. The date given is May 12, but in the work cited the dates of Karl Anton's letters seem to be that of receipt. Bucher sent his reports of April 14 and 20 to Karl Anton on May 8. Bucher to Karl Anton, May 8, 1870, draft in secret file; translation, Bonnin, no. 120.

[70] Bucher to Bismarck, May 2, 1870, secret file; Bonnin, no. 115.

surely known in Madrid. I think none of us will regret this refusal." [71]

At his audience with King William, Versen requested permission to go to Varzin to make an oral report to Bismarck. The king gave his consent but the chancellor refused. He did not see any practical value in the visit; he would read the written report on his return to Berlin. Versen was, therefore, instructed to leave Dresden, where he had gone to escape the observation of the many who knew him in Berlin, and to return to his post at Posen. Instead of doing so, he went to Potsdam to call on the crown prince and to win his support for the revival of the candidacy of Prince Leopold.[72]

Frederick William shared his father's opinion that Versen was inclined to look at the situation in Spain through rose-tinted glasses, and he warned his relatives that they were dealing with an enthusiast who needed more to be repressed than encouraged.[73] Yet he was obviously impressed by the description of the situation in Spain and by the arguments for the acceptance of the crown by a prince of the House of Hohenzollern. He consented to support Versen in an attempt

[71] William to Karl Anton, May 12, 1870, K. Th. Zingeler, *Karl Anton Fürst von Hohenzollern*, p. 243; Fester, *Briefe*, vol. I, no. 162. The letter as published is dated May 12 and says: "Erst heute bin ich dazu gekommen, mir durch Major von Versen das Memoire vorlesen zu lassen." The secret file contains a note from Thile to King William dated May 11 to the effect that Versen said that the king approved his trip to Varzin. At the head, in the king's hand: "Einverstanden. W. 11/5/70." Versen did not go to Varzin, but this note raises the question of the date of his report to the king and the king's letter to Karl Anton. If Versen received permission to go to Varzin from the king personally, it is probable that the interview took place on May 11.

[72] Thile to King William, May 11, 16, 1870; tg., Thile to Eichmann (at Dresden), May 16; tg., Eichmann to Thile, May 17; secret file; Bonnin, nos. 122, 129, 130, 131; Versen's diary; German archives, I. A. (Deutschland) 158g, Bd. 3 (microfilm copy); Bonnin, appendix A, pp. 261ff.

[73] King William to Karl Anton, May 12; Frederick William to Karl Anton, May 19, 1870; Fester, *Briefe*, vol. I, nos. 162, 176. The latter letter in Dittrich thesis, appendix 47, from original in Sigmaringen archives, differs in unimportant details; translation, Bonnin, p. 295.

to renew the necessary contacts and wrote a letter to Moltke, the major's immediate superior, to obtain a leave of absence so that he could go to Düsseldorf to see what he could do with Karl Anton and Leopold. Moltke approved the request. He was "quite vehement" that Prince Frederick would not do as a king for Spain and that it would be damaging to the interests of Prussia if a Habsburg archduke, a Bavarian or an Orleans prince came to the throne there, or if, in default of a monarchical candidate, a republic was set up.[74]

Versen left Berlin on the morning of May 21. At the railroad station in Potsdam, he was given the letters that the crown prince had promised to write to Karl Anton and to Leopold to introduce him. At Düsseldorf, however, he learned that Karl Anton was taking the cure at Nauheim and that Leopold was at his residence at Benrath, some twelve miles to the south, and intended to leave the next morning to visit his sister in Brussels. He had, therefore, only about half an hour, on the train from Benrath to Düsseldorf, to present to the prince and his wife the main points of his impressions of the situation in Spain. It was enough to make Leopold feel that now "it was rather tempting — at any rate very interesting." He still insisted on leaving the matter to his father but agreed that if his father wanted him, he would return from Brussels on receipt of a telegram. At Leopold's suggestion, Versen also discussed the problem with Karl Anton's privy councillor and then tried, but in vain, to convince Leopold's mother, Princess Josephine, that her fears of what might happen to her son in Spain were not justified.[75]

[74] Versen diary, May 19, Bonnin, pp. 261–263.
[75] Versen diary, May 20, 21, Bonnin, pp. 263–265; Leopold to Frederick William, draft, May 21, 1870, Dittrich thesis, appendix 48. The date of the draft is probably correct, though Wertheimer cites the original from the Hohenzollern Hausarchiv with date May 23. *Preussische Jahrbücher*, vol. CCV, p. 292. Frederick William, in a letter to Leopold, refers to Leopold's letter of May 23 from Brussels. Dittrich thesis, appendix 54; Versen diary.

To see Karl Anton, Versen went on from Düsseldorf to Nauheim, where he remained from May 21 to May 23. Karl Anton, too, found the reports "interesting." Versen's impressions might be a little sanguine but the total impression was satisfying and comforting. Karl Anton insisted, however, that he and his son would not take the initiative. To the crown prince he wrote that he would have regarded the whole affair of the Spanish candidacy as dead and buried if he had not had the impression that Leopold had begun to regret his categorical refusal. If, in the judgment of the crown prince and of Bismarck, it was desirable to come back to it, he would, "in the interest of the state and with reverent regard for the undoubtedly great historical moment," put no pressure on Leopold but leave him a completely free hand. It would be for Leopold to express himself freely to the crown prince, who should act as intermediary with the king. To Leopold, Karl Anton wrote that he did not think that the affair was completely closed: the historical moment might come for them to make the great sacrifice. They themselves must consider the matter as ended. There was no need to recall Leopold for a conference — the affair had been discussed more than enough — but only in case that it touched the highest interests of state, could it be taken up under carefully formulated conditions and assumptions. "It must come to us, not we to it." [76]

On the evening of May 22, after two days' discussion with Karl Anton, Versen wrote to Moltke asking him to get Bismarck to write a letter to Karl Anton saying that acceptance of the Spanish crown would be in the interest of the state.

---

[76] Aktennotiz Karl Antons, Dittrich thesis, appendix 49; Karl Anton to Frederick William, Nauheim, May 23, 1870, Dittrich thesis, appendix 50. The text from Zingeler, *Karl Anton*, pp 244–245, as published by Fester, *Briefe*, vol. I, no. 180, is correct as far as ". . . Entscheidung," p. 83, l. 17. The omissions are supplied by Dittrich. Karl Anton to Leopold, May 23 (*sic*, Dittrich), 1870, received Benrath, May 28, Dittrich thesis, appendix 51.

The following noon, a telegram from Moltke invited Versen to come back to Berlin.[77]

Bismarck had returned to Berlin on Saturday, May 21, to take part in the final sessions of the Reichstag. He intervened especially in the debates on the third reading of the bill for a common code of criminal law for the North German Confederation and on the treaty with Switzerland and Italy for a substantial North German contribution to the construction of the St. Gotthard railway. Each debate provided an opportunity for him to go beyond the substance of the bills by calling attention to their national significance. In speaking for the former, Bismarck emphasized his appeal for uniformity and equality of citizenship in the confederation and hinted that this would facilitate the completion of the unity of Germany. For the latter, he spoke of the advantage for Germany of a direct rail connection with "a friendly and, as we believe, permanently friendly country." In the speech from the throne, which closed the session on May 26, the unifying achievements of the Reichstag were stressed. The king specifically mentioned the results obtained in welfare and education, in freedom and order at home, as guarantees to foreign countries that the North German Confederation, in the development of its internal institutions and in its national links with South Germany, would make of German national power not a threat but a strong support to the general peace.[78]

Until the Reichstag was adjourned, Bismarck had to be preoccupied with internal politics. At the same time, however, he was worried about recent developments in France. The plebiscite of May 8 was generally believed to have strengthened Napoleon's position at home and was assumed by many to be the prelude to a more vigorous foreign policy. The appoint-

[77] Versen diary, May 23; Bonnin, p. 265–266.
[78] H. Kohl, *Die politischen Reden des Fürsten Bismarck*, vol. IV, pp. 366–390.

ment a week later of the Duke of Gramont as minister of foreign affairs seemed especially ominous. He had been French ambassador at Vienna and was reputed to be not only strongly anti-Prussia but also ultramontane. General von Schweinitz, now German ambassador at Vienna, who was temporarily in Berlin, tried to reassure the chancellor that there was nothing disquieting in the situation: "Gramont had been ambassador in Vienna for six or seven years and must know that France has no aid to expect from Austria," but Bismarck's anxiety was not overcome, at least for a few days longer.[79]

To Versen, who was taken by Moltke to Bismarck at the Reichstag building as soon as he reached Berlin on May 24, the chancellor seemed tired and depressed.[80] He had lost all real hope of putting a Hohenzollern on the throne of Spain. The king was set against it, and it was too irritating and wearing for him to come into conflict with the king's personal feelings.[81] As a last resort, he talked of sending Versen to Bucharest to see if Prince Charles would consider a move to Madrid. Versen's report of the conversations with the crown prince and the two Hohenzollern-Sigmaringen princes showed that the game was not lost and revived Bismarck's spirits a little. He commissioned Versen to ask the crown prince to fix a time for him — preferably Ascension Day, May 26 — when they would talk it over. "I was to say to the crown prince," Versen noted in his diary, "that [Bismarck's] opinion remained unchanged, especially since he had learned from me that the

[79] *G.W.*, vol. VIb, p. 321; Schweinitz, *Denkwürdigkeiten*, vol. I, p. 258. Schweinitz's statement reflects Moltke's opinion that France was not strong enough alone. The danger signal would be military activity in Austria. *Ibid.*, p. 249.
[80] ". . . ganz matt." In a letter to his close friend, Moritz von Blanckenburg, Bismarck wrote a few days before he went to Berlin: "Viel Politik vermag ich noch nicht zu leisten, meine Beine sind besser als mein Kopf." Varzin, May 19, 1870, *G. W.*, vol. XIV(2), no. 1300.
[81] On May 19, Bucher told Versen that Bismarck had "die Flinte ins Korn geworfen." Versen diary, May 19; see also entry for May 25. Translation, Bonnin, pp. 263, 267.

Spanish army was better, but that the political constellation was less favorable than it had been described to the crown prince two months ago." [82]

Late in the afternoon, Versen went to Potsdam to deliver Bismarck's message and Karl Anton's letter to the crown prince. They talked over the problem, and Versen explained how the negotiation could be taken up again at Madrid.[83]

The crown prince read the letters to his father on May 29. The king was unpleasantly surprised that a matter which he had considered at an end should be raised again, but the fact that the initiative had, to a certain degree, come from Leopold of his own free will was a new element. The king did not reject it offhand, but until he could confer with Bismarck, he declined his son's proposal to have Leopold come secretly to the palace.[84]

Bismarck was already moving to take advantage of the new situation. He had, he wrote to Karl Anton, become acquainted on his return to duty with the last negotiations about the Spanish candidacy,[85] and could not escape the impression that the interests of Germany had not been given due weight. He had, for the first time, the opportunity to discuss Bucher's and Versen's reports directly with the king. They showed, he argued, that the present rulers of Spain had seriously and with some success been exerting themselves to bring order into the finances, the military organization, and the general administration, and that "a nation of seventeen [*sic*] millions, which like us is dedicated to the maintenance of European peace," was, in case of European complications, in the position to throw a certain weight in the scales. He was as certain as before that

[82] Versen diary, May 24; translation, Bonnin, pp. 266–267.

[83] Versen diary, May 24. Versen does not tell anything else about how contact with Madrid could be renewed.

[84] Frederick William to Bismarck, May 30, 1870, *Bismarck Jahrbuch*, vol. IV, p. 96; in Fester, *Briefe*, vol. I, no. 189.

[85] This was at best a half-truth. Bismarck already knew the main facts.

in a crisis the decision could be determined by whether Germany had friends or opponents in Madrid. He had asked the king to consider the problem again, and had obtained the answer that if a prince of the House of Hohenzollern should show any inclination to accept the crown, he would not oppose it. This was, he pointed out to Karl Anton, the only answer that could be expected. The king would certainly never command a member of his house to undertake a mission, the success of which depended so much on the individual's personal sense of vocation. If, he concluded, Leopold, or a younger son, should be disposed to perform the service to both countries and to win the gratitude of Spain and of Germany, he believed that a reply to a telegram sent by Marshal Prim after the last rejection and still unanswered, would provide the opportunity to re-establish contact.[86]

Bucher arrived at Nauheim with Bismarck's letter on May 31 and left that same evening with the reply. Karl Anton's long and difficult conflict between family feeling and higher duty had been overcome. A rejection under existing circumstances would fail to recognize an historic vocation and the will of Providence. He had not communicated with Leopold, but was sure of his readiness to make the required sacrifice. In anticipation of the king's consent and with the express reservation of his son's right to make the final decision, he suggested that Bismarck let Madrid know that the refusal to accept the Spanish proposal might be modified "subject to conditions still to be formulated." Of these conditions, the most important was to win time. "If the Spanish rulers can maintain the *status quo* until fall, this would create an additional moral obligation on the part of the Hohenzollerns to make no further resistance; that is, to accept an election based on a satisfactory number of votes." In the meantime, the members of the family could complete their visits to various spas,

[86] Bismarck to Karl Anton, May 28, 1870. *G.W.*, vol. VIb, no. 1557.

and the Sigmaringen house law could be revised to establish the necessary change in the order of succession.[87]

On the following day, June 1, Karl Anton sent his chief of cabinet to take the papers to Leopold at Benrath. "The die is cast!" he wrote in his instructions to Herr von Weiser. "It is no longer possible to hold back — it is a duty to yield. I would not have answered so categorically if there were not danger in delay and we would have to count Spain among our most determined opponents in the future if we refused absolutely." [88]

Leopold went at once to join his father at Nauheim. He accepted Karl Anton's conclusion that the high Prussian and German interests of state put forward by Bismarck would be harmed by his refusal but as the rejection had been communicated to Spain by the king, they could never take the initiative.[89]

On the afternoon of May 30, Bismarck informed Canitz at Madrid that in a few days a courier would leave Berlin with a reply to Prim's letter of April 24.[90] The excuse for the delay was his illness. The telegram, sent to the telegraph office at 5:15 P.M., was drafted before Bucher left for Nauheim with the letter to Karl Anton dated May 28.[91] It crossed a telegram from Canitz, who reported that, according to present arrangements, the Cortes would meet on June 9 to elect a king. The Duke of Montpensier, he added, had assured his intimates that Prim had promised him his vote and his influence. It was

[87] Memorandum of Karl Anton, Nauheim, May 31; Karl Anton to Bismarck, May 31, 1870, Dittrich thesis appendices 55, 56; Leopold to Frederick William, Benrath, June 4, 1870, secret file; Bonnin, no. 152.
[88] Karl Anton to von Werner, Nauheim, June 1, 1870, Dittrich thesis, appendix 57.
[89] Leopold to Frederick William, copy, Benrath, June 4, 1870, secret file, f. 262; Bonnin, no. 152.
[90] See p. 73 above.
[91] Secret file; Bonnin, no. 137.

doubtful, however, that the duke would receive the required majority.[92]

Bismarck's letter to Prim was taken by the regular courier, Lieutenant Rohrbeck, who left Berlin on June 2 and arrived at Madrid on the morning of June 6.[93] According to a memorandum by Bucher, to which Bismarck agreed, it was decided not to have the letter transmitted to Prim by Canitz. The courier was instructed to ask by written note when he could bring it to Prim's residence. He was ordered to travel in civilian clothes so that he would escape notice.[94] Bismarck's letter was in part an apology for the delay, in part an expression of hope that the candidacy might still be possible.

I avail myself of the first moment of peace and quiet to thank Your Excellency for the letter which you were good enough to write me under date of April 24. I received it only on my return from the country still only partially recovered from a severe illness of a kind that made it absolutely impossible for me to attend to business. I hope that in spite of such a long delay, Your Excellency will not doubt my eagerness to give you an account of the steps which I have taken for realizing the projects which agree so well with the sentiments which inspire me towards you and for the future of your country. Having come to the conclusion that Prince Frederick is out of the question, I have resumed the

[92] Secret file; Bonnin, no. 139.

[93] Tg., Canitz to Bismarck, June 6, 1870, 2:30 P.M., secret file; Bonnin, no. 155.

[94] Bucher's memorandum with Bismarck's notes, June 1, 1870, secret file; Bonnin, no. 144. Bucher's statement to Busch in 1891 (Busch, *Bismarck: Some Secret Pages from His History*, vol. III, p. 378): "He denied the letter to Prim until I reminded him that I myself handed it to the general in Madrid" was an error of memory. I make no reference in the text to the document published by the Spanish historian Pirala and often said to be a memorandum of instructions for Bucher. It could not have been written before June 21, too late to affect the negotiations, and, I believe, it was composed not by Bismarck but by Bucher himself. See L. D. Steefel, "Bismarck and Bucher. The Letter of Instructions," in *Studies in Diplomatic History and Historiography in Honour of G. P. Gooch, C.H.*, ch. xii.

negotiations with the hereditary prince [Leopold], and today it seems to me that despite his first refusal, we have succeeded in convincing the prince and His Royal Highness, his father, that the prejudices and the anxieties with which they at first looked at the plan and at the state of affairs in Spain were not well founded. But nevertheless the general difficulties which I had the honor to point out to Your Excellency in my letter of April 11, still hinder a positive decision. I have just received from His Royal Highness the prince and father, the certainty that his eldest son, the hereditary prince, no longer holds to his refusal on personal grounds. The prince adds to this notification the promise that his eldest son will accept the result of the vote provided that by that time an agreement has been reached on the conditions and the future position of the king in so far as they are not taken care of in the constitution. Whether or not the Spanish government is in a position to agree to this delay is a question upon which I can have no opinion. In the hope that the presence of Salazar might perhaps accelerate the issue, I have just requested him by telegraph to come to Berlin. Whatever turn this affair may take, I pray Your Excellency to remain convinced that I have done and that I will do all that rests with me and that, if I do not in good time arrive at the result that we both desire, it will be only because of the difficulty of bringing to agreement as promptly as necessary personages in the status of life of those with whom we are concerned.

I am deeply touched by your good wishes for my health and I beg you to believe that I shall be most happy to be of service to you personally and to your fatherland.[95]

For Canitz, Lieutenant Rohrbeck carried a secret dispatch in which Bismarck informed him of the new situation and gave suggestions for his subsequent reports. He was told that the instructions of October 28, 1868, were no longer relevant, now that the proper authorities in Spain had let the wish be known in Berlin that one of the princes of the princely line of the royal house might accept the crown. The highest officials, whom the king had brought together to hear their confidential advice, expressed the unanimous opinion that accept-

[95] Bismarck to Prim, June 1, 1870, secret file; Bonnin, no. 143. The draft by Bucher was revised by Bismarck. See Appendix B below.

ance was demanded in the interest of Germany. The crown prince had also spoken in favor of the project but the king had refused to make a decision between the political considerations and his anxiety for the fate of the princes concerned so long as the latter did not express more definitely their readiness to undertake the difficult and dangerous mission. Bismarck, in his official position, took account only of the political aspects of the problem and represented them in anticipation of the royal decision. Canitz was requested, therefore, to keep in mind in his reporting the interests of the Prussian state and the international relations of Prussia and Spain. He was, as a matter of course, to report all important facts that needed to be taken into account in reaching the decision but warned to avoid conjectures that might have an adverse effect.[96]

Salazar was notified of the new developments by a telegram sent on June 1 via Hanover addressed to one of his cover names: "Pedro Sierra, Concepcion Geronimo, 28, Madrid." The message, in French, announced that the two machines would be delivered together by Tuesday [97] if possible. It was signed by Bucher's code name, "Braun." [98] Salazar replied that the engineer could assemble the machines on the agreed date if there was real hope of casting at Hanover pipes of the diameter numbers 4 and 6.[99] Bucher answered at once that the mold for pipe number 6 no longer existed and that the manufacture of pipe number 4, which had been started, would be greatly accelerated by the personal direction of the fitter.[100] The fitter, however, insisted that it was indispensable for the

[96] Bismarck to Canitz, June 1, 1870, secret file; Bonnin, no. 145.
[97] June 7.
[98] To telegraph director, Hanover, June 1, 1870, secret file; Bonnin, no. 142.
[99] Canitz to Bismarck, June 2, 1870, 9 P.M., secret file; Bonnin, nos. 147, 148.
[100] To Canitz for Sierra, June 3, 1870; to telegraph station, 12:05 P.M., secret file; Bonnin, no. 149.

successful manufacture that the doctor come at once to compare "the state of our machines with the dimensions of the pipes." This cooperation, he said, would facilitate the task of the engineer. They could then go back together.[101] On June 5, Bismarck, who had just returned from Ems, authorized Bucher to go and the telegram, "The doctor will come," went off to Madrid.[102]

Bismarck had left Berlin on the evening of June 1 to accompany King William to Ems to pay their respects to Tsar Alexander. On the return trip, on June 4, Karl Anton met them for a conference when the royal train stopped at Giessen. "The king is in agreement with us," Karl Anton wrote to Leopold, "that is, he yields to Bismarck's political necessities. The latter is triumphant. If we had again refused, we should have had to pay for it — for the Spanish throne candidacy is a big factor in his political calculations. I have repeated the conditions to the king clearly and he agrees to our point of view." King William was still at heart opposed. He felt compromised by the telegram of refusal to Prim and would do nothing on his part to reopen the question. Should Karl Anton really want to put his hand to the task, if Prim would state that he could wait until fall, if then the proposal came from father and son that they for their part had decided to undertake the hazardous enterprise, then he would think it all over again before he could give a decision. Now as before, he was against it and he would not persuade, much less command, any one to accept it.[103]

The last half of May and the first week of June were a time of political confusion and maneuver at Madrid. Under in-

---

[101] Canitz to Bismarck, June 4, 1870, secret file; Bonnin, nos. 150, 151.

[102] Bismarck to Canitz, June 5, 1870, 8:15 A.M., secret file; Bonnin, no. 153.

[103] Major von Schreckenstein to Karl Anton, Ems, June 3, 1870; Karl Anton's memorandum, June 4; Karl Anton to Leopold, June 5; Dittrich thesis, appendices 60, 61, 63; King William to Queen Augusta, June 5, *G.W.*, vol. VIb, p. 331.

creased pressure to establish the public power on a definitive basis, the cabinet found agreement difficult. Without a candidate for the throne acceptable to the leaders of the cabinet, Prim seemed to be moving to consolidate the provisional organization with the Regent as its nominal head. The partisans of the Duke of Montpensier were doing all in their power to block the interim, and the duke with his eldest son returned to Madrid to be close to the center of action. They believed that they could depend on about a hundred members of the Cortes, and the duke, after a courtesy visit to Prim, spread the word that he could count on the influence and the vote of the president of the council. If the duke really believed this, he was mistaken. "I have seen Marshal Prim since this visit," Mercier de l'Ostende, the French ambassador, reported, "and I have heard him repeat in the most positive tone that the Duke of Montpensier did not have the slightest chance." [104]

The North German minister doubted that the duke would get the necessary majority, for he had heard that some of the ministers and the "monarchical Democrats" planned to make the election impossible by walking out of the meeting.[105] Prim's plan, as he outlined it to the French ambassador, was to gain time "to prepare some new combination" by adjourning the Cortes on June 15 and thus to prolong the interim by default.

I will lay before the Cortes all that I have done to find a king at the foreign courts and the small success of my efforts. If the Montpensierists and the Esparterists want to use the occasion to put forward their candidates, we will take a vote. The result is certain, and then we will see that there is no alternative to the interim. By following this procedure, I shall have paid my respects to the authority of the Cortes and have thrust upon it the responsibility for the uncertainties of which they complain.[106]

Serrano, whose sympathies leaned to Montpensier, was more

[104] *O.D.*, vol. XXVII, p. 338, n. 2, and nos. 8156, 8183.
[105] Tg., Canitz to Bismarck, May 30, 1870, secret file; Bonnin, no. 139.
[106] Mercier to Gramont, May 29, 1870, *O.D.*, vol. XXVII, p. 339 n.

pessimistic. The situation, he told Mercier, was becoming more and more critical, and he could not foresee anything in the next few days that could get them out of it. People were getting stirred up and the debates scheduled to open on June 9 could lead to God knows what incidents. The interim, if they fell back on it, would put the Alphonsists, the Carlists, and the republicans into such open opposition that it would soon come to shooting.[107]

The immediate practical problem was to provide by law the procedure for electing a king. In April, Karl Anton had insisted on a two-thirds majority if one of his sons should be a candidate. At the end of May, there was, of course, no Hohenzollern candidacy, and the supporters of Montpensier dominated the committee responsible for the bill. Their draft provided that if a majority of the qualified deputies were present, they could proceed to the election and a majority of those present would elect. With a total membership of 350 deputies, the presence of 176 would produce a quorum, and in that case, 89 members could choose a king. As Montpensier was believed to have the support of 100, his chances were favored by this bill.

On June 3, however, one of Prim's political friends, Rojo Arias, presented an amendment to Article 7 of the proposed electoral law. This would require for an election the absolute majority of the qualified deputies, that is, instead of a minimum of 89, a minimum of 176. The amendment was passed on the evening of June 7 by a vote of 138 to 124. It was a defeat for Montpensier, whose partisans did not try to cover up their vexation. In the present mood of the Cortes, it was unlikely that any of the current candidates could be elected; the interim would have to continue and Prim would have time to prepare his "new combination." [108] It was becoming more

---

[107] *O.D.*, vol. XXVII, no. 8183.
[108] *O.D.*, vol. XXVII, nos. 8183, 8190, 8195.

certain every day that this could be Leopold of Hohenzollern-Sigmaringen.

"The law for the election of the king was approved yesterday," Salazar telegraphed triumphantly to Bismarck. "It requires an absolute majority of the 350 qualified deputies. This clause takes away all hope for the partisans of Espartero and Montpensier. The latter is going to leave. Letter received. I am waiting for Doctor. Next week will be decisive for the monarchical principle. Immediate election of the king will not prevent the time asked for for preliminary arrangements. Game postponed, game lost. Almost all of the deputies are at hand in expectation of a decision. Their fatigue is very great and a large number will not come back." [109]

Bucher arrived in Madrid on the morning of June 9. He found Salazar and Prim ready and eager to conclude the negotiations and to proceed with the election. "Doctor [is] here," Salazar telegraphed to Bismarck.

Moment has come to transform the confidential *démarches* into official negotiations. The Spanish government will address the Prussian government officially as soon as Bismarck has notified the minister of foreign affairs through his representative at Madrid that he is ready to receive [official] communications in the sense of the informal *démarches* of the president of the Council. I confirm telegram of yesterday. Reply is therefore urgent. Election completed, three months at least will be conceded for arrival. According to the law, the private fortune of the prince will always belong to him personally, not to the crown. Civil list planned for the king will be five million francs. [110]

A few hours later a second telegram asked Bismarck to send by telegraph the instructions for Canitz. [111]

[109] Salazar to Canitz, June 8, 1870, transmitted by Canitz to Bismarck, tg., 2:15 P.M., secret file; Bonnin, nos. 156, 157. Cf. Mercier to Gramont, June 6, 1870, *O.D.*, vol. XXVII, no. 8186.

[110] Salazar to Canitz, June 9, 1870, transmitted by Canitz to Bismarck, tg., 4:30 P.M., secret file; Bonnin, nos. 161, 162, 163.

[111] Salazar to Canitz, June 9, 1870, transmitted by Canitz to Bismarck, tg., 6 P.M., secret file; Bonnin, nos. 164, 165.

Bismarck, at Varzin, scrawled on the margin of the longer telegram that the Prussian government had nothing to do with all this, and sent Thile his instructions for the reply:

Count Bismarck, after receipt of the two telegrams of the ninth, requests me to telegraph to the doctor, in reply to the urgent entreaties of his friend, that he is absent from Berlin, that he has no cipher with him, and that a result can only be obtained through direct communications with the person directly concerned, who at present is free to make decisions and is animated by the best of will. The count adds that the affair would probably be already arranged if Alonso, instead of demanding the doctor, had followed the suggestion made a week ago to come to Berlin.[112]

A third message from Salazar on June 10 stated that the vexation of the partisans of Montpensier might hasten the election of a king to within the next ten days. Under these circumstances, formal official communications would take too long. It would be enough to bring forward the candidacy if Bismarck would send by special courier — on condition that he could arrive by June 17 — a letter to Prim accepting the vote on the basis of the agreed conditions. Longer indecision would lose everything. The dispatch of this letter could be notified on the same day by Canitz to the minister of foreign affairs. A reply from Leopold would aid the success of the plan, even if it were merely announced.[113]

Bismarck received this message from Thile on June 12, and the reply amplified the instructions of the day before.

For the doctor. The chief charges you to tell Alonso as follows: the only way to accomplish the business is for someone to go at once to the hereditary prince at Reichenhall, to do with him whatever can be done. The prince is of age and ready to negotiate. The objections on the part of his family have been removed.

---

[112] Tg., Bismarck to Thile, Varzin, June 11, 1870; Thile to Canitz, June 11, 1870, secret file; Bonnin, nos. 168, 169.

[113] Salazar to Canitz, June 9, 1870, transmitted by Canitz to Bismarck, tg., June 10, 1:35 P.M., secret file; Bonnin, nos. 166, 167.

The Prussian government has no orders to give him but our chief has read some private letters which prove that the prince wants to accept. The doctor must say all this as the personal opinion of the chief. Versen is leaving tomorrow morning for Reichenhall.[114]

During the debates on the law for the election of a king, Canovas de Castillo had delivered an eloquent appeal in favor of Isabella's son Alfonso. Shortly afterwards, a private meeting, said to include about a hundred deputies, prepared a request to the government to bring the provisional regime to an end. It was therefore expected that Prim would make his long-awaited report to the Cortes on June 9.[115] It was postponed until the afternoon of June 11, undoubtedly at first because Prim hoped that Bucher would bring the last word on the Hohenzollern candidacy, and then, to await an answer to Salazar's telegrams to Bismarck of June 9.

The Cortes was tense but silent when Prim at about half past three asked for the floor. He began by assuring the deputies that the government was as ardent as the Cortes to finish with the provisional status and contradicted vigorously the reports that he had a personal interest in prolonging it. It was, however, not so easy to crown the constitution with a king as he and his friends had believed when they were in exile. He then sketched in general terms the efforts made to find a suitable king, naming Ferdinand, Amadeus of Savoy, and the Duke of Genoa. Negotiations had followed with a fourth candidate whose name he would not mention because it might lead to complications and because, in addition, he had given his word not to. This candidate, whom he could not name, had the qualifications needed and which had been put forward by many deputies: he was of a royal line, a Catholic, and of age. But after all their efforts, the government had not been

[114] Tg., Thile to Canitz, June 12, 1870, 10:10 P.M., secret file; Bonnin, no. 175.
[115] O.D., vol. XXVII, no. 8195.

fortunate: they had no candidate at present. "They have none at this moment, they have none today, and I cannot tell if they will have one tomorrow." They could not fix a time or a date, but they would continue their efforts in the hope that some day fortune would bring them a candidate who would fulfil the mentioned conditions and would bring unity to the parties and an end to the interim which the government as well as the Cortes recognized as the first need of the country.[116] Prim's opponents continued to emphasize the duty of the government to do its best to escape from the impasse, but did not press hard.[117] An attempt of the supporters of the Duke of Montpensier to force the immediate election of a king or a vote of censure was blocked.[118]

With the critical session past and the Cortes sitting only for routine business, Salazar was free to leave Madrid. Together with Bucher, he started on June 14 to confer with Leopold at Reichenhall.[119]

Versen had already left Berlin on the evening of Monday, June 12, and reached Reichenhall on the morning of June 14.[120]

---

[116] Prim's speech summarized in Fester, *Briefe*, vol. I, no. 203.

[117] Mercier to Gramont, June 12, 1870, *O.D.*, vol. XXVII, no. 8206.

[118] Tg., Canitz (for Salazar) to Bismarck, June 12, 1870, 12:13 P.M., secret file; Bonnin, no. 176. The text, as deciphered at Berlin and sent on to Varzin, has the meaningless phrase: "vote caracteristique"; the draft has "vote censure." Bonnin translates "decisive vote."

[119] Salazar to Canitz, June 13, 1870; transmitted by Canitz to Bismarck, tg., 5:10 P.M., secret file; Bonnin, nos. 178, 179.

[120] My account of Versen's mission and the discussions at Reichenhall and Sigmaringen is derived from Versen's diary (translation in Bonnin, pp. 268–281); Versen to Bismarck, June 8, 1870; Bismarck to Versen, June 11; Bismarck to Thile, June 11; Versen to Bismarck, June 12; Thile to Bismarck, June 13; tg., Thile to Versen, June 15; tgs., Versen to Thile, June 15, 5 P.M., 10:10 P.M.; letter, June 15; June 17; Versen to Bismarck, June 19; Karl Anton to Bismarck, June 19; secret file; Bonnin, nos. 159, 172, 173, 177 and n. 5, 180, 183, 184, 185, 186, 189, 192, 193; Karl Anton to Queen Augusta, undated copy, Dittrich thesis, appendix 72; memoranda, Karl Anton, Leopold, Dittrich thesis, appendix 64, 68, 65.

Leopold arrived on the following morning. Versen had brought copies of the telegrams from Salazar to Bismarck which urged that the candidacy be made official. He begged the prince to consent to this and to write a letter asking the king's approval, for him to take to Berlin, if possible, that day. Leopold refused both requests. He would not do anything without his father. In any case, it had been agreed, with the approval of the king, that there would be a period of three months before any further steps were taken. Until then, he wanted to be left in peace. He had, as Versen knew, yielded reluctantly to the pressure of the Prussian government, and had announced his eventual acceptance of the Spanish crown under conditions to be definitely formulated. He had many reasons for wanting the election put off until fall. Finally, he agreed to Versen's pleas, and on June 16 the two men left for Sigmaringen. Karl Anton, after a night on the train from Heidelberg to Ulm, was surprised to meet them the next morning, and they all went together to the castle.

The negotiations continued to be long and difficult. Karl Anton had read a newspaper report that the Cortes had already adjourned and concluded that time was no longer pressing. Finally, Versen persuaded him to draft a letter for Leopold to send to the king in which the prince, "in conformity with the family law," asked His Majesty for permission to accept the proffered crown. A telegram from Reichenhall on June 18 announced that Bucher and Salazar were on their way, and they arrived on the morning of June 19. They declared that the newspaper report about the adjournment was false, "a French intrigue," and described the situation at Madrid as demanding quick action. It was necessary to telegraph to Madrid at once that Leopold was ready to accept the crown. The Cortes was soon to disperse. The decisive argument was that the last moment for a Hohenzollern candidacy had come. The Archduke Salvator was being considered, and the French and Austrian ambassadors at Madrid were "intriguing" on his behalf.

It was agreed then that Bucher would leave as soon as possible that day to carry the letters from Leopold to King William. In the meantime, Salazar sent a telegram to Manuel Ruiz Zorilla, president of the Cortes, that Leopold was willing to accept and that only the formal approval of the king was needed. The message was filed at the telegraph station at Mengen in the code phrase: "Carlistes conspirent de nouveau — surveillance sur Deputé No. 3." A letter from Karl Anton to Bismarck was taken by Versen that night. Salazar was to wait at Sigmaringen for the king's answer and then to take Leopold's letter of acceptance to Madrid. "This great affair will therefore soon be under way," Karl Anton wrote at the end of his letter to Bismarck, "and my son and I hope that, in view of the great sacrifice we have made, Your Excellency will guide it in a safe channel."

At Ems, on the morning of June 21, in an audience lasting an hour and a quarter, Bucher "not without difficulty" won the king's consent to send the telegram "Einverstanden" to Karl Anton at Sigmaringen.[121]

King William had been unpleasantly surprised, some ten days earlier, to learn that the question of the Spanish throne had shown new signs of life, but at that time he had not asked Thile any questions about details that might have been embarrassing to answer. Before he set out for Ems, on June 18, he had extracted from the crown prince the information that Bucher had gone to Spain again; that Versen, whose return to his post at Posen had long ago been decided, was traveling around with commissions from Bismarck; and that Salazar was coming back to Germany. Of all this, he had known nothing and he found it very strange that such things could happen

[121] Bucher to Karl Anton, June 23, 1870; Dittrich thesis, appendix 71.

without his assent. His own position was unchanged, he told Thile. He would never command, or even express the wish, that a Hohenzollern prince should accept the Spanish crown, but if one felt a definite calling to undertake it, he would not stand in his way. In any case, he did not want anything to be done behind his back, and he instructed Thile to let Bismarck know that His Majesty wanted to know everything that was done about it. "All this the king expressed not without some touchiness," Thile wrote, "but he added at once that everything must be avoided that could upset Your Excellency or excite your nerves." More reassuring was Thile's opinion that the king's curiosity could be satisfied by somewhat general allusions, so that there would be no need to disturb the negotiations.[122]

Bismarck's nerves were not soothed by the king's demands. He underlined the words, "von allem was Salazar mündlich oder schriftlich bringen werde," and added at the top of the page: "S.M. will also die Sache *mit amtlicher* allerh[öchster] Einmischung behandelt haben?!!" After "es müsse alles vermieden werden dass Euer Excellency verstimmen oder nervös aufregen könne," he inserted: "u[nd] was nach *Kön*[iglich] *Preuss*[ische] *Einmischung* aussieht." At the head of the letter, he wrote that the whole affair was possible only if it remained "princely Hohenzollern"; it must not become Prussian. The king must be able to say without lying, "I know him not." [123]

To Bucher, King William remarked that it now seemed as if Princess Antonia was better disposed toward the affair but that he did not know what had brought about the change of mind. Bucher, never at a loss for an answer, explained that it might have been the *coup d'état* of Marshal Saldanha and the way it had been received in Spain; perhaps she had been led

[122] Thile to Bismarck, June 19, 1870, secret file; Bonnin, no. 191.
[123] Bismarck's marginal notes, Thile to Bismarck, June 19, 1870.

to the conclusion that her relatives at Lisbon would be safest if she was residing in Madrid. The king also spoke of his doubts that the acceptance of the crown was really as important for Prussian interests of state as Bismarck and the Sigmaringen princes assumed. In answer to this, Bucher asked permission to give the impressions about this that he had brought back from Spain. He had often observed, he said, and could prove it by examples, that the Spanish statesmen, with whom he had contacts, were completely unoriented to the relations of the great powers, their relative weights, and the nature of their intercourse; they tried to get acquainted with these things from the newspapers and discussed their contents as dilettantes. This state of affairs allowed the possibility of providing a real service for Spain without any additional expense. The Prussian government needed only to provide the North German minister at Madrid with copies of important dispatches, as was done with other ministers and ambassadors, and to authorize him to make confidential communication of them. Through the passing on of accurate information, by providing an antidote to influences from other quarters, this procedure would also be of service to Prussia, for the interests of North Germany and Spain did not collide anywhere. At the most important point, the relations with France, they coincided. In Spain, the memories of the war of liberation against Napoleon were as vivid as they had been in Prussia forty years ago.

King William was never really convinced, yet no matter how much he might continue to dislike the candidacy, he was committed not to oppose it if Leopold indicated that he felt the call to accept. He promised, therefore, to send the telegram of consent, "Einverstanden," to Sigmaringen. In addition, Bucher, who suspected that Salazar's private telegrams might be garbled in France, received permission to have Prim informed by a telegram to the North German legation that

Salazar was now in position to send him the telegram that had been agreed on.[124]

Three telegrams from Salazar brought by Versen had already been transmitted by Thile, all dated Tuesday 21, Sigmaringen Castle.[125] The first, to Prim, confirmed the telegram announcing the acceptance by the prince. The third, to "Anastasio Alonso" and signed "Gama," was to Salazar's family. The second, to Ruiz Zorilla, president of the Cortes, read in the draft: "Je confirme télégramme avant hier. Les Carlistes conspirent de nouveau. Surveiller deputé no. 3. A revoir vers le 26." In the Madrid copy, the last sentence read, "A revoir vers le 9." It was a code phrase. If the date of Salazar's return was given as before July 1, the Cortes was to be held together so that it could proceed to the election of a king; if later, the Cortes was to be adjourned until fall. On June 23, therefore, the session was formally ended, and the delegates went to their homes.

When Salazar reached Madrid on June 28,[126] he learned that the Cortes was no longer in session, and that the message as received by Zorilla read *nine* instead of *twenty-six*. The investigation showed that his draft read *twenty-six* and had been correctly encoded at Berlin. The responsibility was laid on the legation at Madrid, but it was impossible to be certain whose fault it was; the original figures had been destroyed in accordance with current regulations as soon as a fair copy of the decipher had been made.[127] The mistake in decoding

[124] Bucher to Bismarck, June 22, 1870; Abeken to Bismarck, June 22 and 24; King William to Leopold, June 21; King William to Karl Anton, June 21; secret file; Bonnin, nos. 209, 210, 216, 203, 204; Bucher to Karl Anton, June 23; Dittrich thesis, appendix 71.

[125] Secret file; Bonnin, nos. 199, 200.

[126] The date is generally given as June 26; see Fester, *Briefe*, vol. I, no. 245. H. Leonardon, *Prim*, has June 28, which is confirmed by Salazar to Canitz, June 28, 1870, secret file; Bonnin, no. 220.

[127] The full report of the investigation is in the secret file; translations in Bonnin, nos. 220, 221, 222, 225, 227, 229, 230, 231, 232, 235, 247,

made impossible the *fait accompli* of a quick election in secret session. Reports that a candidate had been found by Salazar began to circulate in Madrid and passed quickly from Madrid to Paris.[128]

254, 287. This was the most serious mistake in the correspondence; examination of the texts in the secret file shows many others.

[128] On the spread of the secret, see Fester, *Briefe,* vol. I, no. 245.

-⟦ III ⟧-

The Candidate is Lost

Prim returned to Madrid the evening of July 1. He was met at the railroad station by political friends who told him how pleased they were that he had a candidate who accepted. The marshal asked, in surprise, how they knew. "Everybody in the political world of Madrid knows the name of the candidate and that he has accepted" was the answer, whereupon Prim knitted his eyebrows, crushed the glove that he held in his hand, and exclaimed: "Labor lost, candidacy lost — and God grant that that is all!" [1] The news was given wider publicity by an article in the Alphonsist newspaper *Epoca*.[2] This was contradicted in other newspapers and might have had no greater importance than previous reports of the same kind but now that the candidacy of Leopold was at last a fact, and with so many people in possession of it, Prim concluded that the secret could no longer be kept. He could not even wait until the visit to Vichy which he had planned for the second week of July to inform Napoleon and to try to convince him that there was no better alternative.[3]

[1] V. Balaguer, *Memorias de un Constituyente*, cited in Fester, *Briefe*, vol. I, no. 248; Ollivier, vol. XIV, pp. 9–10.
[2] Cf. Fester, *Briefe*, vol. I, no. 249; *The Times*, London, July 4, 1870, p. 9, col. 4.
[3] Mercier to Gramont, June 25, 1870, *O.D.*, vol. XXVII, no. 8229.

When the French ambassador called on him on the evening of July 2, Prim seemed more agitated than usual. He said to Mercier,

I have to talk to you about something that I fear will not please the emperor and you must help me to keep him from taking it in too bad part. You know our situation; we cannot prolong the interim indefinitely nor even appear before the Cortes without a solution to propose to them. You know what I have done to avert what would not have suited the emperor. I had only to relax my grip and Montpensier would have been elected; I did not yield to any of the advances made to win me to the side of the republic. What I wanted above all was a Portuguese combination or in default of that, an Italian. Recently I turned again to Lisbon and to Florence, but in vain. Nevertheless we need a king and now, at the moment of our greatest difficulty, one has been proposed to us who has all the qualifications which we want. He is Catholic, of royal line, he is thirty-six years old, of excellent personality, and a soldier. He has two sons, and his marriage to a Portuguese princess will win many to his support. You will understand that I could not let pass the only chance that remained to save the revolution, especially when presented in such a form. How do you think the emperor will take it? [4]

The news of the Hohenzollern candidacy had already reached Paris. Before noon on Saturday, July 2, Viscount Walsh, a well-known Legitimist, sent to Gramont a document whose authenticity, he wrote, he would guarantee.[5] The source of his information is not certainly known, but it seems probable that it came from Carlist circles. Prince Leopold, it is said, had informed his aunt, Princess Marie of Baden, that he had accepted the Spanish offer, and she telegraphed the news to Vevey to the wife of Don Carlos, pretender to the Spanish throne.[6] The text of the document is also unknown, but it probably corresponds to the message transmitted by

[4] Mercier to Gramont, July 3, 1870, *O.D.*, vol. XXVIII, no. 8243.
[5] Ollivier, vol. XIV, pp. 20–21.
[6] Fester, *Briefe*, vol. I, no. 250.

The Candidate is Lost

Walsh to the editor of the Legitimist newspaper, the *Gazette de France*:

Deputation sent by Prim arrived at Sigmaringen to offer crown to Prince Leopold Hohenzollern, who is married to a Portuguese princess. Acceptance given will be announced in about two weeks. Assert [this], unmask this Prussian-Spanish-Portuguese intrigue.[7]

The message was published that evening with sensational additions:

A King of Spain. — At this moment, we learned the following news: "A delegation of Marshal Prim's cronies has been sent to Sigmaringen to offer the crown of Spain to young Prince Leopold of Hohenzollern, who is married to a Portuguese princess. As soon as acceptance given, Marshal Prim will make a *coup d'état* and proclaim [the accession of] this Prussian prince. In order to hurry up the issue, he has decided to by-pass the intervention of the Cortes." [8]

The same evening, at 7:30, the Havas Agency received a telegram from Madrid:

According to several papers, the government is opening negotiation with new candidate for throne. Prim, Zorilla are reported to have postponed journey in order to take active part in negotiation.[9]

On the following day, the agency not only confirmed the news of the negotiations, but also named the candidate:

A delegation sent to Prussia by Marshal Prim has offered the crown to the prince of Hohenzollern, and he has accepted it. This candidacy will be announced without the cooperation of the Cortes.[10]

---

[7] Tg., Walsh to Voillet for communication to the *Gazette*, *O.D.*, vol. XXVIII, p. 19, no. 8238, n. 2.

[8] *O.D.*, vol. XXVIII, p. 19, no. 8238, n. 2.

[9] *O.D.*, vol. XXVIII, p. 19, no. 8238, n. 2.

[10] *O.D.*, vol. XXVIII, p. 19, no. 8238, n. 2. See P. de la Gorce, *Histoire du second empire*, vol. VI, pp. 218–221.

Mercier's telegram, sent from Madrid at 10:40 in the morning of July 3, reached Paris at 12:30 P.M. It reported the bare fact that the Hohenzollern matter seemed to be well advanced, perhaps already decided. The information came from Prim, and the details would be carried to Paris by the secretary of the embassy.[11] Gramont was given the message at once. He telegraphed to St. Cloud to ask the emperor to receive him and to Berlin to request Benedetti, if still there, to postpone his departure for Wildbad, as he had received serious news from Spain. At about 4:30 he was with the emperor. Napoleon was completely surprised by the news. He had, he told Gramont, received no hint of it from Prince Leopold, Prince Charles of Rumania, or Prince Karl Anton.[12] He had been sure that if there had been anything to the earlier reports of the candidacy, he would have been informed, and he was moved by their apparent disloyal action. It was agreed that Gramont should send dispatches to Madrid and Berlin to seek further information and that on the following day they would begin "a prudent but effective" campaign in the newspapers.[13]

The "prudent but effective" campaign in the press began with a note to the editor of the *Constitutionnel*, published by him on July 4.

It follows from information which appears worthy of belief that agents of Marshal Prim have gone recently to Prussia to the prince

[11] Tg., Mercier to Gramont, July 3, 1870, 10:40 A.M., received 12:30 P.M., *O.D.*, vol. XXVIII, no. 8238.

[12] According to a sometimes well-informed source, "One of the Emperor's aides-de-camp has left this inedited statement concerning the machinations of this period: 'The Emperor, who had been rather ill, was visited in October 1869, by Prince Charles of Roumania, with whom he discussed his pacific intentions. We learned that Prince Anthony of Hohenzollern had been approached on the matter, would give no positive answer, and it was believed that the conditions made by Prince Leopold were equivalent of a refusal of the proffered honor' " (Maurice Comte Fleury, *Memoirs of the Empress Eugenie*, vol. II, p. 204). Internal evidence suggests that the statement was not written before July 1870.

[13] Ollivier, vol. XIV, pp. 21–27; *O.D.*, vol. XXVIII, p. 21, n. 3.

of Hohenzollern to offer him the crown of Spain and that he has accepted. We do not know if Marshal Prim, in undertaking this *démarche*, was acting on his personal responsibility or if he had received any kind of mandate from the Spanish Cortes or Regent. Therefore let us wait for fuller details to judge an event whose gravity is obvious to everyone. If, as everything leads us to suppose, the marshal has acted without authority, this incident reduces itself to an intrigue; if, on the contrary, the Spanish nation sanctions or advises this *démarche*, we must above all regard it with the respect due to the will of a people regulating its own destiny. But in doing homage to the sovereignty of the Spanish people, sole judge of such an affair, we cannot suppress an emotion of surprise in seeing the scepter of Charles V conferred on a Prussian prince, the grandson of a princess of the Murat family, whose name is associated in Spain with such sore memories.[14]

This reference to the ruthless repression by French troops of a popular rising in Madrid on May 2, 1808, was rebuked by Napoleon III when he noticed it in the instructions to the ambassador at Madrid, but it remained an element in the French propaganda against the candidacy.[15]

Gramont instructed Mercier at Madrid to combat "this intrigue hatched by Prim and Prussia against France" with all his tact, prudence, and reserve but with ingenuity and vigor. "Act on the press and through your friends but without compromising yourself. Make use of the date of May 2." [16] Gramont informed Georges Le Sourd, who was in charge of the French embassy at Berlin, that "we have learned that a deputation sent by Marshal Prim has offered the crown of Spain to the prince of Hohenzollern who has accepted it. We do not take this candidacy seriously, and believe that the Spanish nation will reject it. But we cannot see without some surprise a Prussian prince try to seat himself on the throne of Spain.

[14] Ollivier, vol XIV, pp. 27–28.
[15] Ollivier, vol. XIV, p. 28. A well-known painting by F. Goya (in the Prado at Madrid) portrayed executions by a French firing squad.
[16] *O.D.*, vol. XXVIII, no 8241.

We should like to think that the cabinet of Berlin is not a party to this intrigue; if it should be, its conduct suggests to us reflections of a nature too delicate to be entrusted to a telegram." The news had made a bad impression at Paris, and Gramont ordered Le Sourd to let the Prussian government know it.[17]

At the beginning of July 1870, in Germany as in France and elsewhere in Europe, the international situation appeared to be completely tranquil. Most of the political and diplomatic world had dispersed for the summer vacation. The king of Prussia was taking his cure at Ems, with only Geheimrat Heinrich Abeken as representative of the Foreign Office at his side. Bismarck was at Varzin with Bucher as his aide. The Foreign Office was in the charge of Secretary of State Thile. Benedetti, the French ambassador, had just departed for his vacation at Wildbad. Karl Anton was at Sigmaringen, Leopold at or near Reichenhall in the Bavarian or in the neighboring Austrian Alps. Nevertheless, it is impossible to believe that Bismarck and his immediate staff, Thile, Bucher, and Abeken, were taken so much by surprise as has sometimes been claimed.[18] By July 2, Bismarck had learned from Salazar's telegram, forwarded by Thile to Varzin, that it was doubtful that the secrecy of the candidacy could be kept; that as soon as Prim returned to Madrid, the Council of Ministers would meet to be formally notified of Leopold's acceptance; and that it was hoped that an *ad hoc* meeting of the Cortes could be summoned.[19] From this Bismarck must have concluded that the crisis was close — the formal decision in Spain and an out-

[17] *O.D.*, vol. XXVIII, no. 8242; sent at 10:30 P.M.

[18] Lord, *The Origins of the War of 1870*, p. 29; E. Fitzmaurice, *The Life of Granville*, vol. II, pp. 30–32; Bismarck to Crown Prince Frederick William, Varzin, June 30, 1870, *G.W.*, vol. VIb, no. 1564.

[19] Tg., cipher, Salazar to Canitz, June 29, 1870, Canitz to Thile, June 29, 1870, 6:50 P.M., received June 30, 2:30 A.M., transmitted to Varzin July 1, presented to Bismarck July 2, secret file; Bonnin, nos. 223, 224.

burst in France. He must have anticipated that the French government would make representations at Berlin as well as at Madrid. No precise instructions could be given to meet the French action, but both Thile in Berlin and Abeken at Ems were well acquainted with his position.[20]

At about noon on July 4, Le Sourd, the French chargé d'affaires, called upon Thile at the Foreign Office, told him of the news that had come to Paris and of the bad impression it had made. It was important, therefore, to know if the Prussian government had anything to do with these negotiations. Thile replied that the Prussian government knew absolutely nothing about this affair and that for it, it did not exist.[21] As Le Sourd pointed out, Thile, who seemed to him visibly embarrassed, had tried to clear his government of any responsibility, but he had avoided a categorical affirmation that the cabinet of Berlin did not have *actual* knowledge of the negotiation and its result. It was obvious, however, that the Prussian government was not willing even to discuss the problem.

That same afternoon, even before Le Sourd's telegram was received, Gramont undertook a second *démarche* to the king of Prussia himself. Baron Karl von Werther, who had been Gramont's colleague at Vienna for several years, was about to go to Ems to pay his respects to King William. On the eve of his departure, he called on Gramont for the customary farewell but did not find him in. Gramont, in turn, called at the embassy, and as Werther was absent, left a note that he wished to see him before he left. Werther went back to the Foreign Office a little after six in the evening and found Gra-

---

[20] Lord, pp. 29–30, is undoubtedly correct in this, although not on the testimony of the so-called "letter of instructions" to Bucher. Cf. L. D. Steefel, "Bismarck and Bucher. The Letter of Instructions," in *Studies in Diplomatic History and Historiography in Honour of G. P. Gooch, C.H.*

[21] Tg., cipher, Le Sourd to Gramont, July 4, 1870, P.M., received 8 P.M., *O.D.*, vol. XXVIII, no. 8246. A letter, with fuller detail, was sent by mail. *Ibid.*, no. 8247 (direction politique, July 11).

mont and Ollivier waiting for him.[22] The two Frenchmen made it clear that the news of the candidacy was deeply resented by the French government. The emperor was so moved that he had said he would prefer even the Duke of Montpensier on the Spanish throne to a Hohenzollern prince. They did not know, they stated, if the Prussian cabinet was involved, but French public opinion would certainly believe that it was. The secrecy of the negotiations appeared as an unfriendly procedure not just of General Prim but especially of Prussia. In Paris, they insisted, there was a sincere desire for good and friendly relations with Prussia, but there could be no doubt that a Hohenzollern on the Spanish throne would inevitably change these relations for the worse. If the candidacy became an accomplished fact, it would compromise the peace. Such a solution of the Spanish problem was more than public opinion could put up with and, in the long run, Emperor Napoleon would not be able to accept it. The two ministers counted on the wisdom of King William not to give his consent to this project and suggested that the king use his influence to confirm the peace and to improve the relations of Prussia and France. Gramont gave as his opinion that a prince of Hohenzollern would not last more than six months at Madrid. Civil war or the coalition of various parties would drive him out. Ollivier emphasized the feeling in parliamentary circles that the candidacy would mean a resounding defeat for the Empire. Werther could reply in all good faith that he had known nothing at all about the whole affair. He was visibly affected by their statements and by the excitement of the newspapers, and agreed to bring these impressions to the attention of the king.[23] He left Paris on the evening of July 5 and arrived in Ems the following morning.

[22] On the sources and time, see Lord, p. 32, n. 15.

[23] This paragraph is based on Werther's report but the language of the French ministers, as told by them to foreign diplomats, was in some respects even stronger. See Lord, p. 33, especially n. 21.

Bismarck learned of Le Sourd's *démarche* on the afternoon of July 4. He found the French inquiry "very impertinent" and gave Thile's reply his full approval. He advised that if the question were repeated, Thile should ask for it in writing so that he could take the king's command for the answer. He also asked that Werther in Paris be informed of the interpellation and be instructed "to express our surprise and to say that the prince and the Spanish government were masters of their own wills." [24]

On the following morning Bismarck learned something of the second French *démarche*. Two brief telegrams from Werther alluded to the emotion at Paris, intimated that he had had a talk with Gramont and Ollivier, and announced that he was coming to Ems, intending to lay directly before the king the "extremely grave impressions" of the French ministers. For a moment, Abeken at Ems and Bismarck at Varzin thought of ordering Werther to remain at his post. But there were obvious objections to forbidding a journey which had already been announced. It could be interpreted as a tacit admission that Prussia was involved in the affair and alarmed at the French attitude.[25]

It would have created an even greater sensation if Bismarck had hurried from Varzin to Ems to stand by the king's side. He had, therefore, to depend on telegrams, letters, and Abeken to counteract the influence of Werther and the queen on the king's conciliatory disposition,[26] and to impress on the royal mind once more the principles upon which his strategy was based. Werther ought to have refused any discussion of questions that concerned only Spain and the prince of Hohenzol-

---

[24] Lord, p. 34 and document nos. 1, 4, 5.

[25] Lord, p. 34. In the telegram sent to Ems on the afternoon of the 5th, Bismarck did, indeed, hint at the inconvenience of Werther's journey at such a moment, but made no positive suggestion that it be countermanded.

[26] See Lord, p. 39.

lern. In a phrase which Prussian diplomats were henceforth to use on all occasions, Bismarck declared: "Respecting the independence of Spain and not called upon to interfere in Spanish constitutional questions, we leave the latter to the Spaniards and to those who wish to become such." If France wished to intervene in such matters, that was her affair and no concern of Prussia. "The acceptance of a discussion [on such a question] would weaken our otherwise unassailable position." Above all things, Prussia must avoid giving the impression that she could be intimidated.[27]

Werther reached Ems on the morning of July 6. His first words to Count Waldersee,[28] who met him at the station, were: "The devil is loose at Paris: it looks very much like war." He was informed by Abeken of Bismarck's standpoint and promised "not to worry the king." He was then received by King William in a long audience.[29]

Werther's oral report, which added such unpleasant details as Ollivier's threat that Leopold might well meet the fate of Maximilian of Mexico, intensified King William's concern at the premature explosion of the bomb. Now, only a few days after the revelation, all France was talking of war with Prussia. He regretted, he wrote to Karl Anton, that they had dropped the condition put forward in February that they should make sure of France, partly because Prim had asked for complete secrecy and partly because Bismarck had expressed the opinion that no one had a right to interfere when a nation chose a king for itself. It was to be foreseen that

[27] Lord, pp. 34–37.
[28] Military attaché at Paris. He had recently been appointed aide-de-camp and had been ordered to report to the king at Ems rather than immediately at Berlin. He left Paris on June 28 and arrived at Ems on July 3. He learned of the Hohenzollern candidacy from Paris telegrams received while he was dining with Queen Augusta at Coblenz on the evening of July 5. Waldersee, *Denkwürdigkeiten*, vol. I, pp. 70–71.
[29] Tg., Abeken to Bismarck, July 6, 1870, Lord, no. 21; Waldersee, p. 71.

this was not so, given France's centuries-old position toward Spain. He passed on to Karl Anton Bismarck's suggestion that Leopold try to win the confidence of Paris to head off the use of gold and influence to stir up conspiracies in the Spanish army. How this should be done King William left to the judgment of the Sigmaringen Hohenzollerns. He was convinced that France would do all in her power to block the election by the Cortes. If, in spite of this, the vote was favorable, Leopold should stop off in Paris on his way to Madrid, if the agitation there was not still too great, although even then his reception would probably be unfriendly.[30]

That evening, an even more disturbing telegram was received at Berlin and at Ems from the chargé d'affaires at Paris. Count Solms reported that Gramont had just replied in the Chamber of Deputies to an interpellation on the candidacy of the prince of Hohenzollern. Solms himself had not been present to hear it, but both the Russian chargé and the British ambassador had told him of the stormy applause and their alarm at the attitude of the Chamber.[31]

Le Sourd's telegraphic summary of his conversation with Thile had reached Paris at about eight o'clock on the evening of July 4. The next morning, Ollivier and Gramont were called to confer with the emperor at St. Cloud. "If we had merely been seeking a pretext for war," Ollivier has written in his apologia, "the conversation would have been short: we

---

[30] William to Karl Anton, July 6, 1870, Dittrich thesis, appendix 79. See Abeken to Karl Anton, July 6, 1870, secret file; Bonnin, no. 241; tg., Bucher to Thile, July 6, 1870, quoting tg. to Abeken, Lord, no. 19; Bismarck to crown prince, July 6, 1870, cited by Wertheimer, *Preussische Jahrbücher*, vol. CCV, p. 300. Lord's conjecture (p. 41) that "the really significant part of the King's letter, apparently, was the inquiry, the exact form of which we do not know, as to what the Sigmaringen princes intended to do in the face of this situation" is not confirmed by the full texts which have come to our knowledge since Lord wrote. See J. Dittrich, "Bismarck, Frankreich und die Hohenzollernkandidatur," *Die Welt als Geschichte*, vol. XIII, p. 52.

[31] Tg., Solms, July 6, 1870, Lord, no. 22; Waldersee, vol. I, p. 72.

had the pretext and it would not have been difficult to take advantage of it. But though we had decided to repel the Hohenzollern candidacy, even by war, we were passionately eager to have the candidacy disappear without war." [32] It was agreed that a formal statement of the attitude of the French government should be made, and the emperor instructed Gramont to prepare a draft for the approval of the Council of Ministers.

A suitable occasion for making the statement public was provided that very afternoon. At the suggestion of Thiers and with the approval of Ollivier, Adolphe Cochèry, a deputy of the left center, decided to interpellate the government on the eventual candidacy for the throne of Spain of a prince of the royal family of Prussia.[33]

On the morning of July 6, the emperor presided over a meeting of the Council of Ministers, the first since the news of the Hohenzollern candidacy had reached Paris. The specific business for which the meeting had been called was to approve the text of a reply to the interpellation. Before doing so, the Council examined the military and diplomatic situation. To most of those present, the question about the army was put only as a matter of form: they were confident of its readiness and superiority. Marshal Le Boeuf, the minister of war, merely confirmed the general opinion when he answered that the struggle would be difficult, but that as it was inevitable sooner or later, France could, now that the occasion offered, face it without fear. The army was admirable, disciplined, trained, valiant; its rifle better than the Prussian, its artillery commanded by crack officers, and its machine guns, which the Prussians did not have, "would produce as devastating effects as our rifles." Mobilization and concentration, on

[32] Ollivier, vol. XIV, p. 85.
[33] On the background of the interpellation, see Lehautcourt, *La candidature Hohenzollern*, pp. 235–236 and notes.

principles established by Marshal Niel, would be rapid, and if decided on with resolution and without loss of time, would catch the Prussians in the midst of their preparations.[34]

The Council then took up the question of alliances. "All of us, especially the emperor and I," Ollivier recorded, "were in favor of fostering close friendship with Great Britain. But under the circumstances, we had no material aid to expect from her, for we had nothing to offer her. We did, on the contrary, have something to offer to Italy, Austria, and Russia: to Italy, the evacuation of Rome and the opportunity to demonstrate her gratitude for services rendered; to Austria, revenge for Sadowa; to Russia, the revision of the Treaty of Paris." [35] Ollivier spoke in favor of seeking the Russian alliance; Gramont pointed out the obstacles and argued for Austria as the principal ally. While Ollivier was trying to rebut Gramont's points, the emperor got up, went to a desk, opened a drawer, took out and read aloud the letters which the emperor of Austria and the king of Italy had written to him in September 1869.[36] They were obviously not a binding treaty, but Napoleon implied that they were a promise of eventual aid in the situation in which France then found herself. He did not read the report of General Le Brun on his mission to Vienna and the plan of campaign of Archduke Albrecht, which he also held in his hands, but he spoke with confidence of the support to be expected. Napoleon did not explain the circumstances under which the letters had been written and was asked no embarrassing questions.[37]

With confidence in the military and diplomatic position of France, the ministers then moved to the reading and revision of the draft of Gramont's reply. In its final form, amended

[34] Ollivier, vol. XIV, pp. 99–101.

[35] Ollivier, vol. XIV, p. 101.

[36] Ollivier, vol. XIV, p. 105; H. Oncken, *Die Rheinpolitik* vol. III, nos. 728, 733.

[37] Ollivier, vol. XIV, pp. 101–106.

by both the emperor and Ollivier, it was approved by unanimous vote of the Council.[38]

The session of the Chamber was called to order at two o'clock, but in the state of excitement that prevailed, it was impossible to carry on routine business, and the meeting was practically suspended until Gramont appeared. Before the crowded floor and galleries, he read the official statement.

It is true that Marshal Prim has offered the crown of Spain to Prince Leopold of Hohenzollern and the latter has accepted it. But the Spanish people have not yet pronounced themselves and we still do not know the exact details of the negotiation which was kept secret from us. A debate now cannot, therefore, end in any practical results. We invite you, gentlemen, to adjourn. We have not ceased to manifest our sympathy for the Spanish nation nor to avoid everything that could give the appearance of any intervention at all in the internal affairs of a great nation carrying out its full sovereign rights; we have not departed from the most strict neutrality toward the various candidates for the throne and we have not shown for any of them either preference or aversion. We will continue this line of conduct. But we do not believe that respect for the rights of a neighboring people obliges us to endure that a foreign power, in placing one of its princes on the throne of Charles V, may upset to our disadvantage, the present balance of power in Europe and place in jeopardy the interests and the honor of France. This eventuality, we firmly hope, will not be realized. To prevent it, we count both on the wisdom of the German and on the friendship of the Spanish people. If it should be otherwise, gentlemen, strong in your support and in that of the nation, we shall know how to discharge our duty without faltering or weakness.[39]

The response to Gramont's statement was mixed. To many,

---

[38] The story that a violent draft was softened by the Council is not borne out by the evidence. See Ollivier, vol. XIV, pp. 107–108, 568–573; La Gorce, vol. VI, pp. 226–227.

[39] Solms reported that the version in the *Journal Officiel* had been toned down; that Gramont had actually said "mais nous ne souffrirons pas que" or "mais jamais nous ne souffrirons" and had emphasized this. H. Oncken, vol. III, p. 396, n. 1.

it seemed more like a first step to war than to negotiation. It was welcomed by the groups on the right, and the most excited acclamation came from them. In the left center and in part of the right center, the dominant impression was one of astonishment and anxiety. On the left, the questions suggested a belief in the warlike policy of the government and a welcome opening for the opposition to attack. The general impression of observers was one of enthusiastic support for the cabinet, but both Gramont and Ollivier seemed surprised at the intensity of the emotion in the Chamber and tried to soften the belligerent interpretation. To a deputy who rushed to him and exclaimed, "But this is war! This is a challenge that you are hurling at Prussia!" Gramont answered, "It is peace if that is possible; it is war if that is inevitable." Ollivier entered the debate to deny that Gramont's words were a declaration of war. "The government," he insisted, "wants peace — passionately wants peace — but peace with honor." He denied that the government, in giving vigorous expression to its views on a situation that touched the security and prestige of France, was compromising the peace of the world. In his opinion they had used the one remaining means of strengthening peace, "for every time that France has shown herself firm . . . in the defense of her legitimate interest, she is sure to have the moral support and the sanction of Europe." [40]

A generation later, Ollivier still held to this opinion. "The declaration which France received, in great majority, with impassioned approval, stirred up neither surprise nor shock in Europe except on the part of a few timorous diplomats who were scared of everything that rose above their usual cackling." It is true that a few influential foreign papers approved what had been said, but the leaders of British, Austrian, and Russian foreign policy did not.[41]

[40] Lehautcourt, pp. 247–253.
[41] Lehautcourt, pp. 258–261.

The first news of Gramont's statement to the Chamber of Deputies reached Bismarck at Varzin on the morning of July 7. Two telegrams were forwarded from Berlin: the one from Solms in which he told that Gramont had made a very stiff declaration in the Chamber, "amicable toward Spain but unfriendly toward us," and one from Bernstorff that it was believed in London that war was inevitable unless the candidacy were withdrawn.[42] The full text of the declaration from the Wolff telegraph agency, was telegraphed by Thile to Varzin at about 1:15 P.M., and Solm's telegram with the text from the *Journal Officiel*, received at Berlin at 3:23, was also sent on, probably that same afternoon.

In his *Erinnerungen und Gedanken*, Bismarck stated that the very fact that the French cabinet undertook to call Prussia to account for the candidacy, especially in a form that was interpreted by the French press as an open threat, was an act of international insolence that made it impossible to yield an inch.[43] Other sources, unreliable in detail but probably correct in substance, reported "stormy outbursts and wild projects; an explosion over the breakfast table on seeing Gramont's speech in the newspapers; a first impulse to demand that minister's dismissal, or to propose to the King the mobilization of the army and an immediate attack on . . . France." [44] A few weeks later, at the beginning of August, Bismarck told his table companions that after Gramont's speech, he had considered war as probable.[45]

War may have seemed probable and a sudden attack on

[42] Tg., Thile to Bucher, July 7, 1870, to the telegraph Station 9:15 A.M. The time of arrival is not given. Lord assumes, probably justly, that Bucher's telegram of 11:45 A.M. was in reply. It is clear, however, that the news had come from another source as well — which and in what detail, I do not know — for Bucher's telegram refers to "Cochèry's interpellation," which was not mentioned in the telegrams that we know went to Varzin.

[43] *G.W.*, vol. XV, p. 305, ll. 11–29.

[44] Lord, p. 45. See also A. O. Meyer, *Bismarcks Glaube*, pp. 35–38.

[45] [L. Bamberger], *Bismarcks grosses Spiel*, p. 141.

France might make victory certain, but Bismarck did not yield to unripe impulse. It would, in the first place, have been hard, probably impossible, to win the king's consent to a preventive war. In the second place, such action would have been disadvantageous. It would have stamped Prussia rather than France as the disturber of the peace. It would have cost valuable sympathies on the part of the public and governments of the other powers; and, perhaps most important of all, it would have wrecked the chance of rallying South German opinion to the support of the North. In 1867, the threat from France in the Luxemburg crisis had made easier the consolidation of the North German Confederation; in 1870, there was ample reason to expect that French menaces, even if they did not lead to war, would stimulate the national movement. Even if we should accept the opinion that Bismarck had taken up the Hohenzollern candidacy in order to provoke France to war, there was no real danger in waiting. As Lord has pointed out, Bismarck had also just learned, first, that in spite of the French remonstrances, the Spanish cabinet had decided to convoke the Cortes for July 20 in extraordinary session, to put through Leopold's election; and, second, that Benedetti was on his way to Ems on some kind of mission to the king. "After the French had burned their bridges behind them on the 6th of July, and with this terrifying date, the 20th, staring them in the face, it might be presumed that they would soon plunge into some new act of folly." [46] If France wanted war, then as Bismarck had often said, Germany was prepared. There was no political advantage in changing tactics now. If war did result, it was essential that Germany be attacked; otherwise, it was not certain that Bavaria and Württemberg would accept the *casus foederis*.

Whatever Bismarck may have thought in the first flush of indignation, the first thing that he did was to begin a cam-

[46] Lord, p. 46.

paign in the press. He instructed Thile that Gramont's answer to Cochèry's interpellation should be commented on in the sense of the telegram of July 5, with the added question: what has this all to do with the German people? [47] A second telegram, obviously an attempt to stir up Spanish national pride and to counteract Gramont's distinction between the responsibilities of Spain and Prussia, gave Busch directives for continuing the campaign. The semi-official papers were to point out that discussion of the problem of the Spanish crown was premature; only the Spanish Cortes had any standing for this and it had not yet acted. The German governments had respected the independence of Spain and would continue to do so. The unofficial press should express surprise over the fact that the French Chamber had taken this up "as if it had any right to dispose of the Spanish throne." The concluding sentence raised a specter: "Does Eugénie want a new War of the Spanish Succession?" [48]

On the copy of Solms's telegram which contains Gramont's words, Bismarck wrote: "Die Sprache ist doch sehr roh! Das kommt davon, wenn man solche Leute zu Ministers macht; spricht nur parti pris aus"; (opposite the phrase "Négotiation qui nous a été cachée"): "Haben die Franzosen uns etwa ihre Absichten mitgetheilt? Wir hatten fremde Geheimnisse zu wahren, für die Prim Schweigen verlangt hatte"; (opposite the phrase "qui une puissance étranger en plaçant un de ses princes sur le trône de Charles Quint," etc.): "Nicht wir, sondern die Cortez wählen den König für Spanien et le placent sur le trône." [49]

[47] Tg., Bucher to Thile, Varzin, July 7, 1870, 11:45 A.M., Lord, no. 28. The telegram of July 5 is Lord's document no. 13. See p. 109 above.

[48] Bucher to Foreign Office, Varzin, July 7, 1870, 1:50 P.M. Lord comments (p. 45, n. 66): "Bismarck's willingness to stoop to any means appears in his quite gratuitous singling out of the Empress Eugénie for attack." It was certainly not chivalrous, but Eugénie's hostility to Prussia and her support for the war party in Paris are established.

[49] Lord, p. 138, n. 2.

Official action by the German Foreign Office would have weakened the position which Bismarck insisted on, that the question concerned only Spain and the Hohenzollern-Sigmaringen family.[50] In a telegram to Secretary of State Thile, sent late on the evening of July 8, Bismarck merely said that he found the language "insolent and bumptious beyond all expectation," but that he disliked to make international protests over a parliamentary speech. "The newspapers, however, must be very rough, and as many of them as possible." [51] The press campaign was continued,[52] and Bismarck did nothing to relieve the tension. Gramont's speech was a convenient excuse to explain why Prussia could make no concessions to threats,[53] although, as Lord has convincingly shown, it was Bismarck's attitude from the beginning of the crisis that she would not even negotiate.[54]

King William's first reaction to the report of Gramont's declaration was that the ministers had spoken very sensibly in persuading the Chamber to return to the order of the day. No one, he said in a letter to the queen, could object that they had spoken of the honor of France and of their determination to defend it with vigor. It was a question, however, how the choice by Spain of a king other than one that France wanted could offend French honor so much that it must lead to war. France would certainly not be justified in making war against Prussia just because Spain sought a king from the princely branch of the Prussian royal house. It was, he concluded, a case of offended vanity, just as it had been after the Prussian

[50] See, for example, tg., Bismarck to Thile, Varzin, July 8, 1870, 5:15 P.M., Lord, no. 46.

[51] Lord, p. 46.

[52] See Lord, p. 45; M. Busch, *Bismarck: Some Secret Pages from His History*, vol I, pp. 35-46; and E. Schulz, *Bismarcks Einfluss auf die deutsche Presse (Juli 1870)*. On the French press, see especially L. M. Case, *French Opinion on War and Diplomacy during the Second Empire*, ch. x.

[53] Lord, p. 47.

[54] Lord, p. 37.

victories of 1866 — Napoleon had not made war at that time. The prince of the Asturias (the future King Alfonso) was now, William believed, the candidate favored by France. He could not see how Napoleon hoped to put him through in the face of the formal exclusion of the House of Bourbon, but he could see that it must be very unpleasant for Napoleon personally to have his plans crossed by the election of a Hohenzollern. It was to be foreseen that the French would try to turn the election even if it should cost them a million and it should not be too difficult for them to succeed. Prussia and the Hohenzollerns, on the other hand, would not spend a dollar to buy votes. He himself would not be sorry if Leopold failed to get the necessary majority.[55]

To some extent, no doubt, this letter was intended to reassure the queen. It was, however, becoming clear that the situation was serious and that, if the prince of Hohenzollern were elected king of Spain, it might not be possible to avoid war. In a long conference with Werther and Abeken, it seems to have been agreed that it would be desirable that Leopold renounce his candidacy. It must happen, however, without any pressure from the king.[56] "That we are now suddenly facing serious complications," the king told Count Waldersee,

is most disagreeable to me. I have to thank Bismarck for this; he made light of it, just as he did in many another case.[57] I cannot,

[55] William to Augusta, July 7, 1870, W. Oncken, *Unser Heldenkaiser*, pp. 185–186; Fester, *Briefe*, vol. II, no. 320. It is probable that this letter was written on the basis of press (Wolff agency?) reports of the proceedings in the Chamber of Deputies. The king's letter was being written when a telegram from Thile at Berlin to Abeken at Ems (Lord, no. 32) was received. Solms telegraphed the full text of Gramont's speech at 1:15 P.M. on July 7 (Lord, no. 31), and it was received at Berlin at 3:23 P.M. The duplicate to Ems would have arrived before that time, but I doubt if it could have been deciphered, copied, and presented to the king before he finished his letter.

[56] Waldersee, *Denkwürdigkeiten*, vol. I, p. 72.

[57] ". . . Ich verdanke dass jedenfalls Bismarck, der die Sache auf die leichte Achsel genommen hat, wie schon manche andere." Waldersee noted in the margin "Wörtlich." *Denkwürdigkeiten*, vol. I, pp. 72–73.

above all, intervene in the affair; I am holding firm to my original standpoint which is the only correct one. I cannot deny that I am playing two parts, but I can keep them completely separate. Never [in this affair] have I negotiated with anyone, directly or officially, and I have not committed myself to anything. I can only refer the French government to the prince of Hohenzollern and will not use any influence on him. But if France is seeking a pretext for war, — well, she will find us ready! [58] The world will have to believe me, that at my advanced age, I don't have any wish to lead in another great war and that it is not I who have lightly brought about such serious complications. But if war is forced on me, I will carry it on in firm reliance on my excellent army.[59]

In the meantime, Gramont had begun his appeal to the other powers. Lord Lyons reported:

The Duc de Gramont told me this afternoon [July 5] that the French Government had received positive intelligence that the Crown of Spain had been offered by General Prim to Prince Leopold of Hohenzollern, and has been accepted by the Prince. "To this," continued M. de Gramont, "France will not resign herself, and when I say that we will not resign ourselves to it, I mean that we shall not permit it, and that we shall use our whole strength to prevent it. . . ." M. de Gramont proceeded to observe to me that nothing could be further from the wishes of the French Government than to interfere in the internal affairs of Spain, but that the interest and dignity of France alike forbade them to permit the establishment of a Prussian dynasty in the Peninsula. They could not consent to the existence of a state of things which would oblige them, in case of war with Prussia, to keep a watch upon Spain which would paralyze a division of their army. The proposal to set the Crown of Spain upon a Prussian head was nothing less than an insult to France. With a full consideration of all that such a declaration implied, the Government of the Emperor declared that France would not endure it.

To the Austrian and Italian ambassadors, Gramont spoke in

[58] "Diese Worte wurden mit grossem Nachdruck gesagt." Waldersee's comment, *Denkwürdigkeiten*, vol. I, p. 74.

[59] July 8, before Waldersee's return to his post at Paris. *Denkwürdigkeiten*, vol. I, pp. 72–74.

much the same tone. "It won't come to pass; we will oppose it by every means, even by war against Prussia." He asked for diplomatic support to bring the candidacy to an end.[60] The British and Italian governments, also, were asked to use their influence at Madrid "to make clear to the Regent [Serrano] the perils in the scheme of which Marshal Prim is the real author." [61]

During the cabinet meeting on the morning of July 6, Napoleon passed to Gramont the draft of a telegram to be sent to Count Fleury at St. Petersburg: "I think it will be useful to send in cipher just this telegram: 'Inform Prince Gorchakov that if Prussia insists on the accession of the prince of Hohenzollern to the throne of Spain, it will be war.'" He was convinced, he explained orally, that the Russian emperor did not want a war to break out and would bring about the withdrawal of the candidacy.[62]

The major French diplomatic campaign and all of the threats of war were directed against Prussia, but the government did not overlook the possibility of blocking the candidacy in Spain. Every effort was made, however, to avoid wounding the national pride of the Spaniards by public statements or open menace.

Napoleon received the Spanish ambassador, Olózaga, at St. Cloud early on the afternoon of July 6 and made no secret of his own and France's dislike of the Hohenzollern candidacy.[63]

[60] Lyons to Granville, July 5, 1870, extract; Fester, *Briefe*, vol. I, no. 273; W. E. Mosse, *The European Powers and the German Question*, p. 382; Metternich to Beust, July 8, 1870, H. Oncken, vol. III, no. 847; tg. and dispatch, Nigra to Visconti-Venosta, July 5, 1870, cited by W. S. Halperin, "Visconti-Venosta and the Diplomatic Crisis of July 1870," *Journal of Modern History*, vol. XXXI, no. 4, pp. 295–296.

[61] Gramont to La Valette and to Malaret, July 7, 1870, *O.D.*, vol. XVIII, nos. 8300, 8296; Halperin, *Journal of Modern History*, vol. XXXI, no. 4, pp. 296–297.

[62] Ollivier, vol. XIV, p. 108; draft tg., Gramont to Fleury, July 6, 1870, *O.D.*, vol. XVIII, no. 8273.

[63] Tg., Napoleon to Gramont, St. Cloud, July 5, 1870, 10:25 P.M., *O.D.*, vol. XXVIII, no. 8252. Metternich, who went in to see the em-

Gramont, in his telegrams to Mercier at Madrid of the same date, emphasized that the Spanish people were masters of their own destiny and that France "today as before" would respect their sovereignty. Nevertheless, he instructed Mercier to say to Prim that the worst possible choice had been made and that the injury to France was deeply resented by the emperor. "Those who bring it up and advise Spain to accept it assume a considerable responsibility before their country and before Europe." [64] "Nothing is farther from our thoughts," he wrote a few hours later, "than to infringe on the liberty of the Spanish nation but the ordeal is very hard on us." [65] On the following day, after learning that the Cortes was to be convened in special session, Gramont responded with a veiled threat.

In spite of the circular of Marshal Prim and the communication which M. Olózaga has just made to me, we have too much condence in the [friendly] feelings of the Spanish nation to admit that they will persist at Madrid in the only solution which injures at the same time our interests and our honor. We will persist in our friendly conduct and *will continue to observe the vigilance on our Spanish border which is necessary to divert anything that might stir up troubles in the peninsula.* We will be faithful in our sympathies up to the last moment and we will certainly not be the first to break the bonds which have been dear to us and which we hoped we had made indissoluble.[66]

At the same time, Gramont and the emperor tried to exploit the differences in the Spanish government. It was known that Serrano, the Regent, had not been in full agreement with Prim. "The secretary of M. Olózaga has gone on his behalf to see the Regent to beg him not to assume the responsibility

peror as Olózaga was leaving, reports that he found his Spanish colleague "ayant l'air très mortifié" (H. Oncken, vol. III, no. 844).

[64] Tg., Gramont to Mercier, July 6, 1870, sent 4:05 P.M., *O.D.*, vol. XXVIII, no. 8269.

[65] 6:15 P.M., *O.D.*, vol. XXVIII, no. 8270.

[66] Tg., Gramont to Mercier, July 7, 1870, *O.D.*, vol. XXVIII, no. 8290. My italics.

of an affair that will be the signal for a war," Gramont informed Mercier. "See the Regent, act in the same sense, you will be seconded by the British ambassador and probably by those of Russia, Austria and Italy. Tell Serrano not to convoke the Cortes, that is the essential point." [67] Bartholdi, the secretary of embassy who had brought Mercier's dispatches, was sent back to Madrid with personal messages from Napoleon.[68] But even before this pressure had been exerted, news came of the first small break in the Spanish position. At the end of a long conversation with Mercier on the afternoon of July 7, Prim finally said, "How can we get out of this? I see only one way: let the prince say that he has met obstacles in the consent of the King, and then, instead of pressing him, I will facilitate his withdrawal." Prim declined to take the initiative and begged that his suggestion remain absolutely confidential.[69] On July 9, Gramont sent another telegram to Mercier and instructed him to see Serrano again. "Tell him that at the point where matters are now, he alone can save the peace of Europe by using his influence with the king of Prussia and the prince of Hohenzollern. Add that France and the whole world will be grateful to him, and that the government of the emperor will never forget so generous an action." [70]

Serrano was reluctant to act. He admitted to Mercier that if Prim had realized the danger involved in the candidacy, he might have told the prince that with all the good will on both sides, the best thing to do would be to renounce it. But from the moment that the secret was out, this would have been politically impossible. It was necessary to carry it through.

[67] Tg., Gramont to Mercier, July 7, 1870, 4 P.M., *O.D.*, vol. XXVIII, no. 8289. Cf. Gramont to Malaret, July 7, 1870, *ibid.*, no. 8292, to La Valette, *ibid.*, no. 8300. See also Olózaga to Sagasta, July 8 and July 9, Conde de Romanones, *Amadeo de Saboya*, pp. 177–179.

[68] Tg., Napoleon to Gramont, July 7, 1870, 1:10 P.M., *O.D.*, vol. XXVIII, no. 8287.

[69] Tg., Mercier to Gramont, Madrid, July 7, 1870, 4:20 P.M., received 11:45 P.M., *O.D.*, vol. XXVIII, no. 8296.

[70] Tg., Gramont to Mercier, July 9, 1870, *O.D.*, vol. XXVIII, no. 8340.

"You are not ignorant," he pointed out to Mercier, "of the extent to which public opinion charges Prim and me with thinking only of our personal ambitions and what would have been said if we had appeared not to take seriously a candidacy which has, after all, much in its favor." [71] On July 10, however, Mercier received a message from Serrano: "He is going at half-past five; keep it secret——." Serrano had sent his nephew and secretary, General Lopez Dominguez, to Sigmaringen.[72]

Officially, the diplomatic campaign was directed against Prussia, and on July 7, Gramont sent a telegram to Benedetti at Wildbad ordering him to go to the king of Prussia at Ems. An attaché would leave Paris the next morning with the instructions and would arrive at Ems at eleven o'clock at night.[73]

In his dispatch, the minister of foreign affairs informed the ambassador that as the question then stood and in consequence of the resentment in France, it was of the greatest interest to have some light on the real intentions of the Prussian government. "If the head of the Hohenzollern family has up to this time been unconcerned with this affair, we demand that he not remain so, and we beg him to intervene, if not by his

[71] He added an assurance that Bismarck had had nothing to do with it. Mercier to Gramont, July 9, 1870, *O.D.*, vol. XXVIII, no. 8365.
[72] "Le Régent m'écrit le mot suivant: 'Il est parti à cinq heures et demi; silence' " (tg., Mercier to Gramont, July 10, 1870, 9 P.M., received July 11, 12:45 A.M., *O.D.*, vol. XXVIII, no. 8380). The Spanish, as reported in Mercier's dispatch, uses the present indicative: "Sale a las cinco y media; silencio —." Mercier translated it to the past tense, no doubt because his telegram was sent after 5:30. Ollivier (vol. XIV, p. 167), gives 9 o'clock, the time of Mercier's telegram, as that of the note which Serrano wrote to Mercier.
[73] Gramont to Benedetti, July 7, 1870. The text as published by Benedetti, *Ma Mission en Prusse*, p. 315, gives the time as 11:45 P.M., that jublished in *O.D.*, vol. XXVIII, no. 8205, gives 11:25. Gramont began his official dispatch: "Ayant accepté l'offre que vous m'aviez faite de vous rendre à Ems. . . ."; the text of Benedetti's offer as we have it announces his arrival at Wildbad "yesterday" and adds: "Si vous avez des ordres à me donner, je m'y conformerai immédiatement" (*O.D.*, vol. XXVIII, no. 8294).

commands, at least by his advice to Prince Leopold." By exercising a decisive influence on the determinations of the prince and thus bringing the candidacy to an end, the king would also put an end to the disturbance caused by it, would spare Spain the bloodshed of a civil war, and would make a contribution to the cause of peace and to the good relations of France and Prussia.[74]

In a "private" letter, however, Gramont insisted on more than advice from the head of the family. The only thing that would satisfy France and prevent war, he stated, would be the categorical reply that "the government of the king does not give its approval to the acceptance [of the Spanish offer] by the prince of Hohenzollern and orders him to reverse this decision which was made without its permission." The matter was urgent because in case of an unsatisfactory reply, it would be necessary to begin troop movements in two days, on Saturday, July 9, so that the campaign could begin in two weeks. Benedetti was told to give the king the precedents of "certain crowns forbidden to certain princes" for reasons of high politics. He was warned against evasive answers and delaying tactics. "If you secure from the king that he revokes the acceptance of the prince of Hohenzollern, it will be an immense success and a great service. The king, on his part, will have assured the peace of Europe. Otherwise, it is war." [75]

The news that the French ambassador was coming reached Ems early on the evening of July 8.[76] The king decided to

---

[74] Gramont to Benedetti, July 7, 1870, *O.D.*, vol. XXVIII, no. 8297.

[75] Gramont to Benedetti, *lettre particulière*, July 7, 1870, *O.D.*, vol. XXVIII, no. 8298. The statement in the first paragraph of this letter as we have it in print: "Nous savons, par les aveux du prince lui-même, qu'il a combiné toute l'affaire avec le gouvernement prussien. . ." has caused much confusion. There is no known evidence that the prince of Hohenzollern made any communication to the French government. See, for example, Lehautcourt, p. 269, n. 4, and Fester, *Die Genesis der Emser Depesche*, pp. 73–74. If instead of "du prince," we may read "de Prim," the statement makes sense. *O.D.*, vol. XXVIII, p. 90, n. 3.

[76] Probably in a telegram sent by Benedetti en route from Wildbad.

receive him in audience, and Bismarck was informed that His Majesty would speak to him in the spirit of the instructions for the Paris embassy [77] and sternly about Gramont's speech. If, as then seemed probable, Benedetti should suggest a European congress, he would ask him if Spain was willing to have the question of its throne decided by a congress. There was no Prussian question to be submitted to it.[78]

King William received the French ambassador on July 9 at the appointed time, about three in the afternoon. Benedetti appealed to him to advise Prince Leopold to withdraw his candidacy. William admitted that he had authorized the prince to receive the Spanish offer, but he insisted that he had acted throughout in his capacity as head of the House of Hohenzollern and not as king of Prussia. He was in communication with the prince and his father in order to learn their reaction to the excitement in Paris. If they were disposed to withdraw the candidacy, he would approve their decision. He was awaiting an answer and would talk it over more fully when it had been received.[79]

A letter from Karl Anton reached Ems by postal messenger late on the night of July 9 and was presented to King William early the next morning. Karl Anton was obviously impressed by the excitement in Paris, but he assured the king that both his son and he would conscientiously maintain the standpoint adopted by the king, namely, to pass off the candidacy as an

See Lord, p. 49. A telegram from Solms in Paris arrived later. See Lord, no. 48.

[77] Lord, no. 18. See pp. 109–110 above.

[78] See Lord, nos. 43, 49. A European congress was known to be a frequent suggestion of Napoleon III when he needed to escape from a dilemma. Bismarck instructed Thile to use in the press: "Wer Congress will, muss nicht vorher öffentlich Krieg androhen für den Fall, dass seine Wille nicht geschieht." Lord, no. 62.

[79] Tg., Benedetti to Gramont, July 9, 1870, 8 P.M., *O.D.*, vol. XXVIII, no. 8355. The summary contains the essential facts of the conversation. For full details, see Benedetti to Gramont, dispatch no. 1, July 9, 1870, *lettre particulière*, July 9, 1870, "dans le nuit"; *ibid.*, nos. 8357, 8358; and tg., Abeken to Bismarck, July 9, July 10, 1870, Lord, nos. 72, 77.

internal family matter, "a question in which the Prussian government and state have no say." He would observe the strictest silence about His Majesty's consent "as required by family law." For the initiate, he added, this was no secret, and there was no necessity for outsiders to know about it. They would remain silent and let matters take their course. Until a few days ago, he had indulged in the silent hope that perhaps at the eleventh hour, nonacceptance might be based on an insufficient majority in the vote of the Cortes. Now, since the demonstration in the French Chamber of Deputies, he had lost this hope, for it now seemed a point of honor for both Spain and the Hohenzollerns not to yield to intimidation. If, however, the course of events and the good of the state made it advisable to yield, a hint from His Majesty would be sufficient. "In the same submissive spirit as the offer was finally accepted, it will now joyfully be declined, though for reasons of honor, no longer declined of our own free will." [80]

On the afternoon of the tenth, Werther called on Benedetti and told him that the king would probably want to renew their conversations the next morning. His Majesty had heard from Karl Anton, but as Leopold had not yet returned to his father, the news received was incomplete and insufficient.[81] Later, the king met Benedetti on the promenade, stopped him, and said merely that he had no reply from Leopold. Benedetti took the opportunity to impress upon William the urgency of the situation, and it was agreed that they would meet the next morning.[82]

[80] Karl Anton to William, Sigmaringen, July 8, 1870, original in secret file; Bonnin, no. 253. Extracts were published by Zingeler, *Karl Anton*, pp. 251–252, and reprinted by Fester, *Briefe*, vol. II, no. 345. A letter to Abeken was received at the same time. Secret file; Bonnin, no. 252. In it, Karl Anton comments on the French attitude toward the candidacy and agrees with the suggestion that after the election, Leopold should try to reach a personal reconciliation with Paris. See p. 111 above.

[81] Tg., Benedetti to Gramont, July 10, 1870, 8 P.M., *O.D.*, vol. XXVIII, no. 8378.

[82] Tg., Benedetti to Gramont, July 10, 1870, 11:30 P.M., *O.D.*, vol. XXVIII, no. 8381.

At the same time, the latest telegrams from Paris were laid before the king. He found them very alarming. Count Solms, the chargé d'affaires, reported that the situation was becoming more critical every moment. The French, he stated, had begun to arm, and his colleagues in the diplomatic corps and other well-informed persons were convinced that if Prussia did not put an end to the Hohenzollern candidacy within a few days, France would declare war. When Olózaga, the Spanish ambassador, had given Gramont official notice of the candidacy, the latter had simply referred to the statement to the Chamber of Deputies as his reply. France would leave Spain out of the issue but would declare war on Prussia if Leopold did not withdraw. Count Waldersee, the military attaché, added that in the ministries of war and navy, elaborate preparations were under way for a large-scale war. To be sure, the reserves had not yet been called up but it appeared that troop movements would begin "tomorrow [July 10]." It might be that France would strike without waiting for final mobilization.[83]

Abeken telegraphed at the king's command to ask Bismarck's opinion of the news and especially if the king should take measures of precaution or even return to Berlin.[84] This crossed a telegram from Bismarck stating that it was desirable to have Baron von Werther go back to his post since Solms seemed to be much too impressionable.[85] The king was not reassured; Waldersee had confirmed Solms's impressions. At noon, a telegram went off to Berlin to make sure that Bismarck had

[83] William to Augusta, July 10, 1870, W. Oncken, *Unser Heldenkaiser*, p. 186; Fester, *Briefe*, vol. II, no. 398. Tgs., Solms to the Foreign Office, July 9, 1870, sent 2:30 P.M., 3 P.M.; Solms to Bismarck (to Berlin), July 9, 1870, sent 10:40 P.M.; duplicates to Ems. Lord, nos. 64, 65, 70. In his letter to Queen Augusta, King William included details that are not in these telegrams.

[84] Abeken to Bismarck, July 10, 1870, sent to telegraph station, 10:50 A.M., Lord, no. 77.

[85] Bismarck to Abeken, Varzin, July 10, 1870, sent 11:15 A.M., received 12:10 P.M., Lord, no. 78.

the messages from Solms and to order the Foreign Office to lay the situation before the Ministry of State. The minister of war should have his attention called to the French military measures.[86] Early in the afternoon, another telegram to Bismarck asked if Werther might not take an autograph letter from the king to Emperor Napoleon [87] and if Prussia could and should appeal to the powers to use their good offices under the Paris protocol of 1856.[88] To both questions, the reply was "no." [89]

Sometime during that day, the king decided to send a trusted officer, Colonel Karl von Strantz,[90] to carry the latest news to Karl Anton at Sigmaringen. If, as Waldersee reports,[91] the king had agreed with Werther and Abeken as early as July 7 that the withdrawal of the candidacy was desirable if war was to be avoided, it was now essential. William was still firm in stating that he had not commanded Prince Leopold to accept the offer and that he would not command him to give it up, but he emphasized the serious nature of the situation and the military preparations reported to be taking place in France. So, if Leopold did make the decision, the king's "agreed" would again not be wanting. If this hint were not enough, Strantz could supply the necessary commentary by word of mouth [92] in a way that would not contradict the king's deter-

[86] Abeken to the Foreign Office, July 10, 1870, sent to telegraph station, 12:10 P.M., Lord, no. 80.

[87] If Werther, who was still at Ems, knew that the king had made this suggestion, it would help explain his readiness to listen on July 12 to Gramont's suggestion of the "letter of apology." See p. 153 below.

[88] Abeken to Bismarck, July 10, 1870, sent to telegraph station, 3 P.M., Lord, no. 82.

[89] Bismarck to Abeken, July 10, 1870, sent 7:17 P.M., received 9:30 P.M., Lord, no. 88.

[90] Strantz had visited Spain in December 1868. See p. 15 above.

[91] *Denkwürdigkeiten*, vol. I, p. 72.

[92] Fester, *Briefe*, vol. II, no. 399. The text of King William's letter as communicated to Fester by Dr. Zingeler may be a summary. The draft is apparently no longer in the Sigmaringen archives (it is not published by Dittrich), and the original is not in the secret file. Perhaps it was in the Hohenzollern Hausarchiv. That there was a letter is confirmed by

mination not to give orders. The statement to Benedetti that he was awaiting a reply from Sigmaringen made it necessary to get one as soon as possible.

The king did not inform Bismarck that he had sent Strantz to Sigmaringen; Abeken's draft of a telegram was canceled. Instead, Bismarck's suggestion that he was now well enough to come to Ems was answered by the request to do so as soon as possible.[93]

The telegram from Benedetti, which summarized his first conversation with King William, was delayed in transmission and was received at Paris with the middle third so garbled that it was impossible to determine its sense. The parts that could be read, however, made an unfavorable impression on the French ministers. It was now clear that King William had authorized Prince Leopold to accept the Spanish offer, that he had refused to order the prince to withdraw, and that a possible explanation for the position taken by the king was his desire to gain time for military preparations.[94] In reply, Gramont informed Benedetti by telegram of what had happened to his message and impressed upon him that he must obtain a definite response from the king. France could not wait while Prussia began military precautions. He added that it had been learned from Madrid that Serrano, the Regent, wanted Leopold to renounce. In a second telegram, Benedetti was told

---

Karl Anton's reply in the secret file. The paragraph referring to it was omitted from the earlier published version. Karl Anton's reply, secret file; Bonnin, no. 295.

[93] Bismarck to Abeken, telegram, July 10, 1870, sent 5:28 P.M., received 7:40 P.M.; Abeken to Bismarck, July 11, 1870, sent to telegraph station, 5:30 A.M. Abeken received the instructions from General Tresckow, chief of the military cabinet, at about 10:30 P.M. on July 10 (Lord, nos. 86, 101).

[94] Tg., Benedetti to Gramont, July 9, 1870, 8:55 P.M., received July 10, 11 A.M., *O.D.*, vol. XXVIII, no. 8355. The explanation given for the delay and the garbling was a violent electrical storm in the Rhine valley (*ibid.*, no. 8379). In the part that could not be read was Benedetti's preferred explanation: that the king really intended to leave the formal initiative to the Sigmaringen Hohenzollerns.

to write a dispatch which Gramont could read to the Chamber or make public in some other way "in which you show that the king knew of and authorized the acceptance by the prince of Hohenzollern and say especially that he [the king] has asked you [for time] for him to reach an understanding with the prince before he informs you of the decision." [95]

Ollivier felt that Benedetti's telegram confirmed his worst presentiments: the alternative of a dishonorable backdown or war. He invited his colleagues to meet at the Foreign Office at two o'clock; war was being forced upon them and there seemed nothing left but to resign themselves to it fearlessly, like men. His colleagues judged the situation as he did and, pending the decisions of a formal council to be held the next morning under the presidency of the emperor, they urged Gramont to keep up the pressure on Benedetti. Under the sting of public opinion, they were counting the hours. It was necessary to insist on a reply from the king tomorrow; the day after would be too late. [96]

The emperor, too, was impatient. Though Gramont's suspicions of Prussia's military activity were exaggerated, [97] Napoleon had begun precautionary measures. In consultation only with the minister of war, Marshal Le Boeuf, he had sent Colonel Gresley of the general staff to Algiers to order Marshal MacMahon to embark his troops as soon as possible. In addition, artillery and engineer officers were sent in civilian dress to examine the state of preparations of the fortresses in northeastern France. The generals commanding brigades were ordered to investigate the readiness of the recruiting stations to expedite eventual orders for the recall of the reserves and the adminis-

[95] Tgs., Gramont to Benedetti, July 10, 1870, "minute à chiffrer," 12:35 and 12:55 P.M., *O.D.*, vol. XXVIII, nos. 8368, 8369.

[96] Ollivier, vol. XIV, pp. 189–190.

[97] See tg., Le Sourd to Gramont, July 11, 1870, 4:48 P.M., received 7:30 P.M., transmitting the report of the military attaché in Berlin, Colonel Stoffel (*O.D.*, vol. XXVIII, no. 8401).

trative director of the war ministry was authorized to exceed the credits voted for his office.[98]

On the morning of the tenth, Napoleon talked with Count Ottaviano Vimercati, the special agent of King Victor Emanuel in the secret alliance negotiations. He explained that he had not summoned the ambassador because he did not want to hinder Italy's pacificatory endeavors. If the candidacy were renounced in any form, there would be no war. If, however, the Prussian answer which was expected on the eleventh should be unsatisfactory, he would send for Nigra and ask him to inform his government that the French government was counting on the "alliance" with Italy. The French troops would be "immediately" withdrawn from Civita Vecchia;[99] in return, he would ask Italy to send an army of 100,000 men via Vienna. "Hitherto Italy had been able to rely on him personally. Henceforth, if she joined France, she would be able to depend on the entire French nation."[100]

Gramont followed his telegrams to Benedetti with a "private" letter that was more detailed and more vehement: "If the king won't advise the prince of Hohenzollern to renounce, well, it's immediate war and in a few days we'll be on the Rhine."[101] Finally, late at night, Gramont sent off another telegram which informed Benedetti of the excited state of public opinion and insisted on a reply "negative or affirmative" from the king "tomorrow."[102]

[98] Ollivier, vol. XIV, p. 190. *The Times*, London, for July 11, 1870, prints a Paris report from the evening of July 9: "Ministers of War and Marine conferred with Emperor yesterday and today, and orders have been sent to concentrate a portion of the troops in Algeria."

[99] Where they were stationed to maintain the defense of the Papal States.

[100] Nigra to Visconti-Venosta, July 10, 1870, cited by Halperin, "Visconti-Venosta and the Diplomatic Crisis of July 1870," *Journal of Modern History*, vol. XXI, no. 4, p. 301.

[101] Gramont to Benedetti, July 10, 1870, *O.D.*, vol. XXVIII, no. 8382.

[102] Tg., Gramont to Benedetti, July 11, 1870, 1 A.M. Although dated July 11, it was obviously drafted on July 10 and "tomorrow" meant the 11th. *O.D.*, vol. XXVIII, no. 8378. Benedetti was also told that Serrano

The Council met on the morning of July 11, prepared to consider the military measures. Except for the minister of war, none of them knew that some steps had already been taken. The telegrams received from Benedetti and communicated to the Council showed that the ambassador had obtained no satisfaction from the king. He had, however, been told by the king in person that he would have another audience, and this justified the hope that there would be an answer "negative or affirmative." In addition, Benedetti had emphasized the opinion that if observable military measures were begun, war was inevitable. It was decided therefore to postpone everything except the authority for the minister of war to add a fourth battalion to the regiments and to recall to the colors troops presently on leave. The minister of marine, Admiral Rigault, also asked permission to call up six thousand sailors. When the Council refused, he threatened to resign and the decision was reversed.[103]

In the afternoon, the government faced the Chamber of Deputies. On the preceding day, Gramont had drafted a statement in which he traced the history of the candidacy and the state of the negotiations and made an appeal to the Chamber for an expression of opinion before the ministers made their recommendation to the emperor, "who alone, according to the constitution, has the right to declare war."[104] The statement could not be used. Indeed, there was really nothing to report except that negotiations were still in progress and that the cabinet was awaiting the reply on which its resolutions would depend. He appealed to "the patriotism and the political sense" of the Chamber to be satisfied for the moment with this incomplete information. Emanuel Arago tried to open a debate

---

was sending someone "to see the king and Bismarck" and to ask for the withdrawal of the candidacy.

[103] Ollivier, vol. XIV, pp. 194–195; Gramont, pp. 77–80; Lehautcourt, pp. 333–335.

[104] *O.D.*, vol. XXVIII, p. 186, n. 2.

by asking if the questions addressed to Prussia were limited to the immediate question of the offer made by Marshal Prim to a Prussian prince or did they cover a wide complex of issues as pretexts for a declaration of war. The discussion was cut off by a storm of protest from the right supported by some of the leaders of the left. A vote of closure passed easily and the ministers had no further chance to explain their policy. The general interpretation was that powerful groups in the assembly would not be satisfied simply by the end of the candidacy.[105] The war spirit seemed to be uncontrollable and that evening the Austrian ambassador and the military attaché, who were at St. Cloud until late at night, were convinced that the emperor had made up his mind to order mobilization the next day unless a completely satisfactory answer had been received from Ems.[106]

The formal action of the French minister of foreign affairs was seconded by the conversations of Ollivier with foreign diplomats and by the personal diplomacy of the emperor.

Ollivier had visited Werther again on July 5, shortly before the German ambassador's departure for Ems, and told him the additional news that the French ambassador at Madrid had reported Prim's words: "We were offered the candidacy of the prince of Hohenzollern-Sigmaringen without our having asked for it." At his official reception that evening, Ollivier spoke to Lord Lyons "at some length and with considerable emphasis." His language was similar to that of Gramont, but he entered into rather more detail and spoke with even more precision of the impossibility of permitting the prince to become king of Spain. "Public opinion in France," he said, "would never tolerate it. Any cabinet — any government — which acquiesced in it would be at once overthrown. For his own part, it was well known he had never been an enemy of Germany, but with

[105] See Ollivier, vol. XIV, pp. 198–201; Gramont, pp. 80–83; Lehautcourt, pp. 343–345.
[106] Lord, p. 63; H. Oncken, vol. III, nos. 872, 873.

all his good will toward the Germans he must confess that he felt this proceeding to be an insult, and fully shared the indignation of the public." He assured Lyons, however, that the declaration to be made on the following day would be "as mild as was compatible with the necessity of satisfying public opinion in France." [107]

Napoleon, on the afternoon of July 5, had invited Baron Alfons, the head of the Paris branch of the House of Rothschild, to come to St. Cloud and had told him that, as there was at the moment no secretary of state for foreign affairs in England,[108] he wanted a message conveyed to the prime minister, William E. Gladstone. He wanted him to know that the Council of Ministers at Madrid had decided to propose Leopold of Hohenzollern for the Spanish throne, that his candidacy would be intolerable for France, and that he hoped Gladstone would try to secure its withdrawal.[109]

Prince Richard Metternich, the Austrian ambassador, with whom Napoleon was accustomed to talk more freely than with most of the other diplomatists, found the emperor engrossed with "l'affaire Hohenzollern." He seemed to be delighted, and was inclined to be skeptical at the ambassador's confidence that Bismarck would be happy to be of service to France in this question — in return, probably, for reciprocity in something of more direct interest to Prussia. Empress Eugénie, Metternich reported, hoped that Prussia would not yield, and she seemed to have grown ten years younger at the thought of a political triumph or a war.[110]

[107] Lyons to Granville, July 7, 1870, Fester, *Briefe*, vol. II, no. 313. For Ollivier's conversation with Metternich, see Metternich to Beust, July 8, 1870, H. Oncken, vol. III, no. 850.

[108] Lord Clarendon died on June 27 and his successor, Lord Granville, was formally installed on July 6.

[109] The message was telegraphed to Lionel Rothschild in cipher and taken to Gladstone on the morning of the sixth. John Morley, *Life of William Ewart Gladstone*, vol. II, p. 325.

[110] The conversations took place at St. Cloud late on the afternoon of July 6. Tg., Metternich to Beust, Paris, July 6, 1870, 7:10 P.M.; letters, July 8, 1870; H. Oncken, vol. III, nos. 844, 848, 849.

The emperor was less belligerent than the empress. He continued to talk to Metternich and to Vimercati, the Italian military attaché, about the support that France might expect from Austria and Italy — both men had been active in the secret negotiations for a triple alliance — but he also continued his efforts, through indirect channels, to bring an end to the crisis by the withdrawal of the candidacy. He refused to permit Benedetti to see Prince Leopold,[111] it would have been beneath his dignity to send his ambassador to a prince who, he felt, had behaved so unfairly towards him. He did, on the other hand, request the king of the Belgians to write personally to Prince Leopold, and King Leopold suggested to Queen Victoria that she write a parallel letter.[112]

In his move to bring an end to the Hohenzollern candidacy, Napoleon found his most effectual ally in the Spanish ambassador at Paris. It may be, as Ollivier, who knew him well, says, that Olózaga was displeased that he had been kept in ignorance of the decision to offer the crown to Prince Leopold and that his personal sympathy for France and the emperor made him want to spare them the risk of a terrible war.[113] It is more probable that his action was inspired by his concern about the effects of the candidacy on Spain. He was afraid that if Leopold were elected, France would use every means to encourage civil war which would devastate the country and probably mean the end of the revolution.[114] He never

[111] See tg., Gramont to Benedetti, July 8, 1870, 1 A.M.; tg., Napoleon to Gramont, July 8, 1870, *O.D.*, vol. XXVIII, nos. 8308, 8314; Ollivier, vol. XIV, pp. 137–138; Gramont, pp. 66–67.

[112] Leopold of Belgium to Queen Victoria, copy, July 10, 1870, *The Letters of Queen Victoria*, 2d ser., vol. II, pp. 25–27; to Leopold of Hohenzollern, July 9, 1870, secret file (frames 911–913). Queen Victoria wrote, instead, to the Count of Flanders, the brother of King Leopold and the brother-in-law of Prince Leopold. Copy, July 11, 1870, *Letters of Queen Victoria*, vol. II, p. 28.

[113] Ollivier, vol. XIV, pp. 138–139.

[114] See especially his letter to Sagasta, July 9, 1870, in Conde de Romanones, *Amadeo de Saboya*, pp. 177–178. Arnim to Bismarck, Paris, January 14, 1873, reporting a conversation with Olózaga, Bonnin, no. 307.

had any doubt, he claimed,[115] that the Cortes and the Spanish nation would take up arms against France in defense of the elected king, but he was reluctant to have his country risk so much for the sake of the Hohenzollern dynasty. He went, secretly, to see Napoleon and, after assuring himself that the emperor would be satisfied if the candidacy were withdrawn, he agreed to appeal to Prince Leopold.[116] He was, he wrote to the prince, not only an ambassador but also a deputy in the Cortes. In this capacity it was his duty to go to Madrid to vote for Leopold and also to call upon the country to take vigorous action on his behalf. He knew that by doing so, Spain would embark on a course which would end in a great misfortune. At the same time, Olózaga took it upon himself to try to revive the candidacy of Ferdinand of Portugal.[117]

Olózaga's letter was taken to Sigmaringen by J. Strat, the Rumanian envoy at Paris, who was concerned over the effect that French hostility might have on the position of Prince Charles. Exposed as the prince was to the intrigues of rival political factions and of revolutionary exiles in Paris who were reputed to be in close touch with Russia, his position would have been intolerable if his opponents came to the conclusion that France, too, would look with favor on his downfall. It was rumored that Gramont regarded Prince Charles as an accomplice of his brother and was threatening to work to overthrow him. Strat believed that Gramont had already made contact with the conspirators. In return for his consent to use his influence at Sigmaringen, Strat asked and received from Napoleon the assurance that if the mission was successful,

[115] To a German ambassador, Bonnin, no. 307.
[116] According to his statements to Arnim, it was on the evening of July 7. This may be inaccurate; the other dates Arnim reports certainly are. Lord, p. 65, n. 6.
[117] Ollivier, vol. XIV, pp. 141–142; Carnota, *Saldanha*, vol. II, p. 407. Ferdinand had been his preference. See *O.D.*, vol. XXVIII, p. 141, n. 1; and Olózaga to Sagasta, Paris, July 1, 1870; Conde de Romanones, *Amadeo de Saboya*, p. 176.

Karl Anton, instead of having to fear the bad will of France, could count on her support for his son at Bucharest.[118]

Strat left Paris on the morning of July 10 and arrived at Sigmaringen on the following evening. He found Karl Anton both disconcerted and vexed by the declaration of the French government. His first response to Strat's suggestions was a flat refusal: his son was no longer a free agent; he was bound; he had given his word; he could not honorably withdraw. What would be the use of this dishonorable retreat, he argued. The emperor was only seeking a pretext for war and if this one were removed, he would create another. In reply, Strat succeeded in convincing the prince that he was mistaken about Napoleon's intentions; the emperor had no ulterior motives, and his desire for a peaceful settlement was serious and sincere. Strat then laid before Karl Anton the consequences of persistence. He described in the darkest colors the situation in which Leopold would find himself in Spain. He would have to struggle against the plots of the Alfonsists and of the Carlists who would be favored by France; against the intrigues of his defeated competitors, especially the Duke of Montpensier, and against republican revolts. When his candidacy had been first announced, Strat continued, there had been an immense majority of the Cortes in his favor, but, under the influence of fear or hatred, this was shrinking day by day. The best that could occur now would be a majority large enough to im-

---

[118] The most detailed account of Strat's mission is in Ollivier, vol. XIV, pp. 139–141, 206–210. Though Ollivier obtained his information from Olózaga and Strat, much of his account is, as Lord (p. 65) has shown, inaccurate. Lord's conclusion that Strat did not leave Paris until the morning of July 10 and arrived at Sigmaringen on the evening of July 11 is supported by the telegram of Horlock to Lasser, Paris, July 9, 1870, sent 11:38 (P.M.), received at Sigmaringen, July 10: "Wollen Sie gefälligst anzeigen dass Herr Strat morgen abend kommen wird" (Dittrich thesis, appendix 82). In addition to the sources cited by Lord, see Bamberg to Karl Anton, Paris, July 9, 1870, Fester, *Briefe*, vol. II, no. 381; and Strat to Olózaga, Paris, July 18, 1870, *O.D.*, vol. XXIX, no. 8635.

pose on him the duty of coming to Spain, but not enough to provide the force needed to maintain him. He might not even have time to limp to the throne; he would be overturned while mounting it. He would be lucky if he got out of the mess alive. He was being summoned to a catastrophe, not to a reign. As for Charles of Rumania, the situation was equally dark. A formidable conspiracy had been organized against him. The threads of it ran to Paris and it depended on the emperor whether they were to be cut off or extended. If Leopold renounced his candidacy, Napoleon would cut them; if not, he would not interfere. By his refusal to withdraw the candidacy, Karl Anton would be risking a throne that could be made secure in order to conquer one that was doubtful.[119]

Strat's arguments finally prevailed. They were supported, he told Ollivier, by the tears of the candidate's mother. In Karl Anton, too, political decisions were sometimes mixed with emotion. In a letter to Leopold from Nauheim, he had written after his meeting with the king and Bismarck on June 5:

> First of all, I want you to have a written welcome from me on your arrival at Sigmaringen. It is, *perhaps*, the last occasion for a long time to come on which you will greet the city of your fathers and your native land. I don't like it — I cannot bear to think about it! My heart breaks when I do. But in this situation in which we are, fits of emotion count for nothing — the day demands realism and the time of idealistic contemplation gives way within me to the categorical imperative of the present. . . . The king is in agreement with us, that is, he yields to the political compulsion of Bismarck. . . . *Perhaps, though, some European happening or other will still arise as an obstacle — if so, so much the better!* [120]

[119] Ollivier, vol. XIV, pp. 206–208. Although many of the details given by Ollivier are inaccurate, I see no reason to doubt the substance of his account of the arguments. It is consistent with Karl Anton's letters to King William and others as well as with the general situation.

[120] Dittrich thesis, appendix 63. The italics are mine. He admitted to King William that he had indulged in the silent hope that at the eleventh hour, nonacceptance might be based on the pretext of an in-

The "European happening" had come to pass. With France on the verge of mobilization and King William steadfastly refusing to order the withdrawal of the candidacy, it had become clear to the courts and diplomats of most of Europe that the decision for war or peace must be made at Sigmaringen. Voluntary renunciation by Prince Leopold offered the best hope of averting war between France and Prussia without compromising the dignity of either power. The prince, however, was "most unaccountably" lost somewhere in the Austrian Alps, and the inability of even his family to communicate with him seemed incomprehensible and even sinister. In his absence, the responsibility fell upon his father.[121]

It was not an easy decision for Karl Anton to make. On the one hand, his son had given his word to the Spanish government; on the other, he felt that it would be dishonorable for a Hohenzollern and a Prussian officer to give way before the threats of France. Above all, he hesitated to take political responsibility. He had agreed to the candidacy only because he had been persuaded that it was a matter of high political importance. He wanted the king to give him a hint if the course of events and the interests of state made it advisable to yield.[122] To meet the first obstacle, the obligation to Spain, Olózaga had provided a formula.[123] To meet the others, the mission of Colonel Strantz implied that a hint from the king was on its way.

Colonel Strantz, the officer sent by King William to Sigmaringen, left Ems on the evening of July 10. He missed his

---

sufficient majority in the Cortes but that since the reception of Gramont's speech in the Chamber of Deputies, he had given up this hope. It now seemed a point of honor for Spain and for the Hohenzollerns not to be intimidated. July 8, 1870, secret file; Bonnin, no. 253.

[121] See Lord, pp. 64–65.

[122] Karl Anton to King William, July 8, 1870, secret file; Bonnin, no. 253.

[123] Lord, p. 66, n. 9; and Arnim's report of a conversation with Olózaga, Arnim to Bismarck, Jan. 14, 1873, Bonnin, no. 307.

connection at Bruchsal in the morning and reached his destination so late at night that he did not give the king's letter to Karl Anton until the morning of the twelfth.[124]

Even before he opened the letter, Karl Anton told Strantz that he had decided, the night before, to renounce the candidacy on behalf of his son and had prepared the telegrams. "The thought of an imminent *casus belli* because of a purely family matter," he wrote to King William, "had become so unbearable that I had to hold myself in leash not to publish the decision already yesterday. But I thought it my duty first of all to await Colonel von Strantz's arrival." [125] Shortly after nine o'clock that morning, Strantz sent off the news to Abeken at Ems: "Found everybody favorably prepared. My arrival turned the scales, induced betrothed to renounce alliance; returning noon tomorrow." [126]

An hour later, the telegrams announcing the withdrawal of the candidacy were sent off in French. The first was addressed:

To the Spanish Ambassador, Paris. I deem it my duty to inform you as the ambassador of Spain at Paris that I have just dispatched to Madrid to Marshal Prim, the following telegram: "In view of the complications which the candidacy of my son Leopold for the throne of Spain seems to meet, and the difficult situation which recent events have created for the Spanish nation by placing it in the dilemma in which [its action] can be guided only by its feeling of independence, [and] convinced that in such circumstances its vote cannot have the sincerity and spontaneity on which my son had counted in accepting the candidacy, I withdraw it in his name. — [signed] Prince of Hohenzollern.

[124] Tg., Abeken to Karl Anton, Ems, July 11, 1870; tg., Strantz to Abeken, Bruchsal, July 11, 10:35 A.M., received at Ems, 6:15 P.M. (!); tg., Abeken to Karl Anton, July 11, to telegraph office at Ems, 8:10 P.M.; Karl Anton to King William, July 12; all in secret file; Bonnin, nos. 273, 274, 282, 295. A note by Karl Anton gives the time of Strantz's arrival as 1 A.M. on July 12; Fester, *Briefe*, vol. II, no. 448.
[125] Karl Anton to King William, July 12, 1870, secret file; Bonnin, no. 295.
[126] Tg., *en clair*, July 12, 1870, 9:15 A.M., Bonnin, no. 290, with misprint "3:15" as time of filing.

This was dispatched a few minutes before that to Prim, "that being the best way . . . to bring its contents to the knowledge of the French government." The *Schwäbische Merkur* at Stuttgart and the *Allgemeine Zeitung* at Augsburg were notified that "In order to restore to the Spanish government its freedom of initiative, the hereditary prince withdraws his candidacy for the throne, firmly determined not to let a minor family matter become a pretext for war." [127]

[127] Karl Anton to King William, July 12, 1870, enclosing texts of telegrams, secret file; Bonnin, no. 297. The telegram to Olózaga was dispatched at 10:28 A.M.; that to Prim at 10:35; *O.D.*, vol. XXVIII, p. 252, n. 1.

·⟨IV⟩·

The Demand for Guarantees

On the morning of Tuesday, July 12, Emperor Napoleon
came to the Tuileries to preside over the Council of Ministers.[1]
The first important business was to consider the instructions
to be sent to Benedetti in reply to his telegram of the preceding
afternoon. The ambassador had informed his government that
King William still intended to leave to Prince Leopold complete freedom of decision and was determined not to depart
from the role he had followed from the beginning of the affair.
The king had urged Benedetti to telegraph in his name to Gramont that the prince expected to join his father at Sigmaringen.
He, the king, would then not delay in giving a final answer.[2]
This was less than had been asked, but the Council agreed to
wait. Gramont was authorized to telegraph to Benedetti that
it had never been the intention of the French government to
provoke a conflict but only to defend the legitimate interests
of France; that the Council could not accept the king's reasoning as just but, reserving the claims already made, they would
not refuse the requested delay; and that they hoped that it
would not be for more than one day.[3]

[1] He left St. Cloud at 8:45 A.M. The time needed to reach the Tuileries was about 45 minutes. *O.D.*, vol. XVIII, p. 249, n. 4; and nos. 8426,
8427.
[2] Tg., Benedetti to Gramont, Ems, July 11, 1870, 1:30 P.M., dispatched
3:35 P.M., received 6:15 P.M., *O.D.*, vol. XVIII, no. 8395.
[3] Tg., Gramont to Benedetti, July 12, 1870, 12:45 P.M., Benedetti,

After reaching this important decision, the Council took up other items of current business. While this was going on, a chamberlain entered and in a low voice said a few words to the emperor. Napoleon rose and left the room for a few minutes. He had gone to receive Olózaga, the Spanish ambassador, who had come to inform him of a cipher telegram received during the night from Strat at Sigmaringen, which reported that telegrams announcing the renunciation would be sent out on the morning of the twelfth. As Olózaga insisted on secrecy, Napoleon did not pass the news on to the Council.[4] The meeting adjourned at about 11:30 and the ministers separated.[5]

Karl Anton's open telegrams to Olózaga and Prim, which had been dispatched from Sigmaringen at about half past ten on that morning, were intercepted in Paris at the Ministry of the Interior. Copies were brought to the emperor at the Tuileries at about quarter to two [6] and to Ollivier, a few minutes later, as he was crossing the Tuileries Gardens on his way to the Chamber of Deputies. So long as he had only a copy, the source of which he could not reveal, Ollivier kept the secret. In response to questions, he answered that there was still no news but that Gramont was about to have a conference with Werther, and they hoped, by the end of the day, to have something specific to report. Then Olózaga himself appeared in the lobby. Ollivier has left a vivid picture of the scene. "With animation in his countenance and waving a piece of paper in his hand, he rushed towards me and drew me into a corner. 'Is Gramont here?' — 'No, he is at the Ministry of

Ma Mission en Prusse, p. 369; Gramont, *La France et la Prusse*, pp. 102–103. The text, *O.D.*, vol. XVIII, no. 8420, differs from the version given by Benedetti and Gramont in a number of ways, most important of which are the omission of the objection to the king's reasoning and the reservation of the French claims.

[4] Ollivier, vol. XIV, pp. 227–228, 266. See Olózaga's account, with incorrect dates, in Arnim to Bismarck, Paris, January 14, 1873, Bonnin, no. 307.

[5] *O.D.*, vol. XXVIII, p. 5; Ollivier, vol. XIV, pp. 227–228.

[6] *O.D.*, vol. XXVIII, p. 252, n. 1.

Foreign Affairs in conference with Werther.' — 'I have good news to give you,' and he read me the telegram which I already had in my pocket. 'Then the news is reliable?' I said to him. 'Yes, yes, don't have any doubts about it; the affair is finished.' " [7]

The foreign diplomats at Paris generally considered the renunciation as an unquestionable and striking diplomatic victory for France. Nigra, the Italian ambassador, saw the emperor and congratulated him enthusiastically: "It's a great moral victory for France, the more valuable because it has been won without bloodshed." [8] Lord Lyons, the British ambassador, advised Gramont to be satisfied with his diplomatic triumph.[9] As soon as he learned of it, Beust, the Austrian chancellor, sent Metternich a telegram in which he urged the French government to rest on its laurels and to stop with the diplomatic success which it had unquestionably won.[10]

Among the French, Benedetti thought that France had received adequate satisfaction. Thiers, who was notorious for his opposition to Prussian gains, was triumphant: "By forcing Prussia to back down in an enterprise which the whole world believes was deliberately undertaken, we have a tremendous advantage. . . . We emerge from an embarrassing dilemma with a victory; Sadowa is almost avenged." In an oft-quoted statement, Guizot, historian and long-time minister of foreign affairs of the Orleans monarchy, said, "Those fellows have unheard-of luck: this is the finest diplomatic victory I have ever seen." Of the cabinet ministers, at least four — Esquirou de Parieu, Charles Plichon, Charles Louvet, and Emile Ségris — agreed with the opinion of Thiers.[11] Ollivier, the historian, in

[7] Ollivier, vol. XIV, pp. 228–231.
[8] Fester, *Briefe*, vol. II, no. 464.
[9] Lyons to Granville, July 12, 1870, Fester, *Briefe*, vol. II, no. 482.
[10] Tgs. Beust to Metternich, July 13, 1870, 1:25 P.M.; July 13, 4:30 P.M., H. Oncken, *Rheinpolitick*, vol. III, nos. 877, 880.
[11] Muret, "Emile Ollivier et le Duc de Gramont," *Revue d'histoire moderne et contemporaine*, vol. XIII, pp. 306–308.

the fourteenth volume of *L'Empire libéral*, gives eloquent expression to the same point of view. He alludes to Bismarck's account of the failure of his plan and of the bitterness with which he received the news of the renunciation on his arrival at Berlin from Varzin.

In a flash, he saw its lamentable consequences for himself. He was disappointed, crushed, humiliated, left in the lurch by his king, by his candidate; he would become the laughing stock of Germany and of Europe. His structure of falsehoods was falling to pieces about his head. . . . We said on July 6: "We will not tolerate a Hohenzollern candidacy"; and on July 12, the Hohenzollern candidacy had vanished. We had not fallen into the pit which Bismarck had dug for us; we had shoved him into it.[12]

It was tragic for France that Ollivier, the minister and statesman, did not see this clearly in 1870 and hold to it firmly.

In the first flush of excitement after receiving the text from Olózaga, Ollivier made no secret of the happy news to the journalists and deputies who surrounded him. He soon realized, however, that this might not be enough. He had just learned that Leon Gambetta, in a speech at a meeting of the "irreconcilable left," had declared that they must consider the Hohenzollern candidacy as a mere detail and demand the complete execution of the Treaty of Prague and the demolition of the German fortresses that menaced the French frontier. From the ranks of the moderates came the warning that if the cabinet did not go beyond the question of the candidacy, its fall was certain. From the right there was a storm of angry protests. As soon as the minutes of the previous meeting had been read to the Chamber of Deputies, Clement Duvernois presented an interpellation on behalf of a group of his colleagues: "We ask to question the cabinet about the guarantees which it has stipulated or which it intends to stipulate in

[12] Ollivier, vol. XIV, pp. 218–220, 238.

order to prevent the return of further complications with Prussia." At this moment, Ollivier was called out to receive a message from the emperor inviting him to come to the Tuileries. "You know the telegram of Prince Anton to Marshal Prim. If we announce this news to the Chamber, we must get as much as possible out of it and give the impression that it was at the order of the king of Prussia that the candidacy has been withdrawn. . . . The country will be disappointed. But what is there to do?" Ollivier did not dare to make the formal announcement without consulting his colleagues and, especially, without knowing what Werther had brought from Ems. He went at once to the emperor.[13]

Napoleon seemed satisfied because the candidacy was removed but worried that the public would feel that the quarrel with Prussia had not been definitely brought to an end. The emperor admitted to Ollivier that King William had not ordered the renunciation. It was due entirely to the initiative of Olózaga, who had acted without the knowledge of Prim though with his, Napoleon's, authorization. Under these circumstances, no communication could be made to the Chamber. They would risk a blistering *démenti* from Bismarck which could reopen the whole question. Moreover, if Olózaga was acting on his own responsibility, who could tell what Madrid would think of it? Olózaga was the ambassador of Spain, not of Karl Anton. Napoleon and Ollivier agreed, therefore, that no further decisions should be reached before a meeting of the Council the following morning at St. Cloud.[14]

That the emperor at this time seemed ready to accept the withdrawal of the candidacy as a satisfactory and final solution is confirmed by other testimony. In a telegram to King Victor Emanuel, Nigra quoted Napoleon as saying, "It is peace and I have invited you to come to me so that you can tele-

[13] Ollivier, vol. XIV, pp. 230–237.
[14] Ollivier, vol. XIV, pp. 239–241.

graph this to your government. . . . I know that public opinion in France, in its present exaltation, would have preferred . . . war, but I see in the renunciation a satisfactory solution which deprives us of any pretext for war, at least for the moment." [15] Later in the day, however, he changed his mind.

Gramont, in the meantime, had gone to his ministry at the Quai d'Orsay where he drafted and dispatched the telegram of 12:45 P.M. that informed Benedetti of the decision of the Council to wait another day.[16] He then drafted and dispatched at 1:40 P.M. a second and "very confidential" telegram. He urged Benedetti to use all his skill and ingenuity to establish beyond any doubt that the renunciation by the prince of Hohenzollern was "announced, communicated, or transmitted" by the king of Prussia or by his government. It was of the utmost importance, he added, that the participation of the king must at all costs be admitted or at least be manifest from perceptible facts.[17]

In his own account of the events of the day, Gramont asserted that these two telegrams were based on the impressions produced by a telegram, a dispatch, and a "private" letter received from Benedetti in the course of the morning.[18] This could not be true of the telegram of 12:45 P.M., which merely reproduced a decision reached by the Council at a time when it could not have had the new documents before it, but only of the one of 1:40 P.M.[19] Benedetti's telegram acknowledged

[15] Nigra, "Souvenirs diplomatiques 1870," *Bibliothèque universelle et revue suisse*, vol. LXV, pp. 454-455.

[16] See p. 144.

[17] Tg., July 12, 1870, 1:45 P.M., *O.D.*, vol. XXVIII, no. 8421. The decipher at Ems differs in a few respects from Gramont's draft. See Gramont, pp. 104-106.

[18] Gramont, p. 102.

[19] Benedetti's telegram, July 12, 1870, dispatched at 8:30 A.M., reached Paris at about 10:15. Even if it had been deciphered and brought to the Council, there is no reason to believe that it would have influenced the decision. The long dispatch in cipher and the letter were brought by

receipt of Gramont's urgent message of the preceding evening, which informed the ambassador that his language was not vigorous enough to represent the position taken by the emperor's government, and which concluded with a virtual ultimatum: "We demand that the king forbid the prince of Hohenzollern to persist in his candidacy, and, if we do not have a final answer tomorrow [July 12], we will regard silence or ambiguity as a refusal to do what we ask." [20] In answer to this rebuke, Benedetti stated that he had already used firmer and more pressing language and warned that he could not accentuate it without harm to the object of his mission.[21] The dispatch and the letter reproduced the main points reported in telegrams already received in Paris, but the fuller description of the conversations made it clear that the king's decision was firm and that the ambassador had been unable to modify it.[22] It had become useless to demand that the king forbid Leopold to persist in his candidacy. The king would not do it. It was useless even to demand that the king advise Leopold to withdraw. He would not do even that. All that Benedetti had obtained was the hint that the renunciation of the offered crown must be the spontaneous act of the prince and that, when the decision was made, the king would approve it. When Gramont drafted his second telegram to Benedetti, he had then, by implication, dropped his stern demands of the

---

Baron Bourqueney (Benedetti to Gramont, letter, July 11, 1870, 6 P.M., Gramont, appendix 15; *O.D.*, vol. XXVIII, no. 8410 — Gramont's text, p. 96, says by Count Daru, an error which has generally been repeated) on the train that normally reached Paris at 10:15 A.M. It is improbable that they could have been carried from the railway station to the Foreign Office, deciphered, copied, and taken to the Tuileries before 11:30 A.M. when the Council adjourned. Gramont does not mention the Council at all, but there is no reason to suppose that he did not attend the meeting. I conclude, therefore, that he found all three documents, the telegram, the dispatch, and the letter, at his office when he went there after the Council meeting.

[20] *O.D.*, vol. XXVIII, no. 8399.
[21] *O.D.*, vol. XXVIII, no. 8418.
[22] *O.D.*, vol. XXVIII, nos. 8409, 8410.

preceding evening and indicated that he would accept, as a final solution to the controversy, the indirect and implicit participation of the king of Prussia in the withdrawal of the candidacy.[23]

During the next hour, as he prepared for a meeting with the German ambassador, Gramont came to the conclusion that indirect and implicit participation by the king would not satisfy the Chambers, the press, and the public. He felt more certain than ever that the Prussian government was deeply involved in the affair and that the king himself, "forgetting for a moment his usual discretion had explained [to Benedetti] the details of the intrigue." Prussia, he was convinced, had created the problem and must not evade the responsibility for it. It is probable that he, too, soon after two o'clock had learned from the intercepted telegram that the candidacy had been given up and that the announcement of this had come not from the king at Ems but from the candidate's father at Sigmaringen.[24]

In his testimony before the Commission of Inquiry in 1871 and in his book in 1872, Gramont tried to demonstrate that the revelation of the telegram from Karl Anton to Olózaga

[23] See Gramont, pp. 93–97; Muret, pp. 323–325.
[24] Ollivier (vol. XIV, p. 229) says, "Chevandier [Minister of the Interior] me l'envoyait [the intercept] en même temps qu'à l'Empereur et à Gramont." He adds (p. 243), "Gramont reçevait lui aussi, de la main d'un envoyé du Ministère de l'Intérieur, la copie de la dépêche en clair du prince Antoine à Olózaga. Il n'accueillit pas la nouvelle avec la même joie que moi." Gramont, on the other hand, claimed that he did not learn of the telegram until Olózaga brought it to him at about 3 o'clock. His statement is not convincing. He had made it a point of honor not to reveal in his book any confidences that were not already known from other sources, and his statement — "nous apprenions le désistement par une dépêche publique de la compagnie Havas, expédiée en clair, et par conséquent connue sur son passage par bien d'autres avant de nous arriver" — is an obvious evasion (Gramont, pp. 112–113, *after* he has described the receipt of the news from Olózaga). It is difficult to believe that an intercept of such importance was not delivered to Gramont, the minister of foreign affairs, at the same time that it was to the emperor and to Ollivier.

made impractical the expedient of indirect and implicit participation. "Everything that had taken place," he argued, "had been between the prince of Hohenzollern and Spain. Not only had the king of Prussia not communicated anything to us but we were to learn about the withdrawal from a Havas agency report sent out unciphered and therefore known to many others before reaching us." The very text of the message from Karl Anton was offensive to France; it implied that by her protest France was infringing on the independence of the Spanish people. There was nothing in the transaction to atone for the slight to France's legitimate interests and dignity. Gramont planned, therefore, to try to get what he wanted from Werther. "While Werther was with us," he testified, "I said to him: 'This renunciation of the prince of Hohenzollern did not come about without the advice of the king. . . .' If Werther had admitted this, I would have taken formal note of his answer. I was within my rights for the word of an ambassador to a minister of foreign affairs is an official act." As an additional way to associate the king of Prussia with the renunciation, Gramont prepared the text of a letter to be sent by King William to Emperor Napoleon:

By renouncing spontaneously the candidacy for the throne of Spain which has been offered to him, my cousin the prince of Hohenzollern has brought to an end an incident whose origin has been badly interpreted and whose consequences, exaggerated. I attach too high a price to the friendly relations between the North German Confederation and France not to be happy about a solution which is of a nature to safeguard them.[25]

Werther arrived at the Foreign Office at about a quarter to three and was received by Gramont in the friendliest manner, as was customary with old friends. Ten or fifteen minutes later, they were interrupted by a message: the Spanish am-

---

[25] Gramont, pp. 112–115, 123; Lehautcourt, *Les Origines de la guerre de 1870*, pp. 382–383.

bassador asked to be received immediately since he had a communication of the utmost importance to make. Werther did not object to the exceptional procedure and went into a neighboring room while Gramont received from Olózaga the text of Karl Anton's telegram. After a few moments, Olózaga left and Werther came back into the room. The discussion then dealt especially with the theme that King William had authorized the candidacy of a prince of his royal house without consulting the French government. As a neighbor of Spain, it was obvious that France must have important interests in the matter and the failure to attempt any kind of understanding with the imperial government could not be anything but offensive. If, however, as Benedetti had reported and as Werther emphasized, the slight to France had not been intended, could not the king make this clear? The renunciation by Prince Leopold was of secondary importance, for the French government would never have allowed him to ascend the throne; but the procedure threatened to create lasting bad feeling between the two countries. This could be averted by a letter from King William to Emperor Napoleon. It could say that, in authorizing Prince Leopold of Hohenzollern to accept the throne of Spain, the king had not believed that he was giving offense to the interests or the honor of the French nation, and that His Majesty associated himself with the renunciation by the prince of Hohenzollern and wished that every ground of discord between the two governments would from this time disappear. At about this time, Ollivier arrived and joined the discussion. The French ministers urged Werther, in the interest of peace, to bring their suggestion to the king and said that if he did not, they would instruct Benedetti to do so.[26]

Gramont has left no explanation of why he did not use

[26] Gramont, pp. 107–124; Ollivier, vol. XIV, pp. 244–251; Werther to King William, Paris, July 12, 1870, Lord, *The Origins of the War of 1870*, no. 150; Muret, pp. pp. 178–191.

his original draft of a letter from King William to Emperor Napoleon. It may have been because of his growing irritation at the way, as it seemed to him, that the king through his ambassador was evading responsibility; it may have been that he felt that the milder form would have been ineffective in calming the deputies and the press; it may have been that he was encouraged by Werther's insistence that the king, in authorizing the candidacy, had never had the intention of offending the emperor or had supposed that it would give umbrage to France.[27] It was an unfortunate change. The early draft might perhaps have been accepted by King William. He had himself suggested a letter to Napoleon but had been dissuaded by Bismarck. He had sent Werther back to Paris to discuss the Prussian position with the emperor.[28] At any rate, the early draft was less obviously a "letter of apology" than the second one. As Lord has conclusively shown, however, the influence of Werther's report of this incident was less than had long been supposed.[29] It did not reach Ems until the afternoon of July 13 and could not have affected William's attitude toward Benedetti in the morning.[30] The interview with Werther and the letter pressed on him by Gramont and Ollivier had, on the basis of our present knowledge, no major effect on the course of events. Its significance is rather that it shows the French ministers, and especially Gramont, moving away from the policy outlined in Gramont's telegram of 1:40 P.M. to Benedetti [31] and towards the fatal decision that followed, to demand additional guarantees from the king.

[27] Werther (Lord, no. 150) does not report that he admitted this. Gramont (p. 120) asserts it and in this case, I am disposed to accept his testimony.

[28] William to Augusta July 12, 1870, W. Oncken, *Unser Heldenkaiser*, pp. 188–190; Fester, *Briefe*, vol. II, p. 93.

[29] Lord, pp. 81–83.

[30] See pp. 178–182 below.

[31] See p. 149 above.

After the German ambassador took his leave, Ollivier returned to his ministry, and Gramont went to the Tuileries to report to the emperor.[32] Ollivier, apparently, believed that it was understood between them that no further decisions would

[32] Gramont puts the end of the meeting at the Quai d'Orsay at about 3:30 P.M. (Gramont, p. 127); Ollivier at about 4 (Ollivier, vol. XIV, p. 251). The latter hour seems more accurate. According to both Gramont and Ollivier, the former went to St. Cloud where he found the emperor moved by the attitude of the empress and the court to agree to stronger action. The situation is described in detail by Ollivier, vol. XIV, pp. 251–263. Gramont gives fewer details but concludes with the statement that on his return from St. Cloud, he sent a telegram to Benedetti at 7 P.M. In 1906, Empress Eugénie told Paléologue that she was with the emperor and Gramont when the telegram was drafted (M. Paléologue, *The Tragic Empress*, pp. 133–134).

We now have evidence that make it impossible to accept the traditional account of events. A telegram from the Tuileries to the cabinet at St. Cloud, received at 4:30 P.M., states that the departure from the Tuileries had been delayed and asks that dispatches judged to be of sufficient interest be transmitted to the Tuileries. It is a fair conjecture that the delay was caused by the arrival of Gramont. An hour later, a telegram, received at St. Cloud at 5:31, announced the departure of the emperor from the Tuileries at 5:30, and another, received at the Tuileries at 6:16, reports the arrival of the emperor at St. Cloud at 6:15 (*O.D.*, vol. XXVIII, nos. 8424, 8426, 8427). The draft of Gramont's telegram is marked 6:15 P.M. According to Gramont (p. 131) and Paléologue, who examined the file at the Quai d'Orsay (p. 132), it was sent at 7 P.M. It took at least three quarters of an hour for the emperor to travel between the Tuileries and the Palace of St. Cloud. If Gramont had gone with the emperor at 5:30, it is impossible to admit that he could have conferred with the emperor and empress and then drafted a telegram at 6:15. It is equally doubtful that Gramont could have returned from a conference with the emperor at St. Cloud in time to have sent a telegram from Paris at 7. It has been suggested that the telegram may have been sent from St. Cloud. Against this hypothesis, it may be pointed out that at 7:55 P.M., Lord Lyons sent off a telegram to London telling that he had just returned from an interview with Gramont (W. E. Mosse, *The European Powers and the German Question, 1848–71*, p. 384). If Gramont had sent the telegram from St. Cloud at 7, he could not have returned to Paris in time for a long conversation with Lyons before 7:55. In spite of Eugénie's testimony, I am forced to the conclusion that, as stated in the text, Gramont did not go to St. Cloud at all but had his conference with the emperor at the Tuileries between 4:30 and 5:30. On the problem of the time required for drafting and sending telegrams, see the valuable comments in Lord, pp. 82–83.

be made before the Council met on the next morning. Gramont either did not understand this or disregarded it. Convinced as he was that press and public as well as the Chamber of Deputies would not be satisfied without additional guarantees,[33] he persuaded Napoleon to let him instruct Benedetti to ask King William for the assurance that he would not give his consent to the candidacy if it should arise again. The emperor left the Tuileries at half past five, and Gramont drafted and sent this telegram:

> We have received from the hands of the ambassador of Spain, the renunciation by Prince Anthony, in the name of his son Leopold, of his candidacy for the throne of Spain. In order that this renunciation by Prince Anthony produce its complete effect, it seems necessary that the king of Prussia associate himself with it, and [that he] give us the assurance that he will not authorize this candidacy again.
>
> Will you go immediately to the king to request from him this statement, which he cannot refuse if he is truly without ulterior motives. In spite of the renunciation, which is now public knowledge, the agitation is such that we do not know if we will be able to dominate it.[34]

It is doubtful that the emperor was conscious of the full import of the decision he and Gramont had reached. As he left the Tuileries to return to St. Cloud, he appeared calm and satisfied. To his aide-de-camp, General Bourbaki, he said, as he had to Nigra, that there would be peace. Spain had given up the Hohenzollern candidacy and a war that was not necessary would be absurd. On his way from the Tuileries to St. Cloud, however, he is reported to have been impressed by the acclamations of the crowds along the way, and at the palace,

---

[33] See P. de la Gorce, *Histoire du second empire*, vol. VI, p. 250.

[34] Gramont, pp. 129–131 (with time as 7 P.M.); *O.D.*, vol. XXVIII, no. 8428 (draft dated July 12, 6:15). Benedetti received this during the night (*ibid.*, no. 8458). Gramont did not inform Benedetti of the conference with Werther.

he entered an even more excited milieu.[35] The empress and the belligerent courtiers were surrounded by a group of right-wing politicians, who arrived at the palace early in the evening. For a while, Napoleon wavered, vacillating between his own pacific inclination to consider the incident closed and the displeasure of his entourage, which wanted to seize the opportunity to settle the quarrel with Prussia once for all.[36] Finally, he resisted the pressure to widen the grounds of controversy.[37] "My dear Duke," he wrote to Gramont,

on thinking over our conversation of today and on rereading the dispatch of Father Anthony,[38] I see [39] that we must limit ourselves to accentuating more emphatically the dispatch which you have sent to Benedetti by making the following points stand out:

1. Our concern is with Prussia, not with Spain;

2. The dispatch from Prince Anthony, addressed to Prim, is not as far as we are concerned an official document and no one has been commissioned to communicate it to us;

3. Prince Leopold has accepted the candidacy for the throne and it is his father who renounces it;

4. It is necessary then that Benedetti insist, as he has been

[35] Among the more picturesque anecdotes of the day is the one told by Mme. Ollivier ("L'Epouse de l'empereur," *Revue de Genève*, February 1921, p. 180): "Comme on venait d'apprendre que l'empereur allait se contenter du désistement notifié par le prince Antoine, le prince impérial, tout affaré, s'élance vers l'amiral Duperré, de service auprès de lui: 'Venez, venez! crie-t-il, je ne sais pas ce qu'a maman!' Elle avait une attaque de nerfs et criait: 'La couronne de France est tombée en quenouille!'"

[36] Dugué de la Fauconnerie, *Souvenirs d'un vieil homme (1866–1879)*, p. 156.

[37] So I interpret the words in the first sentence of the following to Gramont: "qu'il faut se borner à accentuer davantage la dépêche que vous avez dû envoyer à Benedetti . . ." The limitation makes no sense unless we can assume that the emperor and his entourage had talked of a general settlement of the grievances felt against Prussia. See Lehautcourt, p. 410. On the preceding evening, Napoleon himself had raised this problem with the Austrian ambassador. Tg., Metternich to Beust, Paris, July 12, 1870, 2:20 A.M., H. Oncken, vol. III, no. 872.

[38] Ollivier, vol. XIV, p. 267, inserts the phrase "comme l'appelle Cassagnac," which, he asserts, was omitted by Gramont.

[39] Ollivier, vol. XIV, p. 267, has "crois" instead of "vois."

ordered to do, on a categorical reply by which the king binds himself, for the future, not to permit Prince Leopold (who is not bound) to follow the example of his brother [40] and to set out one fine day for Spain;

5. As long as we do not have an official communication from Ems, we cannot be supposed to have a reply to our just demands;

6. So long [41] as we do not have this reply, we will continue our military preparations;

7. It is impossible to make a statement to the Chambers until we are better informed.[42]

Ollivier happened to be with Gramont when the emperor's letter arrived. He had been, he tells us, less anxious about what might happen at Berlin or Ems than at Madrid, fearful that the appeal to Spanish national pride would have its effect and that Prim would proclaim Leopold as king without waiting for the election.[43] In company with his wife, he had, therefore, gone to the Spanish embassy and talked with Olózaga.[44] The ambassador was reassuring: as far as Spain was concerned, the affair was finished; the renunciation would be accepted. He added a warning against precipitate decisions. Although it was late, after eleven o'clock in the evening, the Olliviers hurried to Gramont's office to let him know what Olózaga had said and to see if any word had come from Ems. Gramont showed Ollivier the telegram to Benedetti with the demand for guarantees, and he had just finished reading it when the letter from St. Cloud was brought in.

Gramont was correct in his judgment that this letter did not go beyond the decision that he and the emperor had already made. It put into writing points which they must have taken

[40] In 1866, Prince Charles had evaded the observation of the Powers and had turned up in Bucharest.

[41] Ollivier, vol. XIV, p. 267, has "Faute" in place of "Tant."

[42] Gramont, pp. 136–137.

[43] Ollivier, vol. XIV, pp. 265–266.

[44] It was at this time that he learned of Olózaga's part in securing the renunciation and that the news had been brought to the emperor that morning during the cabinet meeting.

into account in drawing up the instructions to Benedetti but which had not been transmitted to the ambassador, points which explain and to a substantial degree justify the fears of the French government. The examples of Prince Frederick of Augustenburg in November 1863 and of Prince Charles of Hohenzollern-Sigmaringen in May 1866 were there for all to see. Frederick had refused to be bound by an agreement signed by his father "on behalf of himself and his family" on the pretext that at the time it was made he was of age and therefore not included in the term "family." Prince Charles had gone to Switzerland "to join his brother" and had reappeared at Turnu Severin on his way to Bucharest to accept his election as prince of the United Principalities of Moldavia and Wallachia.

To Ollivier, on the other hand, who had only just learned of the new instructions to Benedetti, the letter seemed additional proof of the influence of his political enemies and of an act of personal power by the emperor. He had learned from Olózaga that Napoleon had that morning withheld from his responsible ministers information of the greatest significance. He resented even more the way in which Napoleon and Gramont had made a decision although it had been understood that none would be reached before the next meeting of the council. To be sure, he himself had not held strictly to that decision; he had joined Gramont in the suggestion to Werther of the letter from King William to Emperor Napoleon but this was a minor lapse when measured against the demand for guarantees. No matter how justifiable such a demand may have been, it was a real change in objectives. Ollivier seems to have sensed the danger more clearly than either Napoleon or Gramont, but there was little that he could do about it. It would, he wrote later, have justified an explosion of angry words. He did not, he believed, have the authority to compel Gramont to countermand his orders to Benedetti and the letter from Napoleon made it appear that the responsibility was that of the emperor rather than of the minister of foreign affairs. It was too late at night to hurry to St. Cloud to present his objections. All he could do was to try to attenuate rather than to accentuate the emphasis.[45] He drafted a paragraph to the effect that it was indispensable that the king prevent Leopold from reversing the renunciation communicated by his father. This, with a pacific concluding paragraph, was incorporated in the telegram which Gramont prepared and dispatched to Benedetti in the course of the night.

> The emperor charges me to call your attention to the fact that we cannot consider as a sufficient reply to the just demands we have addressed to the king of Prussia, the renunciation which the Spanish ambassador has communicated to us but which was not addressed to us directly. Nor can we see in it a guarantee for the future. In order that we may be sure that the son will not disavow his father and that he will not arrive in Spain as his brother did in Rumania, it is indispensable that the king have the goodness to tell us that he will not permit the prince to go back on the renunciation announced by Prince Anthony.

The earlier instructions were not specifically canceled, but the emphasis was changed from a general guarantee against the recurrence of the candidacy at any time in the future to an assurance for the immediate present. Unfortunately this message, dispatched in two almost identical texts at 12:15 and 1:45 A.M. on the thirteenth, did not reach Benedetti until after 10:30 A.M., when he had already followed his first orders.[46]

On his return from the Quai d'Orsay to his own ministry, Ollivier found Robert Mitchell, editor of the *Constitutionnel*, waiting to ask how he should present the renunciation. Ollivier

---

[45] Unpublished journal of Mme. Ollivier, quoted by Pierre Saint Marc, *Emile Ollivier*, p. 293, n. 1.

[46] *O.D.*, vol. XVIII, nos. 8437, 8438; Gramont, pp. 137–138 and appendix 18; Ollivier, vol. XIV, pp. 265–272; Lehautcourt, pp. 407–412; P. Saint Marc, *Emile Ollivier*, pp. 292–293.

kept the secret of the demand for guarantees and told Mitchell to state that "we are satisfied and the affair is ended."

Mitchell's article was one of the few calm notes in the Paris press the next morning: [47]

> The candidacy of a German prince for the throne of Spain has been averted and the peace of Europe will not be broken. The ministers of the Emperor have spoken energetically and firmly, as is proper for those who have the honor to govern a great country. They have been listened to; they have received satisfaction to their just demands. We are satisfied. Prince Leopold of Hohenzollern accepted the crown of Spain. France declared that she was opposed to a political combination or a family arrangement which she judged to menace her interests and the candidacy was withdrawn. The Prince of Hohenzollern will not reign in Spain. We demand nothing more; it is with pride that we accept this peaceful solution; a great victory which has cost not a tear, not a drop of blood.

The position of the *Constitutionnel*, that France should be satisfied with the renunciation of the candidacy by Karl Anton, was supported by the *Journal des Débats*, the *Temps*, the *Siècle*, the *Journal de Paris*, and by some five relatively uninfluential papers. It was opposed, sometimes with irony, sometimes with extreme virulence, by the *Soir*, the *Presse*, the *Liberté*, the *Pays* (edited by Paul de Cassagnac, one of the bitterest opponents of the Ollivier ministry), the *Figaro*, the legitimist *Gazette de France*, the clerical *Univers*, and the *France*.[48] The two groups of papers may have been approximately equal in average daily circulation in July 1870, but most of the contemporary observers in the diplomatic corps, the press, and the French Council of Ministers agree that the opponents of Ollivier's position were dominant.[49] The major-

---

[47] Lehautcourt, p. 427; Ollivier, vol. XIV, p. 272; Fester, *Briefe*, vol. II, nos. 488, 490; L. M. Case, *French Opinion on War and Diplomacy during the Second Empire*, p. 256.

[48] Case, pp. 255–256, 313, n. 19.

[49] Case, pp. 255–256. The influence of some of these papers was due more to the reputation of the editor than to the size of its circulation.

ity opinion in the country also, as reported by the prefects to the minister of the interior, favored war rather than an inconclusive settlement with Prussia.[50]

When, as had been agreed, the Council met at nine o'clock on July 13 at St. Cloud,[51] they were told that a demand for guarantees had been sent to Benedetti the night before. There was some criticism of this action that had been taken without consultation, but since it was too late to withdraw it the accomplished fact was accepted. The principal debate was over its consequences. After a formal division, the majority voted that the demand should not be considered an ultimatum. If, as was to be expected, King William refused to commit himself for the future, the government would declare that it was satisfied and that the affair was over and finished. For the moment, the peace party had prevailed, but in the court there was clear evidence of hostility to the decision.

In the afternoon, Gramont read the official statement first to the Deputies and then to the Senate.

The Spanish ambassador yesterday made to us the official announcement that the prince of Hohenzollern has renounced his candidacy for the throne of Spain. The negotiations which we are carrying on with Prussia, and which have never had any other aim [than to secure this], are still in progress. It is therefore impossible to talk about them or to present today to the Chamber and to the country, a general account of the affair.

See table of the average daily printing of the political journals, December 1869 to July 1870, in A. Dupuy, *1870–1871. La Guerre, la Commune et la presse.*

[50] Case, pp. 246–251.

[51] There are two accounts of what took place at the meeting. One is that of P. de la Gorce in volume VI of his *Histoire du second empire*, based on the unpublished papers of three of the ministers, Louvet, Plichon, and Chevandier de Valdrome; the other is that of Emile Ollivier in his volume XIV, pages 284–291. They contradict each other at many points. I have in general followed Muret ("Emile Ollivier et le Duc de Gramont," *Revue d'histoire moderne*, vol XIV, pp. 201–209) in not accepting Ollivier's attacks on the testimony of his colleagues.

The declaration by the minister of foreign affairs was intended to calm the Chamber, but it had the opposite effect. If, as Gramont had stated, the negotiations with Prussia had no other purpose than to secure the withdrawal of the candidacy and if the government had been officially informed that this result had been secured, what was the meaning of the phrase that the negotiations were not yet terminated? Members on the left and on the right attacked the minister and the cabinet at their weakest points: "From whom did the renunciation emanate?" Gramont persisted in his refusal to add to his statement that he had been informed by the ambassador of Spain that the prince of Hohenzollern had renounced his candidacy. Against this, the opposition brought up the rumors that the renunciation was by the father and contested the right of the cabinet to withhold from the Chamber information which Ollivier had already divulged in the antechamber.[52] After a sharp debate and a series of scornful interpellations, it was accepted that the government would answer two days later, on July 15. The attitude of the Senate was equally hostile, in part because the government had appeared willing to limit its action to the Hohenzollern candidacy, in part because the handling of that episode had not satisfied the national honor. In the eyes of the ministers and of outside observers, the war party was getting the upper hand. There were many who agreed with the statement that by avoiding a vote on July 13, the cabinet had merely postponed its fall until the fifteenth. In both houses, in the streets, and in the press, the statement was sharply attacked and the ministers were vividly impressed by the state of public opinion.[53]

After he made his statements to the two houses, Gramont returned to the Foreign Office. The British ambassador, who

[52] Some of the members, of course, also knew that Benedetti had been instructed to ask for guarantees.
[53] See Lehautcourt, chs. xxv, xxvi.

had also attended the sessions, came to speak to him. When Lyons expressed his surprise and regret that the declaration had not consisted of a simple announcement that the whole question with Prussia as well as with Spain was at an end, Gramont summed up his position as before. "King William," he repeated, "had done nothing, absolutely nothing." France would not take offense at this. She would not call upon His Majesty to make her any amends. The king had authorized the prince of Hohenzollern to accept the crown of Spain; all that France now asked was that His Majesty would forbid the prince to alter at any future time his decision to withdraw the acceptance. "Surely it was but reasonable that France should take some precautions against a repetition of what had occurred when Prince Leopold's brother went off to Bucharest . . . Still, France did not call upon Prussia to prevent the prince's going to Spain; all she desired was that the king should forbid him to change his present resolution to withdraw his candidature. If His Majesty would do this the whole affair would be absolutely and entirely at an end." In support of this statement, Gramont gave Lyons a memorandum: "We ask the king of Prussia to forbid the prince of Hohenzollern to go back on his resolution. If he [the king] does this, the whole affair will be terminated." [54]

[54] Lyons to Granville, July 13, 1870, Fester, *Briefe*, vol. II, no. 525.

-❦[V]❦-

The Ems Telegram

Bismarck left Varzin on the morning of July 12. In an open carriage with Keudell at his side, he rode "uncommonly silent but looking cheerful," [1] to the railroad station at Schlawe. As the carriage passed the parsonage of Wussow, he saw his old friend, Pastor Mulert, wave a greeting. In response, he thrust his arm into the air as with a sword "in quarte and tierce." [2] Bismarck arrived at Berlin late in the afternoon. [3] On his

[1] Robert von Keudell, *Fürst und Fürstin Bismarck*, p. 441. Bucher remained at Varzin.

[2] Arnold Oskar Meyer, *Bismarck*, p. 390, is, I think, mistaken in placing this episode at the time of Bismarck's return to Berlin from Varzin on May 21. It is true that Pauline Hahn, *Varzin: persönliche Erinnerungen an den Fürsten Otto von Bismarck*, p. 122, describes it after a letter from Bismarck to Mulert of May 20 and begins the story "Am andern Tag reiste der Fürst." Her book is loosely knit, and the physical location of the episode in her pages does not necessarily mean an inner connection between the two parts. Moreover, Bismarck, as early as December 19, 1870, told the story in connection with his journey of July 12. M. Busch, *Bismarck: Some Secret Pages from His History*, vol. I, p. 405; R. Pahncke, *Die Parallel-Ezrählungen Bismarcks zu seinen Gedanken und Erinnerungen*, pp. 162–163. In the *Erinnerung und Gedanke*, G.W., vol. XV, p. 305, Bismarck says that Pastor Mulert understood "dass ich glaubte in den Krieg zu gehen"; Hahn, p. 122, says, "Herr Prediger wusste sich zurzeit diese sonderbare Bewegung nicht zu erklären; aber der Fürst wusste dass der Krieg da sei, und dass wollte er andeuten."

[3] The *National-Zeitung*, Abendausgabe, July 13, says at 6 P.M. This corresponds to the timetable, *Bradshaw's Continental Railway Guide* for June 1870, cited by Lord. As Lord shows, however, Bismarck's first tele-

arrival, he was given telegrams from which it appeared that
the prince of Hohenzollern had renounced his candidacy in
order to avert the war which France was threatening and
that the king, in spite of the menaces and insults of the French
parliament and press, was continuing to negotiate with Benedetti instead of coolly maintaining his reserve and referring
the ambassador to his responsible minister.[4] In the following
page of his memoirs, Bismarck gives a vivid account of his
feelings as he received the news. His first thought, he claimed,
was to resign. His first action, however, was to send a telegram to Ems stating that he would take the train that night
and imploring the king to make no statements to Benedetti
before he arrived.[5]

Soon afterwards, Roon and Eulenburg, ministers of war and

gram from Berlin was marked as sent to the telegraph station at 5:50
P.M. and dispatched at 6:12 P.M. As Lord suggests, a special train may
have been used for part of the trip. Thimme, *G.W.*, vol. XIb, p. 357,
without citing his authority, suggests that a high Foreign Office official,
perhaps Counsellor of Legation von Bülow, was sent to meet the chancellor with the latest messages, especially Abeken's telegram of July 11.
Lord, *The Origins of the War of 1870*, no. 119. Schweinitz, *Denkwürdigkeiten*, vol. I, p. 48, tells that he went from Berlin to Varzin in November 1869, a "sechsstundige Bahnfahrt." If this is correct, a train leaving
Schlawe at 11:01 A.M. *could* have reached Berlin at about 5 P.M.

[4] *Erinnerung und Gedanke*, *G.W.* vol. XV, pp. 305–306. The text as
published in 1898 is corrupt. See Lord's attempt to give a correct account of the episode, pp. 68–70. Lord is probably correct in listing the
telegrams and dispatches. Bismarck, *G.W.*, vol. XV, pp. 305–306, says
that he received the telegrams as his carriage drove into the courtyard
of his official residence, but Horst Kohl, under date of November 27,
1891, quotes him as saying that the dispatches were handed to him at the
railroad station. This version is supported by Thimme's statement. See
n. 3 above.

[5] Bismarck to Abeken, July 12, 1870, sent to telegraph station at 5:50
P.M., sent 6:12 P.M., received 6:27 P.M., Lord, no. 139. The crown prince
was informed by a telegram from Keudell sent to the telegraph station
at 6:45 P.M., Lord, no. 140. When Lord wrote, p. 68, that Bismarck
arrived at Berlin "intending to stay over a few hours and take the night
train for Ems," he did not know the telegram, Bismarck to Thile, Varzin,
July 11, 1870, requesting the minister of commerce to have a special car
ready on Wednesday morning for his journey to Ems. Secret file; Bonnin, no. 286.

the interior, came to have dinner with Bismarck.[6] The two ministers joined him in a telegram to the king urging him to make no declaration of any kind to Benedetti but merely to tell him that the hereditary prince (Leopold) would inform the Spanish government directly of the decision which he would reach in consultation with his father.[7] It was decided that Bismarck, "worn out by the journey," could not travel to Ems that night. Eulenburg would go in his place.[8]

About an hour later, Bismarck received what, under the circumstances, must have been welcome news: a telegram from Werther reported that Ológaza, Spanish ambassador to France, had brought to Gramont an "official" telegram from Karl Anton announcing the renunciation of the candidacy by his son. To make sure that this would be a matter of public knowledge before the king could make a compromising statement to Benedetti, Bismarck sent a communiqué to the Wolff news bureau: "The Spanish Ambassador Olózaga early this midday officially informed the Duke of Gramont that the prince of Hohenzollern abandons his candidacy for the throne."[9]

[6] They were invited for 6:30 (secret file; Bonnin, no. 286). The *Erinnerung und Gedanke* as published in 1898 incorrectly says "Moltke and Roon."

[7] Bismarck to King William, July 12, 1870, sent to telegraph station, 7:20 P.M., Lord, no. 142. A telegram of the same time to Abeken developed the theme more fully. It concludes with the statement: "Ich glaube eine vollkommen schickliche Form der Rücktritts-Erklärung des Erbprinzen vorschlagen zu können" (Lord, no. 143).

[8] Bismarck to the crown prince, July 12, 1870, sent to the telegraph station at 7:23 P.M.; to Abeken, sent to the telegraph station at 7:37 P.M. The difference in time is probably due to the fact that the telegram to the crown prince was not put into cipher. Lord, nos. 144, 145.

[9] Werther to King William and to the Foreign Office, Paris, July 12, 1870, 4:45 P.M., received at Ems, 6:30 P.M., at Berlin, 8:20 P.M., Lord, no. 138. Bismarck wrote a communiqué on the margin and it was sent to Wolff at 9:10 P.M. Lord's comment that its "deliberate inaccuracy was only a mild foretaste of what he and his supper-companions were to concoct for the press on the following evening" (p. 75) is a little unfair if, as he indicates in note 42, the inaccuracy is in making it appear

In the last telegram of the evening to Abeken, Bismarck stated that the solution of the crisis by the retreat of Prince Leopold had made an unfavorable impression on public opinion which was already irritated by Gramont's threats and expected, at the least, public satisfaction for Gramont's speeches. In response to this feeling, he proposed that the king cause Werther to take leave of absence from his post at Paris and to make no secret of the motives for it.[10]

Bismarck then set out to make a call on the Russian foreign minister, Prince Alexander M. Gorchakov, who had stopped in Berlin en route to Wildbad for his holiday. On his way, Bismarck met the Italian ambassador, Count Edward de Launay.[11] Throughout the day, Launay had been in touch with the Prussian Foreign Office and had been alarmed by the gloomy opinions held there and repeated in the afternoon newspapers. At about eight o'clock, however, he had heard the first rumors of the renunciation and was eager to confirm them. As a possible source of reliable information, he sought out Gorchakov. The Russian had also heard the rumors but was not able to confirm them. Launay did learn that Bismarck was due at the Russian embassy at nine o'clock, so he stationed himself at a point that he was sure Bismarck would pass on his route. While he was waiting, Thile passed by but declined to answer his questions. Then came Eulenburg, who was more willing to

---

as an "official" communication from Olózaga. Gramont himself treated it as official until the emperor objected. See his statements to the Chamber of Deputies, and to Lord Lyons, Fester, *Briefe*, vol. II, pp. 120, 132. A telegram from Abeken, received at Berlin at 8:05 P.M., reported a telegram from Karl Anton to the king that the telegram of renunciation had gone directly to Marshal Prim and a copy to Olózaga. The secret would not be divulged at Ems, and the king would try to let Benedetti be the first to mention it. Lord, no. 141.

[10] July 12, 1870, sent to the telegraph station at 9:45 P.M., received 11:25 P.M. The Ems copy has Abeken's note: "S. M. 13/7 vor d[er] Prom[enade] präsentirt]" (Lord, no. 147).

[11] Halperin, "Bismarck and the Italian Envoy in Berlin on the Eve of the Franco-Prussian War," *Journal of Modern History*, vol. XXXIII, pp. 33–39.

talk. The report that Leopold's candidacy had been withdrawn was "unfortunately" true: the Spanish ambassador at Paris had informed Gramont. Eulenburg added the startling news that he, not Bismarck, was leaving that night to join King William at Ems. A few minutes later, Bismarck himself came along.

Launay had known Bismarck for years and had seen him at times of crisis, but, he reported, he had rarely seen him so serious, upset, and angry. Speaking jerkily and in a tone that suggested heartbreak, the Prussian minister talked about the situation with characteristically calculated indiscretion. Karl Anton, he confirmed, had announced Leopold's withdrawal. They had been intimidated not only by the gravity of the situation but also by the pressure that "foreigners" had brought upon them. The farce, he added bitterly, was played out. His exasperation with King William was equally marked. The sovereign had shrunk from a contest with the French despite his possession of an army of 800,000 men; he had separated himself from the "instinct" of his own people, and the whole sorry business was moving the country a step closer to left-wing radicalism. The sole beneficiary would be the republican movement. Bismarck also seemed apprehensive about the attitude of Spain: he wondered what the Spaniards would say now. What would people think now of Prussia's good faith?

Dolefully Bismarck went on to speak of his own position. He had left Varzin to rush to Ems even though in so doing he had incurred the risk of an apoplectic stroke. He had been forced to interrupt a series of medical treatments and then upon arriving in Berlin in this lamentable condition, he had been taken unaware by the news of Leopold's renunciation. The next morning, he said, he would return to Varzin.

Giving the appearance of making the best of a bad situation, Bismarck suggested that, in spite of everything, the crisis had been instructive. It had provided Prussia with a warning for the future. It had given her an indication of the temper of the powers. They had not been sparing with their advice, and so — he named specifically Great Britain and Russia — they had exerted considerable pressure for the benefit of France.

As for Italy, Bismarck called Launay's attention to the rumors current in South Germany that Italy would help France with an army of 80,000 men and to others which represented the Italian government as undecided about the course to follow in case of war. To both, Launay gave categorical replies. Italy was doing all in her power, he insisted, and without mental reservations, for the preservation of peace. The rumors about Italian military aid for France had come from Bavaria and were undoubtedly part of a deliberate maneuver to deter Prussia from asking the South German states to fulfil their treaty obligations. In the event of a Franco-Prussian war, Italy could follow only one policy: that of scrupulous and absolute neutrality.

With these assurances of the Italian ambassador safely in mind, Bismarck went on to his more important conference with Gorchakov. He told the Russian chancellor that a telegram from Werther had informed him that Olózaga had notified Gramont of the "spontaneous" renunciation of the prince of Hohenzollern. He added that although the king personally was unconnected with the overtures, the reception given to Benedetti at Ems had made a very unfavorable impression on the country. It would have a bad effect on the elections and was weakening royal prestige. All of his colleagues shared that view. Instead of going on to Ems, he was returning to Varzin. In his opinion, the least that they could do was to give Werther an extended vacation in order to demonstrate to the country that they resented the arrogant language of France.[12]

---

[12] Gorchakov to Alexander II, "secret," Berlin, June 30/July 12, 1870. Chester W. Clark, "Bismarck, Russia, and the War of 1870," *Journal of Modern History*, vol. XIV, no. 2, pp. 200–201.

After his visit to Gorchakov, Bismarck returned to his official residence where he conferred with Roon and other generals. At some time in the course of the evening, Moltke, just returned from his estate in Silesia, joined the conference.[13] The military leaders, Bismarck told Gorchakov on the following day, shared his indignation at the French and had recommended an immediate declaration of war. They felt that Prussia would gain every advantage if the outbreak of hostilities were not delayed. Bismarck, however, said that he opposed this precipitate action. He had answered, he told Gorchkov: "Neither right reason nor religion authorize one to speed up the moment for war only because the calculation of chances may be favorable — the outcome is always in the hands of a power above that of men — and from one minute to the next an unexpected contingency could arise that would stamp such a measure as overhasty." [14]

Other telegrams, drafted during the night, were sent to the telegraph station at 5:30 in the morning of the thirteenth. One, a circular to the North German representatives at the principal European and German capitals,[15] informed them that Werther had telegraphed that the Spanish ambassador in Paris had officially notified Gramont of the renunciation. The sec-

[13] In the first edition of Bismarck's memoirs, his name was incorrectly joined to that of Roon as a dinner guest. The correct text does not mention his presence before the dinner of July 13. The only evidence I have found for the statement above is in Gorchakov's letter to Tsar Alexander: "La veille il avait conseil chez lui, composé surtout de militaires entr' autres les Généraux Roon et Moltke" (Berlin, July 1/13, 1870, in Clark *Journal of Modern History*, vol. XIV, no. 2, p. 202). It is possible, but not certain, that this conference took place after Bismarck's visit to Gorchakov, for the latter's account of what Bismarck told him on July 13 has details not included in his telegram of the night of July 12 and is much more belligerent. On the other hand the latter does say, "Tous ses collègues partagent cette opinion" — but this may not include Moltke, who, strictly speaking, was not a "collègue."

[14] Gorchakov to Alexander II, Berlin, July 1/13, 1870. Clark, *Journal of Modern History*, vol. XIV, no. 2, p. 202..

[15] London, Vienna, St. Petersburgh, Munich, Stuttgart, Karlsrube, Dresden, Florence, and Madrid. Lord, no. 156.

ond, to the representatives at the principal German capitals
and Madrid, told that, according to a telegram from Bernstorff,
the British government had used its influence on the Hohenzollern princes to secure the withdrawal.[16] Neither was sent
in cipher.

After a restless night, Bismarck went to work earlier than
usual on the morning of the thirteenth.[17] He began with instructions to Busch to wait until a statement appeared in the
press to the effect that the renunciation of the prince of Hohenzollern was in consequence of pressure from Ems, and then
to contradict it. In the meantime, the *Norddeutsche Allgemeine
Zeitung*, which was generally assumed to be semi-official,
should say only that the prince's present decision had not been
altogether unexpected.

When he accepted the throne which had been offered to him,
he had obviously not foreseen that his decision would occasion so
much excitement in Paris. For more than thirty years past, the best
relations [had] existed between Napoleon and the Hohenzollern
family. Prince Leopold could not, therefore, have apprehended
any antipathy to his candidature on the part of the Emperor. As
his candidature suddenly became known after the Cortes had
been adjourned until November, it may well have been assumed
that there would be time enough in the interval to sound the
Emperor as to his views. Now that this assumption (here the
Chancellor began to speak more slowly as if he were dictating),

[16] Dresden, Munich, Stuttgart, Karlsruhe, Madrid. Lord, no. 157.
What Bernstorff had actually reported was this: "[Lord Granville]
wünscht nämlich dringend, dass der Erbprinz von Hohenzollern frei-
willig zurücktrete, und hat durch alle ihm zu Gebote stehenden Canäle
auf ihn einzuwirken gesucht, aber bisher nicht erfahren können, wo
der Prinz sich aufhält. . . . Als ich Lord Granville eben schon ver-
lassen hatte, liess er mich Zurückrufen, um mir zu sagen, dass er gerade
ein Telegram erhalten, wonach er hoffe dass es besser gehe, man habe
den Erbprinzen gefunden" (Bernstorff to Bismarck, London, July 12,
1870, sent 4:17 P.M., received 9:45 P.M.; Lord, no. 136). Bismarck did
not see Bernstorff's telegram until after his visits to Gorchakov and
Launay.
[17] Keudell, p. 442; "called early to the Chief" (Busch, *Bismarck: Some
Secret Pages*, vol. I, p. 46).

which up to the acceptance of the Crown by the Prince, was still quite legitimate, had proved to be partly erroneous, it was scarcely probable that the Prince would, on his own responsibility be disposed to cope single-handed with the storm that his decision had raised, and might yet raise, in view of the apprehensions of war of the whole European world, and the influence brought to bear upon him from London and Brussels. Even a portion of the responsibility of involving the great European nations, not only in one war, but possibly in a series of wars, would weigh heavily upon a man who could not claim to have assumed it as part of the duty of the Royal office which he had already accepted. That was more than could well be expected of a Prince who only occupied a private position. It was the offensive tone of Gramont that alone prevented Prussia from exercising her influence with the Prince.

The last point was developed in the directive for other papers.

It cannot be denied that a Spanish Government disposed to promote the cause of peace and to abstain from conspiring with France would be of considerable value to us. But if, some fourteen days ago, the Emperor Napoleon had addressed himself confidentially to Berlin, or indicated that the affair was attracting attention, Prussia, instead of adopting an indifferent attitude, would have co-operated in pacifying public opinion in Paris. The situaton has been entirely altered through the aggressive tone of Gramont's speech, and the direct demands addressed to the King, who is staying in privacy at Ems for the benefit of his health, unaccompanied by a single Minister. His Majesty rightly declined to accede to these demands. That incident has created so much indignation in Germany, that many people feel disappointed at Prince Leopold's renunciation. At any rate, the confidence in the peaceful intentions of France has been so thoroughly shaken, that it will take a considerable time to restore it. If commerce and trade have been injured by the evidence which has shown us what a den of brigands we have to deal with in France, the people of that country must fasten the responsibility on the personal *régime* under which they at present live.[18]

[18] Busch, vol. I, pp. 46–48.

The conference with Busch was interrupted by the arrival of the crown prince.[19] For several days, Frederick William had been watching the news with increasing anxiety. The details of the "lengthy" conversation are unknown, but he carried away the impression that Bismarck thought that peace was assured by the renunciation of Prince Leopold and that he, Bismarck, would soon return to Varzin.[20] Gorchkov, whose visit the prince received soon after he left Bismarck, was also optimistic although the Russian chancellor added the ominous information that France had not been satisfied but was demanding guarantees from Prussia that a Hohenzollern would never again seek the Spanish throne.[21]

When extracts of the crown prince's diary were published in 1888, Bismarck denied the accuracy of the entry: "In the very first lines it is stated that on July 13, 1870, I regarded peace as assured and therefore would return to Varzin, whereas there is documentary proof that His Royal Highness already knew that I considered war necessary and would return to Varzin only after resigning from office, if it were averted." As the text of this part of the diary is known only from a late draft, written down in 1871 after the war, it has been claimed that the discrepancy must be explained by a lapse in memory on the part of the crown prince.[22] His version is confirmed, however, by Gorchakov's report to the tsar.

This does not, of course, prove that Bismarck really believed that the incident was closed. He could not afford to give the crown prince any other opinion or destroy the impression that he was surprised by the sudden and menacing turn of events in Paris; he had given too many assurances that the Hohenzollern candidacy did not involve serious risk of armed

[19] Busch, vol. I, p. 48.
[20] Kaiser Friedrich III, *Das Kriegstagebuch von 1870/71*, entries for July 11, 12, 13, pp. 1ff.
[21] *Das Kriegstagebuch*, entry for July 13, pp. 2ff.
[22] *Das Kriegstagebuch*, pp. xv–xviii and appendix 19, p. 487.

conflict. As the day went on, however, his determination not to let the crisis end became more apparent.

Bismarck had already given a hint of his tactics in his telegram sent to Abeken the night before: that public opinion expected at the least a satisfactory explanation of Gramont's speeches.[23] He had suggested that if Paris did not change its attitude, it would be necessary to call the Reichstag into session.[24] He had thought of insisting that the king return to Berlin and order military countermeasures.[25] Shortly after noon, he had learned that King William had agreed to the suggestion that Werther be ordered to take a "vacation" from his post at Paris.[26] He telegraphed at once to Werther that he had hoped that Gramont would have given the ambassador a reassuring explanation of his menacing expressions but none had been reported. Werther, he continued, could not take the initiative in this direction without specific instructions from the king. "As a guide to [his] conduct," however, Bismarck added that if in the next few days he did not receive completely satisfactory statements about the intentions of France, he would recommend to the king that the North German Reichstag be called in special session at the beginning of the week to deliberate on what should be done.[27]

The substance of this telegram was told to Gorchakov with the added point that the Reichstag would be asked to provide funds for total mobilization of the army. Prussia was not rich enough, Bismarck said, to bear the expense of this for months. It could mean war but, in the state of uncertainty imposed on the Prussians by France, they could not act other-

[23] Cf. p. 168 above.
[24] Tg. to Delbrück, Varzin, July 11, 1870, 7 P.M., Lord, no. 118.
[25] Draft tg. to Eulenburg at Ems, undated but filed with documents of July 12, and not dispatched, Lord, no. 149.
[26] Tg., Abeken to Bismarck, July 13, 1870, 10:50 A.M., received 12:25 P.M., Lord, no. 159.
[27] Bismarck to Werther, July 13, 1870, to telegraph station at 2:25 P.M., Lord, no. 162.

wise. He still had some hope of peace, he claimed, and sincerely desired peace. In words that anticipate the sense of the "Ems telegram," he told Gorchakov that Benedetti had asked the king for a statement which could be used to influence the French deputies but that the king had refused flatly to give one and had replied that from then on France had to address herself to Spain only.[28]

Bismarck's tactics stand out even more clearly in the report of his conversation with Lord Loftus, the British ambassador, later in the afternoon.

I had an interview with Prince Bismarck today, and congratulated him on the apparent solution of the crisis by the spontaneous renunciation of the crown of Spain by the . . . Prince of Hohenzollern. He appeared somewhat doubtful as to whether this solution would prove a settlement of the differences with France. He said that the extreme moderation evinced by the King of Prussia under the menacing tone of the French Government, and the courteous reception by his Majesty of Count Benedetti at Ems after the severe language held to Prussia, both officially and in the French press, was producing throughout Prussia general indignation. . . .

Count Bismarck then observed that intelligence had been received from Paris — (though not officially from the Prussian Embassy) — that the solution of the Spanish difficulty would not suffice to content the French Government, and that other demands would be advanced. "If such be the case," said Count Bismarck, "it was evident that the succession to the Spanish crown was but a mere pretext, and that the real object of France was to seek revenge for Königgrätz." The feeling of the German nation was that they were fully equal to cope with France, and that they were equally as confident as the French might be of military success. The feeling, therefore, in Prussia was that they should accept no humiliation or insult from France, and that if unjustly provoked, they should accept the combat.

"But," said His Excellency, "we do not wish for war, and we have proved, and we shall continue to prove, our peaceful disposi-

[28] Secret telegram, Gorchakov to Alexander II, Berlin, July 1/13, 1870; Clark, *Journal of Modern History*, vol. XIV, no. 3, p. 201.

tion. At the same time, we cannot allow the French to have the start of us as regards armaments. I have positive information that military preparations have been and are being made in France for war. Large stores of munitions are being concentrated. Large purchases of hay and other war material are being made, and horses are being bought. If these preparations continue, we shall be obliged to ask the French Government for explanations as to their object and meaning. After what has now occurred we must require some assurance, some guarantee, that we may not be subject to sudden attack; like a stroke of lightning (sic) in perfect darkness which suddenly reveals to sight a band of Robbers, we must know that this Spanish difficulty once removed, there are no other lurking designs which may burst upon us like a thunderstorm. . . ."

Count Bismarck stated that unless some assurance, some guarantee was given by France to the European Powers, or in some official form, that the present solution of the Spanish question was a final and satisfactory settlement of the French demands, and that no further claims were to be made — and if, further, a withdrawal or a satisfactory explanation of the menacing language held by the Duke of Gramont was not made, the Prussian Government would be obliged to seek explanations from France. "It was impossible," added Count Bismarck, "that Prussia could tamely and quietly sit under the affront offered to the King and to the nation by the menacing language of the French Government. I could not," said His Excellency, "hold communication with the French Ambassador after the language held to Prussia, in the face of Europe, by the French Minister for Foreign Affairs. . . ." [29]

[29] Loftus to Granville, July 13, 1870, published in part in the Parliamentary Papers in 1870; reprinted in *British and Foreign State Papers*, vol. LX, pp. 829–832, and often reproduced elsewhere. The extract in Lord Augustus Loftus, *Diplomatic Reminiscences*, 2d ser., vol. II, pp. 274–276, varies a little from the original. The omitted parts are published by H. Temperley, "Lord Acton on the Origins of the War of 1870, with Some Unpublished Letters from the British and Viennese Archives," *Cambridge Historical Journal*, vol. II, pp. 73–74; printed in full from photocopy of the original (Public Record Office, London, F.O. 64/688, no. 27) in E. Walder, *Die Emser Depesche*, pp. 65–68. The telegram in which Loftus reported the conversation in summary was sent at about 3 P.M. (*ibid.*, p. 65, n. 1) and is printed by Temperley, p. 75. The time at which Loftus met Bismarck is not certain but was probably between one and two o'clock. In the telegram, dispatched at about three, Loftus says, "I have just seen Count Bismarck," but if we reckon

Meanwhile, on the morning of July 13, Benedetti was waiting more anxiously than ever for his opportunity to speak to
the king. He had been told that he would be notified when the
message from Sigmaringen arrived, but it seemed probable that
this would not be soon enough. Gramont's telegram of 7 P.M.[30]
had imposed on him an additional most delicate mission and had
warned him that unless the reply were prompt, the government
might no longer be able to dominate the excitement at Paris.
If, as he still expected, Bismarck were to arrive on the 11:15
A.M. train, his chances of success would be diminished. King
William, who now knew that Bismarck was not coming, had
apparently made up his mind not to receive the ambassador
until he had conferred with Eulenburg. He had learned on the
evening before that the fact of the renunciation was known
by the French government and therefore probably by Benedetti.[31] Early in the morning he had received from Abeken
the telegrams that had come during the night; one from Werther with the simple statement that a report of his conversation
with Gramont would be sent by courier; one from Bernstorff
at London that Lord Lyons had reported that the French government was not satisfied by Werther's explanations; and one
from Bismarck that German public opinion might now require
some kind of satisfaction from France.[32]

King William then set out for his customary morning walk
in the *Kurgarten* along the Lahn.[33] Soon afterwards, Benedetti
went up to Prince Anton Radziwill, the adjutant in attendance,
to solicit an audience at the earliest possible moment. In explanation of this request, he intimated that he needed to see

---

the time needed to draft the message, put it into code, and send it to
the telegraph office, an hour is probably not too much. See Lord, p. 82.
[30] See p. 156 above.
[31] From Werther's telegram, Lord, no. 138.
[32] Lord, pp. 83–84.
[33] Usually from 8 to 10 A.M. Lord, p. 84, n. 10. The following account
of the events at Ems on July 13 is based on Lord, pp. 81–94.

the king before the meeting of the *Corps Legislatif* at Paris
that day, in order to obtain from His Majesty a declaration
or communication which could be used at that session. By
this admission the ambassador must have prejudiced his case
from the outset and helped to put the king still more on
his guard. Hence, when Radziwill had hastened over to report
to the king, who was not far away in the park, he returned
with a rather indefinite reply that His Majesty would grant an
audience some time after his promenade. William's intention at
that moment, if we may believe Abeken's ensuing telegram to
Bismarck, was to receive the ambassador only after he had had
a chance to consult with Count Eulenburg, who would arrive
on the 11:15 train. In any case, he would take care to make no
statement that could be exploited before the French Chambers;
he would only say that the answer at last received from Sigmaringen was that Leopold's decision had been announced to
Madrid and Paris; that these capitals were informed of the news
before he himself was; that Benedetti would learn it from his
own government; and that he (the king) had nothing more to
say to him.

This plan of action, however, was then immediately dis-
arranged by William's own impulsiveness. The nine o'clock
train brought the morning papers with the news of the renunciation, and a copy of the *Kölnische Zeitung* was handed to
Abeken, who brought it to the king. Eager to prove that Leopold's decision was known to all the world before he himself
had received his answer from Sigmaringen, William sent the
newspaper by Radziwill to Benedetti, who had remained in the
park. Doubtless a little chagrined at this offhand way of making the long-expected announcement, the ambassador replied
that the news was indeed already known to him from Paris;
and, in proof of this, in returning the newspaper to the king,
he also transmitted a paraphrase of part of Gramont's dispatch
of the previous evening. William, delighted to have this evi-

dence that the French government was now officially informed, sent back his warmest thanks; but this rapid exchange of communications through Radziwill must have aroused in Benedetti's mind the hope that more important business might be transacted then and there, without waiting for the formal audience which might come too late to serve his purpose. At all events, he seems to have maneuvered so as to place himself in the king's path just as the latter was about to leave the park. Whether it was from a too-hasty desire to discuss the news, or because it might have seemed rude to pass by without some friendly words, William approached him and started the conversation, while his brother, Prince Albert, withdrew a few paces, and their adjutants endeavored to hold back the curious crowd of onlookers.

In the most amicable fashion, the king began by expressing his pleasure at this encounter, which enabled him to thank the ambassador orally for the important communication which the latter had just made to him. "You see," he added, "that you are better and more quickly informed at this moment than I am, for I have not received this good news directly. I have only a private telegram which says that it appears that Prince Leopold is renouncing the crown. Thus the affair is ended, which might have embroiled us in complications, in view of the way in which it has been regarded in France."

Benedetti at once began to point out the flaws in the renunciation, especially the fact that his government could feel no security about the matter, as it did not know whether Leopold would ratify his father's action. William protested that there could be no doubt about that and, for the rest, he still had no direct, official communication from the prince, but would probably receive it in the course of the day, and would inform Benedetti of it.

The ambassador then led up to his real object by suggesting that whatever was lacking in Karl Anton's declaration would be supplied if the king would announce to the French government that he promised never to permit Leopold to renew his acceptance, in case the Spanish crown should again be offered to him. Undoubtedly surprised, if not at the appearance of a new demand, at least at the scope of it, William immediately replied that such an engagement, unlimited in time, was impossible for him to undertake. "But who can guarantee," he objected, "that at some future time the Emperor Napoleon himself might not find that the prince of Hohenzollern is the best candidate for the throne of Spain; what should I do in such a case if I have taken the formal engagement that you ask of me?"

"That will never happen," Benedetti replied. "Public opinion is so strongly against this candidacy that the emperor could never dream of letting it arise again; the agitation in Paris and in the country is increasing hour by hour and the worst is to be feared if Your Majesty does not give me the statement that I request."

"By the same title that you assure [me] that the emperor will never come round to the Hohenzollern candidacy, I am sure that the communication made by the prince, the father, has settled the question of this candidacy forever."

Benedetti, who had become more and more urgent — "almost impertinent," King William wrote later — tried to take advantage of this slight opening to secure what he wanted. After a moment's pause he summed up: "Well, Sire, I can, then, write to my government that Your Majesty has consented to declare that you will never permit Prince Leopold to renew the candidacy in question?"

"At these words," the king wrote in his memorandum, "I stepped back a few paces and said in a very earnest tone: 'It seems to me, Mr. Ambassador, that I have so clearly and plainly expressed myself to the effect that I could never make such a declaration, that I have nothing more to add.' Thereupon I lifted my hat and went on."

Benedetti had seen his demand rejected, not without signs of irritation on the king's part toward the close, but he had not been in any way insulted, and he was not yet fully conscious of the gravity of his defeat. Returning to his hotel about ten o'clock, he sent off to Paris a brief report of what had happened, and then received Gramont's second telegram of the night before, which gave further evidence of the importance which the government attached to the demand for guarantees. It was necessary to make a second and supreme effort to put through that demand; and this Benedetti still hoped to do at the audience which had the night before been promised him as soon as the king should receive his official reply from Sigmaringen.

William returned to his lodgings, wrote a short note to Abeken, relating what had happened in the park, and then heard the reports of various officials. At about noon, he received Count Eulenburg in an audience that may have lasted about an hour. What was said on that occasion has never been revealed but can to some extent be inferred from what is known of the background of Eulenburg's mission. There can be little doubt that the king was told of Bismarck's dissatisfaction with the prolonged and conciliatory dealings with Benedetti and the need to adopt a sharper attitude toward France to satisfy the incensed German public. He may also have emphasized the demand that the king return to Berlin and convoke the Reichstag and, perhaps, it was at this time that he told the king of Bismarck's threat to resign.[34]

At about one o'clock, the king received Karl Anton's letter. This raised the question whether or not Benedetti should now be received in audience. Abeken and Eulenburg argued against it and by two o'clock, William had agreed not to receive the ambassador again but merely to inform him through an adjutant

[34] In the *Erinnerung und Gedanke*, *G.W.*, vol. XV, pp. 306–308, Bismarck describes his thoughts about resignation. See also *G.W.*, vol. VIII, pp. 81, 179, 232; vol. IX, p. 175.

that he (the king) had now learned from Sigmaringen of the renunciation and that he considered the affair as definitely settled. William's consent to the change of plan was doubtless due in part to his irritation at the demand for guarantees and to his desire not to give Benedetti a chance to renew that demand; in part to his feeling that his role in the candidacy had been exaggerated and that he had done all that could fairly be expected of him. Yet one may well doubt that William would have taken the grave decision to refuse an audience promised to the ambassador of France, especially in such a crisis, but for Eulenburg's coming and Bismarck's warnings.

The king also authorized Abeken to send Bismarck an account of the day's events, with the permission, if he saw fit, to inform both the press and the Prussian embassies abroad of Benedetti's demand and of the vigorous refusal that it had met with. It is impossible to say who originated this idea. It may have been King William himself, who, as early as July 8, had suggested that "we owe Germany a public statement" and had wondered if Gramont's declaration of July 6 should be publicly rebutted. It may have been Eulenburg, who had come to stiffen the king's attitude. Publication might be justified as a reply in kind to the language of the French ministers in the Chambers, but it was unusual to reveal to the press an account of negotiations that were not yet completed and it could, as Bismarck saw, be dangerous to peace.

At some time between two and three o'clock, Abeken drafted his report, the first version of the famous "Ems Telegram." The first part of it consisted simply of the king's note to him of that morning describing the incident on the *Brunnenpromenade*. In the second part Abeken related — in a text with many changes and insertions — the arrival of Karl Anton's letter, the king's decision not to see Benedetti, and the message which was now to be sent to the ambassador. Finally, there came what turned out to be the most important part of the document: the authorization to publish the French demand and its rejection. It was sent to the telegraph station at 3:10 P.M. and was dispatched at 3:50. On the whole, the events of the day, up to the time of drafting, were summarized with tolerable accuracy, but with a bluntness and acerbity which, while perhaps permissible in a confidential document, were out of place in one destined for publication.

While Abeken was composing his telegram, Prince Radziwill delivered the king's message to Benedetti. The ambassador expressed his thanks for this communication but at once reminded the envoy that he had asked to be authorized to report to his government the king's explicit approval of the renunciation. He added that, in accordance with new instructions from Paris, he was obliged to insist once more on the subject which he had raised in his interview with the king that morning: the guarantees for the future. For both reasons he begged for a new audience.

King William was still unwilling to grant the request for an audience. He did, however, modify his decision of an hour before that he considered the matter as definitely settled. He sent Radziwill back to give Benedetti the formal assurance that he could telegraph to Paris that the candidacy of Prince Leopold had been withdrawn and that he (the king) approved the renunciation "in the same sense and to the same degree in which he had given his approval to the acceptance." On the second point, the guarantee, Radziwill was instructed to call the ambassador's attention to the king's reply of the morning. Benedetti accepted the assurances with gratitude but, pressed by Gramont's urgent telegrams, he repeated his request for an audience.

The answer was delayed by dinner and then by the arrival of news which destroyed the slightest hope of a further concession. Werther's report of his conference with Gramont and Ollivier had reached Ems by the train due at 3:50 P.M. Abeken and Eulenburg read it and then hastened to tell the king that a dispatch had arrived which was not fit to be laid officially before the king of Prussia. William replied that they might assume for a few minutes that they were all private persons. The report was then read with its "demand" for what Abeken styled "a personal letter of apology from the king to the emperor, to pacify the French nation." There can be no doubt that William was highly indignant. "Has anyone ever heard of such insolence?" he wrote to the queen a few hours later. "I am to appear before the world as a penitent sinner, for an affair which was originated, carried on, and directed, not by me but by Prim, and he is now left out of the question altogether." He found such proceedings on the part of the French "inconceivable," the demand "humiliating," its transmission by Werther "very difficult to explain." [35] The report was promptly sent on to Berlin by courier, with the assurance that His Majesty could not be supposed to have taken any official cognizance of it, but that he desired Bismarck's advice at once as to what was to be done about it.

The final reply, which Radziwill carried to Benedetti about 5:30 P.M., was a flat refusal to grant another audience. The king could not consent, it was said, to renew the discussion as to the guarantees for the future, since what he had said that morning must be taken as his last word on that subject. If the ambassador desired to connect other questions with this, he would have to address himself to Bismarck.

After his conferences with Gorchakov and Loftus, early in the afternoon of the thirteenth,[36] Bismarck waited impatiently for news from Paris and Ems. Evidence was multiplying that the French government was not satisfied by the renunciation

[35] Werther may have remembered that the king had himself thought of writing a letter to the emperor. Cf. p. 130 above.

[36] See pp. 175–177 above.

and there were vague hints of additional and presumably humiliating demands. Bernstorff's short telegram from London of the night before [37] was followed early in the afternoon by a telegram, communicated by Gorchakov, from the Russian chargé d'affaires at Paris, and one from the Prussian at Stuttgart. The latter simply referred to "the latest demands of Gramont" but added the welcome news that they were of a nature to irritate the national feeling in Wurtemberg.[38] The former contained the more specific report that Gramont had said to Werther that the renunciation had not ended the affair, there remained still the injurious behavior. Eulenburg was informed of this by telegram: if the news were confirmed, the return of the king and the convocation of the Reichstag could no longer be postponed. Werther was asked if the news was exact; if so, it must have an important influence on the decisions to be made. An hour later, as there was still no direct word from Werther, Bismarck telegraphed to him again. "It is urgently necessary that you telegraph to me at once what Gramont said to you after he learned of the hereditary prince's renunciation; we have indications from Stuttgart, Munich, and Petersburg but still nothing from you." [39] Nothing at all had come from Ems about the king's talks with Benedetti.

There was still no news from either Paris or Ems when Bismarck was joined by Roon and Moltke for supper. From the account of the evening given in the chancellor's memoirs, it appears that the meal began in the most lugubrious fashion, that all three men were extremely dejected, and that the talk turned chiefly on Bismarck's intention to resign. Actually, the temper and the tone were somewhat different. It seems probable

[37] Lord, no. 148; see p. 000 above.
[38] Plain-language tg., Radolinski to Bismarck, July 13, 1870, 2:08 P.M., received 3:25 P.M., Lord, no. 161.
[39] Tg., Bismarck to Werther, July 13, 1870, sent to telegraph station, 4:10 P.M. and 5:10 P.M.; tg. to Abeken for Eulenburg, 4:10 P.M., Lord, nos. 166, 167, 172.

that the conversation dealt with the aggravating vagueness of
the news from Paris, the plans for a diplomatic offensive which
Bismarck had outlined to Loftus, and the impatience of the
three men with the king's relations with Benedetti. First of all,
Bismarck sent off a telegram to Bernstorff in London to ask
Lord Granville for his good offices in communicating with
Werther. "We hear," he wrote, "of new demands of Gramont
on Werther. The latter has telegraphed nothing since yesterday
noon despite our repeated inquiries. We are becoming suspicious that our telegraphic correspondence is being obstructed.
Try to get Lord Granville to telegraph in cipher to Lord Lyons
asking him to find out from Werther when and what he finally
telegraphed." [40] Even more revealing is the telegram which was
doubtless composed at the supper table as the upshot of their
discussions down to that moment, and which was then sent off
over Bismarck's signature to the king.[41] It ran:

In view of the growing exasperation of public opinion over the
presumptuous conduct of France, symptoms of which are coming
in to me from the most diverse parts of Germany, I hold it necessary that we should address to France a summons [42] to explain
her intentions toward Germany. The text of such a document
can be fixed only with the cooperation of Your Majesty's official
and natural advisers. Therefore, jointly with General von Moltke
and von Roon, I venture to renew my respectful request that
Your Majesty will deign to return to Berlin.[43]

Two other sentences were not included in the telegram as
sent: "It is reported from Paris that Gramont declares that
France's complaints against Prussia have not been set at rest by
the renunciation of the prince of Hohenzollern. In consequence, the prompt convocation of the North German Reichs-

[40] To telegraph station, 6:50 P.M., Lord, no. 175.
[41] In cipher, to telegraph station, 8:10 P.M., therefore probably
drafted at about 7 P.M., Lord, p. 99, n. 59.
[42] Bismarck started to write "ulti[matum]."
[43] Tg., Bismarck to King William, July 13, 1870, sent to telegraph
station, 8:10 P.M., Lord, no. 181.

tag is intended." As these sentences add nothing to what had already been telegraphed to Eulenburg, there was no need to repeat them. Lord's conjecture is probably correct, that the three men were not sure that the new French demands would furnish an immediate *casus belli*. Hence, the Reichstag should be informed of the smouldering quarrel; and with the moral support of this assembly, Prussia would then send France an ultimatum, a categorical demand to know what her intentions were, which would pretty certainly produce a war.[44] But however that may be, it was pushed into the background a few minutes later by the arrival of Abeken's telegram from Ems.

As Bismarck studied the telegram, he began to perceive the possibilities offered by its final phrase, the permission to publish the news. He asked Moltke if everything was in such shape that he could count on winning. On receiving the most confident assurances, Bismarck seated himself at a side table, pencil in hand, and by extensive omissions he produced a version of the telegram that suited him and his companions.[45]

From Bismarck's revision, the Ems telegram emerged cut down by half and very much simplified. The various incidents in Abeken's dispatch were reduced to two: (1) Count Benedetti had presented a demand for guarantees "for all future time," and (2) "His Majesty had thereupon refused to receive the French ambassador again, and sent word to him through the adjutant on duty that His Majesty had nothing further to communicate to him." It is true, as Bismarck repeatedly insisted, that he added nothing that was not in the original telegram and changed no significant words. But as he often pointed out, it was possible to change the spirit and sense of the document by

[44] The memory of the Reichstag interpellation and debate of April 1, 1867, which set off the Luxemburg crisis, makes this interpretation plausible. Lord, pp. 99, 229.

[45] The account in Bismarck's memoirs and stories is overdramatic. See William L. Langer, "Bismarck as a Dramatist," *Studies in Diplomatic History and Historiography in Honour of G. P. Gooch, C.H.*, ch. xi.

leaving out things and by bringing together other things which originally had no connection. The spirit of Abeken's dispatch was altered by leaving out every trace of how courteous and correct the king had been toward Benedetti. The sense of it was altered (1) by insinuating that the only answer William made to the French demand was to break off relations with the ambassador; (2) by concealing the primary object of the sending of the adjutant (to confirm the news of the renunciation), and the real meaning of the words "nothing further to communicate"; and, above all (3) by so phrasing things that the public was likely to draw the conclusion — as it actually did — that all relations with France had been abruptly and decisively terminated. In short, the telegram was, in effect, reduced to the one startling assertion, presented with exaggerated emphasis and with misleading implications: the king of Prussia had refused to receive the ambassador of France.[46]

At about nine o'clock in the evening an extra edition of the semi-official *Norddeutsche Allgemeine Zeitung* was distributed gratis on the streets of Berlin. It contained nothing but Bismarck's condensed version of the Ems telegram.

"The effect this bit of printed paper had upon the town was tremendous," the Berlin correspondent of the London *Times* reported,

It was hailed by old and young. It was welcomed by fathers of families and boys in their teens. It was read and re-read by ladies and young girls, and in patriotic glow, finally handed over to the servants, who fondly hoped their sweethearts would be on the march by this time. As though a stain had been wiped out from the national escutcheon, as though a burden, too heavy to be borne for a long time past, had been cast off at last, people were thanking God that their honour had been ultimately vindicated against intolerable assumption. There was but one opinion as to the manly and worthy conduct of the King; there was but one determination

[46] Lord, pp. 101–102. See Appendix C below for the German texts of Abeken's telegram and Bismarck's condensation.

to follow his example, and take up the gauntlet flung into their face. By ten o'clock the square in front of the royal palace was crowded with an excited multitude. Hurrahs for the King and cries "To the Rhine!" were heard on all sides. Similar demonstrations were made in other quarters of the town. It was the explosion of a long-pent-up anger.[47]

The immense effect of this laconic telegram was due in part to the fact that Bismarck evidently supplemented the official communiqué to the press by privately giving out some details — and apparently some exaggerated details — about the interview on the promenade. An example of the rumors found in a Berlin telegram of that evening to the London *Times*: "This afternoon King William was walking with Count Lehndorff, his adjutant, in the *Kurgarten* at Ems, when M. Benedetti accosted him and proffered his last extravagant demand. The King turned around and ordered Count Lehndorff to tell M. Benedetti that there was no reply and that he could not receive him again." Popular fancy embroidered the theme, and incidents at Ems became a legend of almost epic character in the public minds.[48]

To make sure that the revised version of the Ems telegram would have its full effect, it was made official and transmitted shortly after eleven o'clock to most of the capitals of Europe. It was sent in unciphered telegrams directly to governments of the Mecklenburgs, Oldenburg, Brunswick, Bremen, and Lübeck; in the same way to the Prussian representatives at Dresden, Altenburg, and Dessau; Munich, Stuttgart, Karlsruhe, Darmstadt, Hamburg, Weimar, and Meiningen; and in cipher to the North German envoys at London, St. Petersburg, Vienna, Florence, Madrid, Brussels, The Hague, Berne, and Constantinople. In each case, the envoy was ordered to communi-

[47] July 14, 1870; reprinted in Karl Abel, *Letters on International Relations before and during the War of 1870*, vol. II, p. 129.
[48] Lord, pp. 103–104.

cate the telegram (usually it was added "without delay") to the government to which he was accredited. The dispatches to London, St. Petersburg, and Munich contained as a sort of postscript a direct appeal to Lord Granville, the tsar, and the king of Bavaria alleging that Benedetti, in order to present his demand, had in provocative fashion started a conversation with the king on the promenade against the latter's will.[49]

In the meantime, other news had been pouring in, most of it encouraging. Werther, heard from at last, reported that Gramont's declarations in the Chamber that afternoon, while indecisive and ambiguous, were interpreted in military circles as warlike; and that meantime military preparations for war were being pushed on in the most comprehensive fashion. These telegrams left the impression, indeed, that the French cabinet was divided in opinion and the outcome not yet certain, but the balance seemed to be inclining toward war, and Bismarck hastened to telegraph the news of the French military preparations to his envoys at London, St. Petersburg, and Vienna. Gorchakov had written a note to let Bismarck know that he had telegraphed to the Russian representatives at London and Paris that "after the spontaneous and absolute renunciation by Hohenzollern, we cannot understand why the Franco-Prussian difference was not terminated or why new demands were brought up, if as she is assuring Europe, France wants peace."[50] Bernstorff had reported that England had declared at Paris that France must content herself with the renunciation; and Gladstone had said that if France now began a war she would put herself most flagrantly in the wrong. This was further excellent material for a circular, which was sent out the following day. From Stuttgart came the news that the cabinet of Wurttemberg, whose policy had aroused apprehensions, had now decided to adopt a patriotic attitude and appropriated the money.

[49] Lord, pp. 104–105.
[50] Lord, no. 174.

Finally, from Abeken's last telegram of the day, Bismarck learned the concluding chapter of the Ems incidents: that the king had rejected all Benedetti's pleas for an audience; that the Ems negotiations were over.

Well after midnight came a telegram from Werther, announcing that Gramont had just told the Russian chargé d'affaires of the demand for guarantees made at Ems and had added that if this demand were rejected, war was inevitable. About the same time, first from Abeken, and then from two telegrams from the ambassador himself, the chancellor at last learned the substance of the Werther report of July 12: the "demand for the letter of apology."

In the early hours of the morning, Bismarck telegraphed his recommendations to Ems. The king should instruct Werther that his report was considered as *non avenu*, and that he must inform Gramont that he could not carry out the commission. If the French government wished to lay such a proposal before the king, it would have to choose another channel. Werther must then say that he had requested and obtained a furlough, and must at once return to Berlin to explain his conduct. An earlier draft shows that Bismarck had thought of recalling Werther without explanation to Gramont but had given up this drastic measure. As Lord says, he had, after all, done enough for one day.[51]

That war was now inevitable, all Berlin seems to have recognized, and the rest of Germany too as the news of the Ems incident spread through the country. On July 14, crowds continued to wait *Unter den Linden* for the return of the king.[52] The foreign diplomats reported in much the same sense. The Dutch minister added to his telegram transmitting the text of the newspaper extra: "War henceforth certain." The Austrian

[51] Lord, pp. 105–106.
[52] *Allgemeine Zeitung* (Augsburg), July 16, 1870, no. 197, p. 3141.

ambassador informed his government that any attempt at mediation not only would be useless, but would be regarded by Prussia as an affront. The Italian telegraphed that war was inevitable if France persisted in her new demands.[53] The Russian, Oubril, who received a visit from Bismarck on the morning of the fourteenth, was not quite so sure. "Desirous to leave the door open for peace, the federal chancellor has just telegraphed to Werther that he cannot submit his report to the king and that he leaves it to the Duke of Gramont to address his demands to him in an official manner. . . . 'Perhaps,' he said to me, 'he will reflect how impossible these demands are when he finds himself under the necessity of formulating them in this way'." He felt that Bismarck was eager to avoid war but was disturbed by the serious crisis and hampered by the absence of the king. "If the present state of affairs continues, he cannot be responsible for what happens." The French, he insisted, could push to the Rhine without finding sufficient Prussian forces to meet them. For the moment the French armaments had not reached the stage of danger but the activity in the naval ports was alarming. Bismarck asked if the Great Powers could not make vigorous representations in favor of peace; then, if war should nevertheless break out, could Russia permit Prussia to be crushed? [54]

Bismarck's observations to Oubril were obviously intended to convince his listener, but there are additional indications of his uncertainty. He was still worried that the king might waver, especially when he visited the queen at Coblentz.[55] In the calendar, on the margins of which Bismarck was accustomed to give expression to his feelings, he had written on July 12,

[53] Munch-Bellinghausen to Beust, private, July 14, 1870, Lord, no. 253. Launay to Visconti-Venosta, July 14, 1870, cited by Halperin, "Visconti-Venosta and the Crisis of July 1870," *Journal of Modern History*, vol. XXXI, p. 308.

[54] Oubril to Westmann, July 2/14, 1870, nos. 137, 138; Clark, *Journal of Modern History*, vol. XIV, no. 2, pp. 203–205.

[55] Oubril to Westmann, July 3/15, 1870, no. 140; Clark, p. 206.

the day of the renunciation, "peace?"; on the fourteenth, the day after the Ems telegram, the word was "war?" [56] The question mark suggests that he was not yet sure of the effect of the publication. Until the French government acted, he could not be sure.

In the meantime, he could press the king to return to Berlin, he could try to influence the foreign diplomats in favor of Prussia, and he could use the press to inflame public opinion.[57]

[56] A. O. Meyer, *Bismarcks Glaube*, pp. 38–39.

[57] For example, he told Loftus, in a conversation on July 14, that "about four months ago the French Government had sounded the Swedish Government as to their possible cooperation with France in the event of war with Prussia" (Loftus to Granville, confidential, July 16, 1870, no. 33, Public Record Office, London, F.O. 64/688). Cf. Schweinitz to Bismarck, Vienna, July 12, 1870, no. 184; Prussian Foreign Office Archives, B. o. 32, Bd. 4, A 2298, pr. July 13, 1870. Cf. also Lord, pp. 107–108, 111–113, 115–116.

-❦[VI]❦-

The Declaration of War

"The refusal of the king [to give assurances for the future],"
Benedetti wrote in 1871, "put the [French] government face
to face with a public opinion that was deeply offended. The
path of negotiation was henceforth barred and there remained
only two alternatives: [either] to face down the irritation of
the country and to accept the renunciation in the form in
which it was made or to declare war at once." [1] At Paris, after
the stormy session of the Chamber of Deputies on the afternoon of July 13, the excitement increased. Ollivier's estimate
that the public was opposed to his policy of accepting the
renunciation as it stood was confirmed by most observers in
the press and in the diplomatic corps.[2] There could be no mis-

---

[1] Benedetti, *Ma Mission en Prusse*, p. 409.

[2] On the state of public opinion and its influence, see Lehautcourt,
Les Origines de la guerre de 1870, p. 481, and especially the thorough
and thoughtful study in L. M. Case, *French Opinion on War and Diplomacy during the Second Empire*, pp. 225–262. Rudolf von Albertini
agrees in substance with Case's description of the expressions of public
opinion but puts more stress on the part of the "official" press and on
undercover activity of the police and other government agents in
stimulating it. "Frankreichs Stellungnahme zur deutschen Einigung
während des zweiten Kaiserreichs," *Schweizerische Zeitschrift für
Geschichte*, vol. V, p. 360. Jean Stengers argues that the influence of the
police and other government agents in stimulating public demonstrations was not an important factor. "Aux origines de la guerre de 1870:

take about the bellicose attitude of the politicians of the right, and it was reported that on this issue they had the enthusiastic support of Gambetta on the left. Even the leader of the right center, the keystone of the cabinet majority, advised Ollivier to accept the role of "a minister of public opinion" and to lead the country into war. If he did not, right and left would combine to bring the cabinet down.[3]

For two days, however, the government wavered. At first, the pressure merely stiffened Ollivier's determination to be firm, and he believed that most of his colleagues shared his attitude.[4] Gramont, on the other hand, waiting for further reports from Benedetti, continued to interpret in his own way the cabinet decision of the day before that the demand for guarantees should not be regarded as an ultimatum. The national feeling, he reported in another urgent telegram to Benedetti at Ems, was so heated that it was only with difficulty that the government had been able to get a delay until Friday, July 15, for making a statement to the Chambers. He ordered Benedetti to make a last attempt with the king.

Tell him that we limit ourselves to the demand that he forbid the prince of Hohenzollern to withdraw his renunciation. Let him [the king] say to you "I will forbid him" and have him authorize you to write this to me or have him direct his minister or his ambassador to inform me, — that will be enough for us. If it is true that the king has no mental reservations, this will be a matter of secondary significance for him; it is all important for us. Only the word of the king can be considered an adequate guarantee for the future. . . . In any event, leave Ems and come to Paris with an answer, whether it is affirmative or negative . . . , if necessary, by special train. . . . Perhaps when you receive the news of the renunciation of the prince of Hohenzollern from the king, you would say to him: "Sire, Your Majesty, then, guarantees the word

---

Gouvernement et opinion publique," *Revue Belge de Philologie et d'Histoire*, 1956, p. 713.

[3] Ollivier, vol. XIV, 337–342; Lehautcourt, pp. 481–482.

[4] Ollivier, vol. XIV, pp. 341–344.

of the Prince of Hohenzollern, for [Your Majesty] is not unaware that we, as a Power, have no relations with the prince and that, in consequence, our official guarantee [5] is the word of the King." [6]

The confidence that Gramont expressed in his telegram to Benedetti that the other cabinets of Europe regarded his demands as "just and moderate" was hardly justified by the messages coming in. Most impressive of all was a telegram from Stuttgart that any additional insistence on the part of France would be regarded in South Germany as proof of French belligerence and would lend color to the opinion that for France, the Hohenzollern candidacy was simply a pretext to secure war. [7]

In the course of the evening, Olózaga brought to Ollivier and to Gramont the assurance that the Spanish government had acknowledged receipt of Karl Anton's telegram and was no longer concerned with Leopold's candidacy. [8] Ollivier welcomed this news and was planning a pacific statement for the Chambers. Late at night, he went again to the Ministry of Foreign Affairs to find out if there were more reports from Ems. Two telegrams from Benedetti had arrived at eleven, [9] and Gramont had gone to St. Cloud to show them to the emperor. "Dear Friend," he wrote in a note to Ollivier, "I am going to St.

[5] In the decipher at Ems, "guarantie" was read "abri." Gramont, *La France et la Prusse*, pp. 190–191.

[6] Tg., July 13, 1870, 7 P.M., *O.D.*, vol. XXVIII, no. 8463. Gramont, p. 189, gives the time as 8 P.M. Gramont had received Benedetti's first two telegrams of the day. The first, drafted at 10:30 A.M., dispatched at 12:05 P.M., and received at 2:35 P.M., summarized the conversation in the *Kurgarten* and included the statement that the king had absolutely refused to give a guarantee for the future. The second, drafted at 11:30 A.M., dispatched at 1:05 P.M., and received at 4 P.M., said that Benedetti expected at any moment to be called to the king to be told of the message from Sigmaringen and that he would use this opportunity to carry out his orders. *O.D.*, vol. XXVIII, nos. 8458, 8459.

[7] Lehautcourt, pp. 483–486.

[8] Lehautcourt, pp. 486–487.

[9] Tgs., Benedetti to Gramont, July 13, 1870, dispatched 4:25 P.M. and 7:45 P.M., received 11 P.M., *O.D.*, vol. XVIII, nos. 8469, 8470.

Cloud. There is news. He [King William] has communicated the letter from Hohenzollern and approved [it]; it's a little." In Ollivier's opinion, it was more than a little, especially when matched by the communication from Olózaga, and he pleaded with Gramont not to commit himself further, even in his own mind, until another discussion between them. On his return from St. Cloud, well after midnight, Gramont summed up his impressions in another note to Ollivier: "I am just back from St. Cloud. The indecision is great. At first it was war. Then, hesitation because of this approval by the king. The Spanish dispatch might tilt the balance for peace. The emperor charged me to ask you to let all our colleagues know that he expects us tomorrow at seven o'clock for dinner and a Council meeting." [10]

The next morning (the fourteenth), after his first calm night of sleep for many days,[11] Ollivier was drafting his statement for the government to present to the Chambers. Suddenly Gramont entered the room and called out, "My friend, you are looking at a man who has just received a slap in the face." He held out a piece of yellow paper, a telegram from Le Sourd, the chargé d'affaires at Berlin, with the newspaper text of the Ems telegram. Ollivier, too, lost his composure. "There can be no more illusions," he reports that he said, "they want to force us to war." The two ministers sent a telegram to St. Cloud to ask the emperor to come to the Tuileries as soon as possible to preside over a Council meeting, and they summoned their cabinet colleagues to get the bad news.[12]

[10] Lehautcourt, pp. 489–490.
[11] Ollivier, vol XIV, p. 354.
[12] Lehautcourt, pp. 493–495. The reply from St. Cloud was sent at 11 A.M., so the request to the emperor must have been made while Gramont was with Ollivier but before the other ministers arrived and not after, as Ollivier's account states. Ollivier, vol. XIV, pp. 356–357, also says that before the other ministers arrived, Gramont returned to the Foreign Office "ou Werther s'était fait annoncer." Gramont, p. 208, says that soon after he received, at 11 o'clock, the dispatches from Benedetti, Werther came to see him. This is an error. Werther did not see Gramont until evening. See Lord, *The Origins of the War of 1870*, nos. 206,

At about half past twelve, the emperor arrived at the Tuileries and convened the Council. On the way, he, like the ministers, was impressed by the impatient and angry crowds, shouting protests against further negotiations with Prussia.[13] Even against this background, which made calm deliberation difficult, the discussions went on for over five hours.[14] All possible solutions were analyzed and debated until the participants were close to exhaustion.[15]

At the very beginning of the session, Gramont dropped his portfolio on the table and said, as he sat down, "After what has just happened, a minister of foreign affairs who cannot make up his mind for war is not fit to retain his office." Marshal Le Boeuf, the minister of war, told the Council that, according to his intelligence reports, the Prussians had begun to arm, that they were buying horses in Belgium, and that if the French did not want to be anticipated, they had not a minute to lose. He is said to have added, "in a commanding, almost impatient tone," that everything was prepared and France had a start of at least fifteen days over Prussia: if they did not make war at once, they would lose an opportunity that would never come again.[16] In spite of all this, the Council continued irresolute. Several of the ministers were obstinately in favor of peace and one of them, Plichon, took advantage of a lull to point out to Napoleon, privately, that between him and King William the game was not even. The king could afford to lose some battles; for the emperor, defeat meant revolution.[17]

It was generally agreed, on the basis of Benedetti's telegrams

212. It seems probable, therefore, that Gramont went to the Foreign Office to receive the dispatches from Benedetti, which were expected by the train due at 10:15 A.M.

[13] Lehautcourt, p. 497.

[14] It is generally accepted that the session began at 12:30 and adjourned at 5:45 P.M. *O.D.*, vol. XXVIII, no. 8493, n.2.

[15] Gramont, p. 212; tg., Napoleon to Eugénie, July 14, 1870, 4:05 P.M., *O.D.* XXVIII, no. 8493.

[16] Lehautcourt, pp. 497–498.

[17] Lehautcourt, pp. 498–499.

and reports, that King William's conduct had been beyond reproach. He had refused Benedetti's requests for an audience in courteous terms — there was neither an insulter nor an insulted. There was even some feeling that Benedetti had been too urgent in asking twice for an audience after the king had formally notified him that he had nothing more to say to him. But the publication of the "Ems telegram" was another matter. A straightforward refusal had been turned into an affront: the public had been taken into a confidence that should have remained between the ambassador and the king. The document that had appeared in the *Norddeutsche Allgemeine Zeitung* was much more than a paragraph in a newspaper, even in one that was semi-official. It was a special supplement in large type that could be posted on walls and in shop windows. The information contained in it was not in the form of an ordinary newspaper article but reproduced the text of an official document which could have come only from the Prussian government with the settled intention of making it public. This could be interpreted only as a deliberate affront. To accept it tamely would be degrading; the only possible answer to the challenge was war. Marshal Le Boeuf was told that he could call out the reserves.[18] Before doing so, he asked for a roll call. When he put the question, beginning with Ollivier and ending with the emperor, the vote was unanimous.[19]

A few days earlier, Benedetti had warned Gramont that if France began open military preparations, war would be inevitable.[20] It seems, however, that members of the Council did not think of their vote for recalling the reserves as equivalent to a decision for war.[21] After Le Boeuf left to go to his ministry

[18] At about 4 o'clock. Lehautcourt, pp. 499–500.
[19] Ollivier, vol. XIV, p. 362. La Gorce, citing Le Boeuf's testimony before the Commission of Inquiry, says the vote was almost unanimous.
[20] Benedetti to Gramont, July 10, 1870, *O.D.*, vol. XXVIII, no. 8378.
[21] In a letter to Ollivier, written fifteen years after the event, Le Boeuf maintained that the decision was a response to the war preparations reported from Germany, January 8, 1886; Ollivier, vol. XIV, p. 613. This

to have the orders prepared,[22] they continued to bring up expedients that betray irresolution.

Ollivier proposed that the emperor authorize him to inform the *Corps Législatif* that the affair was finished and that they attached no importance to the Prussian revelations. He would defend this without conviction and he would not win it. The cabinet would fall before an overwhelming vote, but it would at least cover the emperor's responsibility, since he would be forced by the Chamber to dismiss a ministry of peace and to accept one of war. Napoleon's enemies could not accuse him of seeking war for personal (i.e., dynastic) reasons. The emperor rejected the suggestion; he would not separate himself from the ministry at a time when it was more than ever needed by him.[23]

Thereupon, the Council began to draft the statement that would be made to the Chambers. No text has been revealed; none was completed.[24] A telegram from Benedetti was brought in to Gramont and the session was temporarily suspended.[25]

The legislative assembly was anxiously awaiting word from the Tuileries. Its formal business was the debate on the budget of the Ministry of Public Works. Several of the ministers appeared for a few minutes in the Chamber, and one of them spoke briefly in support of his budget. They returned to the Council

---

implies that the Council had not reached a clear and final decision for war. In an exchange of letters in the same year, Ollivier and Plichon disagreed as to whether the decision had been reached on the evening of July 14 or the morning of July 15, but neither implies that it was at the afternoon meeting on July 14. Ollivier, vol. XIV (appendix XI), pp. 605–620.

[22] They were sent off by telegraph at 8:40 P.M. Lehautcourt, p. 500, n. 1. At 4:05 P.M., Napoleon sent a telegram to Eugénie at St. Cloud: "Le Conseil dure encore. Je suis content." It is probable that he referred to the vote to recall the reserves. *O.D.*, vol. XXVII, no. 8493.

[23] Ollivier, vol. XIV, pp. 362–363; Lehautcourt, pp. 500–501.

[24] It would surely have announced the recall of the reserves and an explanation of the reasons; it would probably have referred to the Ems telegram.

[25] Lehautcourt, p. 501; *O.D.*, vol. XXVIII, p. 337, n.2.

obviously impressed by the impatience and hostility of the deputies.[26]

Benedetti's telegram showed that although he had failed to secure an audience with King William to renew his demands, he had been treated with full courtesy. He had talked with Eulenburg in the morning, who had agreed to inform the king of his observations. The reply had been as before; that there was nothing more to communicate to him. But in answer to his request to take formal leave, he was informed that the king would receive him at the railroad station before leaving to visit the queen at Coblentz. Benedetti did not know if the king would return to Ems or to Berlin. On the other hand, Benedetti referred to the "Ems telegram" and assured Gramont that he had not revealed any confidences: its information must have come from the cabinet of the king. He had heard rumors, too, that since the day before, the language of the king's entourage had been deplorable.[27]

When the Council resumed its deliberations, it was still looking for a way to escape from the impasse. Someone suggested a European congress, and the members grasped at this last straw. A number of drafts were tried and rejected. There is no testimony that a formal vote was taken, but it was apparently understood that a pacific declaration would be made to the Chambers to the following effect. "In spite of the refusal of Prussia to grant our legitimate demand, we do not consider conflict as imminent. Nevertheless we are compelled to call up the contingent. We are ready to accept a congress in which all the questions at issue will receive definitive solution in view of establishing a lasting peace." As the Chambers had adjourned for the day, it was agreed that the statement would be presented to them when they reassembled the following afternoon.

[26] La Gorce, *Histoire du second empire*, vol. VI, p. 291; Ollivier, vol. XIV, pp. 363–364; Lehautcourt, pp. 501–502.
[27] Tg., Benedetti to Gramont, July 14, 1870, *O.D.*, vol. XXVIII, no. 8496. Gramont places the receipt of this after the Council (p. 221).

The Council adjourned and the members went their several ways.[28]

Within a few hours, however, the situation was reversed. Before he left the Tuileries, Napoleon wrote a short note to Marshal Le Boeuf. He did not directly revoke the order to call up the reserves but did suggest doubt as to the urgency of the measure. He received the Austrian and Italian ambassadors and told them in confidence of the decision of the Council. On his return to St. Cloud, he found violent opposition, especially from the empress, to what had been resolved. Le Boeuf had hurried to the palace after dinner and pointed out the discrepancy between the decision to recall the reserves and the appeal to the congress. He urged the emperor to call the Council together again to decide if they should cancel or maintain the call-up. The emperor agreed and telegraphed to Ollivier to come with his colleagues as soon as he could.[29]

Ollivier has described in vivid language the change that came over him as he left the seclusion in which the Council had debated for so many hours and went from the close atmosphere of the meeting-room into the fresh air. The phantoms of the brain were dissolved and his mind regained its sense of realities. The project that had been adopted began to appear to him as a chimerical failure of courage. On his arrival at the Chancery, he read the draft declaration to his family and his secretaries. Their indignant dissent was unanimous. If they, who had hitherto been advocates of peace, found the proposal impossible, it was clear that it could not possibly satisfy the Chambers and the public.[30]

[28] See supplementary note I at end of chapter.

[29] Ollivier says (vol. XIV, p. 370), "Le Boeuf, qui malgré le billet de l'Empereur, avait expedié les ordres de mobilisation à huit heures quarante, vint à Saint-Cloud après le diner et pria l'Empereur de réunir le Conseil le soir même." As the telegram to Ollivier asking him to bring his colleagues to St. Cloud was sent at 8 P.M., it would have been possible by a telegram to the Ministry of War to have suspended the transmission of the order. *O.D.*, vol. XXVIII, no. 8507.

[30] Ollivier, vol. XIV, pp. 369–370.

Gramont, before he joined his colleagues at St. Cloud, received a call from Werther. The ambassador informed him that the dispatch in which he had reported his conference of July 12 with Gramont and Ollivier must be regarded as *non avenu* and that proposals of that nature could be brought to the Prussian government only in writing and only by organs of the French cabinet. In other words, he had been disavowed by his own government and had been ordered to take leave of absence at once. Count Solms would be chargé d'affaires in his absence.[31] To Gramont, it seemed the premonition of a break in diplomatic relations.[32]

Gramont had also received a number of additional telegrams and dispatches. His own account of the events of the evening is imprecise; he sums up, he says, "one after another the news that came to us *almost simultaneously* in *the evening of the fourteenth and the night from the fourteenth to the fifteenth*." [33] Among them were several from Spain: first, a report from Mercier that up to eleven o'clock on the thirteenth, the principal secretary of state had received no additional communications about the renunciation and still retained some skepticism about it. He was sure, however, that the renunciation would be accepted and that the Council would not recall the Cortes before fall. Then, they would have to begin a new search for a king. A second report stated that the Regent, Serrano, had no doubt about the authenticity of the message from Karl Anton. Prim was equally satisfied and as soon as the word was officially confirmed, they would notify all the cabinets that it was accepted.[34]

[31] "Reçu l'ordre de prendre un congé" is Gramont's rendering, and he claims that his account is "scrupuleusement exact" (p. 208). Werther's telegram to Berlin says, "Ich habe ihm ferner angezeigt, dass ich Urlaub erbeten und bewilligt erhalten, morgen nach Berlin abreise" (Lord, p. 111 and no. 212). Werther may not have told Gramont explicitly that he had been ordered to take leave — he would not dare report that he had — but it was, in any case, an obvious conclusion.

[32] See the discussion in his book, pp. 208–210.

[33] P. 221. My italics.

[34] Tgs., Mercier to Gramont, July 14, 1870; 9:35 A.M., received 3:30

Three telegrams were from Benedetti. One merely reported that it appeared certain that the king would leave tomorrow morning for Berlin, "moving up his return to the capital by several days." The second told that he had just seen the king at the railroad station. His Majesty had repeated that he had nothing more to communicate but made it clear that he did not mean by this that negotiations were at an end: they could be continued at Berlin, i.e., with the minister of foreign affairs. The third transmitted, on behalf of Captain Samuel "on secret mission," some military information for the minister of war.[35]

Most important of all was a telegram from the French minister at Berne: "General von Röder [the Prussian minister] communicated this morning to the president [of the Swiss Confederation] a telegram from Count Bismarck which announced the refusal of King William to commit himself, as king of Prussia, never to give his consent to the candidacy of the prince of Hohenzollern if it should arise again, and the refusal of the king, in consequence of this demand, to receive our ambassador." [36] Not long afterward, a telegram from Munich brought the text of the "Ems telegram" as reported to that capital, including the supplementary paragraph: "the king of Bavaria will certainly be moved by the fact that Benedetti had accosted the king of Prussia on the promenade in a provocative manner." [37]

P.M.; 2 P.M., received 7 P.M., *O.D.*, vol. XXVIII, nos. 8494, 8501. A telegram received at 10:45 P.M., reported that the Spanish government had a telegram from its minister at Berlin confirming the authenticity of Karl Anton's renunciation but that it would be necessary to have some word from Leopold before the news was communicated officially to the foreign courts (*ibid.*, no. 8528).

[35] Ems, July 14, 1870, *O.D.*, vol. XXVIII, nos. 8498, 8499, 8497. The king noted on the margin of a letter from Solms that he had said to Benedetti at the station, "J'apprends que vous partez ce soir pour Berlin; moi je m'y rends demain: tout ce qui a rapport à la politique se traitera dorénavant de ministère à ministère" (*G.W.*, vol. VIb, p. 374, note to no. 1618).

[36] Tg., Comminges-Guitand to Gramont, July 14, 1870, 4:30 P.M., received 7 P.M., *O.D.*, vol. XVIII, no. 8500.

[37] Cadore to Gramont, July 14, 1870, 6:30 P.M., received 8:15 P.M., *O.D.*, vol. XXVIII, no. 8504. Ollivier (vol. XIV, p. 374) says that Gra-

If any lingering doubts may have remained about the official character of the newspaper extra, they were now destroyed.[38]

Gradually the ministers assembled at St. Cloud. Ollivier was the first to arrive. The emperor explained to him in a few words the reason for the unexpected summons. He added that on reflection, he had decided that the adopted declaration was not very satisfactory. Ollivier agreed with him: "If we take that to the Chambers, they will throw mud on our carriages and hoot us down." After a few moments of silence, the emperor replied: "You see in what a situation a government can sometimes find itself: — even if we should have no avowable cause for war, we should still be obliged to decide for it in obedience to the will of the country." [39] Finally, when all but three of the members had arrived,[40] the emperor opened the session. For the first time, the empress sat with them.[41]

---

mont received this just after he finished reading the telegram from Berne.

[38] Gramont (p. 229) wrote: "Cette communication faite aux puissances étrangères n'avait d'autre but évidemment que de combler la mesure et de placer la France en présence d'un affront public." This interpretation is correct; Bismarck's frequent admissions confirm it. But in criticizing Bismarck's communications to the other cabinets of the demand and its rejection, Gramont conveniently disregards the fact that he had informed a number of the German and other governments that France was demanding of the king of Prussia that he forbid the prince of Hohenzollern to go back on his decision to abandon the candidacy. See, for example, draft tg., Gramont to Cadore (Munich) and St. Vallier (Stuttgart), July 12, 1870, 11 P.M., *O.D.*, vol. XXVIII, no. 8432; to Fleury (St. Petersburg), July 13, 1870, Lyons to Granville, July 13, 1870, Fester, *Briefe*, vol. II, no. 525. See also supplementary note II at end of chapter.

[39] This calls to mind Cavour's report of the conversation with Napoleon at Plombieres in June 1858.

[40] According to La Gorce (vol. VI, p. 297), Segris did not receive the call in time; Louvet seems to have been overlooked. Plichon received word so late that he did not arrive until the session was over. See Ollivier, vol. XIV, p. 608.

[41] Ollivier (vol. XIV, p. 380) says that she listened without saying a word. The Earl of Malmesbury records (*Memoirs of an Ex-minister*, p. 665) that Gramont told him that the empress made a strong and most excited address, declaring that "war was inevitable if the honor of France was to be sustained." This could possibly refer to the meeting of

Le Boeuf explained his reasons for asking that the Council meet. The note from the emperor had made him uneasy. Then he had learned of the last decision of the Council. He wanted the Council, therefore, to determine if the new policy was consistent with the decision to call out the reserves. The order had gone out. According to Ollivier, LeBoeuf added that this should not weigh on their resolution. If it was thought necessary to annul the order, he would himself accept the responsibility before the country and resign his portfolio. According to Gramont, the marshal threw down his portfolio and, in a most violent tone, swore that if war was not declared, he would give it up and renounce his military rank.[42] Gramont presented the telegrams and dispatches received. He also argued vigorously against the plan for a congress and, if we may believe Metternich's report of what Gramont told him, threatened to resign if his advice was not followed.[43] Whatever questions there may be about the details, the upshot of the meeting was the decision to maintain the order to recall the reserves. The declaration adopted in the afternoon with its appeal to Europe was abandoned, and it was agreed that Ollivier and Gramont should prepare a new one to be approved at a meeting in the morning. No formal decision to declare war was made, but it became clear in the discussion that war could no longer be avoided.[44]

---

the next morning, but Ollivier (vol. XIV, p. 393) says that then too the empress expressed no opinion and cast no vote. In any case her views were sufficiently known. Mlle. Garets to her mother, Saint-Cloud, July [15?], 1870: ". . . toute le monde ici, l'Imperatrice en tête désire tellement la guerre qu'il me parait impossible que nous ne l'ayons pas" (Garets, *Souvenirs*, p. 187).

[42] Ollivier, vol. XIV, p. 373; Malmesbury, *Memoirs of an Ex-minister*, p. 665. According to Gramont's statements to Malmesbury, Le Boeuf's outburst followed the speech by the empress.

[43] Private letter, Metternich to Beust, Paris, July 31, 1870. See also Vitzthum's account of his conference with Gramont on the evening of July 15. H. Oncken, vol. III, no. 934, and p. 442. Neither Gramont in his book nor Ollivier mentions this.

[44] Ollivier, vol. XIV, pp. 373–381. In 1886, Ollivier and Plichon debated this situation. Plichon claimed that the war was decided on the

The Council convened at nine o'clock on the morning of the fifteenth. All of the members were present and as on the night before, the empress sat with them. In his apologia, Ollivier insists that the ministers were still free agents in their wills and in their votes. No irrevocable public action had been taken. In theory, this was true, but in fact, all that the Council could do was to draw the consequences of what had been, in fact, settled the night before. Ollivier had contributed to this necessity by his change of policy and by his communication to the press. When at the end of the evening, Mitchell, editor of the *Constitutionnel*, had made his usual call at the Chancery, Ollivier had told him, with regret but with determination, that the Council had decided to declare war. He had done his best to avoid a war with Germany but now that it was to be, he could not resign and let another cabinet lead the country through it. "I cannot [resign]," he said, "the country has confidence in me; I am the security of the pact which binds the Empire and France. If I withdraw . . . the situation, already so difficult, will be complicated by internal politics. . . . *War has been decided, it is legitimate, it is inevitable; no human power can today avert it.* Since we cannot prevent it, our duty is to render it popular." [45]

During the day of the fourteenth, the public demonstrations in Paris had become more excited and by the time that five or six of the evening papers had brought the news of the "Ems telegram," the outburst of national feeling had become uncontrollable. This was paralleled by the newspaper commentaries. A few of the more peaceful cautiously risked restraint. Most of them saw a declaration of war as the only honorable

---

evening of July 14; Ollivier insisted that the unanimous vote for war was taken on the morning of July 15; on the evening of the fourteenth, he admits, "the ministers present decided in principle that France ought to reply by war to the outrage which the reports of our agents did not permit us to doubt" (*ibid.*, pp. 605–620).

[45] Ollivier, vol. XIV, pp. 381–382, 391. My italics.

and possible solution. As Edmond About wrote in *Le Soir*: "Our readers do not expect from us an article on the state of affairs. Our ambassador has been publicly affronted. There is not a Frenchman who will not feel the insult. All our hearts will be united to call for and to get an exemplary satisfaction." The boulevards were so crowded that in some cases traffic was blocked and omnibuses had to be detoured. There were frequent cheers for war and shouts of "on to Berlin." A group of over a thousand demonstrators appeared before the German embassy but was persuaded to withdraw without forcing the gates. The occasional groups that paraded in favor of peace found little support or notice. As Albert Duruy wrote in *La Liberté* for the morning of the fifteenth: "The declaration which the Senate and the Chambers of Deputies awaited with patriotic anxiety has not been made. But in return, Paris yesterday evening made its declaration of war against Prussia. Paris has responded with the *Marseillaise* to the new challenge from Bismarck." [46]

The session of the Council was short; it lasted about an hour. Gramont read the declaration which he and Ollivier had drafted. When the reading was finished, the emperor applauded. Even before a vote could be called for, Chevandier de Valdrôme, minister of the interior, asked permission to make a statement. "As up to this time," he said, "I have been one of those who spoke emphatically in favor of peace, I ask now

---

[46] On the demonstrations and the press and public opinion, see Ollivier, vol. XIV, pp. 383–387; Lehautcourt, pp. 524–526; Dupuy, *1870–1871: La guerre, la Commune, et la presse*, pp. 11–12, 35–43; and especially Case, *French Opinion on War and Diplomacy*, pp. 259–269. Jean Stengers does not question the intensity of the warlike demonstrations but believes that until the government made its statements to the Chamber of Depuies and the Senate on July 15, the "Ems telegram" had little influence on the public. He adds his opinion that if the government had not acted as it did on July 15, an explosion of public opinion would probably have been so intense that it would have irresistably dragged the government to war, "et la probabilité, à notre sense, rejoint presque ici la certitude" ("Aux origines de la guerre de 1870," *Revue Belge de Philologie et d' Histoire*, p. 735).

to be the first to express my opinion. When some one gives me a slap in the face, I don't wait to examine the question of how well I know how to fight; I give one back to him. I vote for war." Others expressed the same opinion. Alexis-Emile Segris, who had been absent the night before, turned to Le Boeuf and asked "not if we are prepared, but if we have a good chance to win." No one was surprised at the answer that not only were they ready but they were never in a better position to settle their difference with Prussia.[47] The ministers who had been most urgent for peace kept generally silent: they may have been converted; at least they bowed before the accomplished fact. The vote for war was unanimous.[48]

The constitution left to the emperor alone the right to make war and peace. Nevertheless, Ollivier had promised, in the name of the cabinet, that if they should believe that war was inevitable, they would not engage until they had asked and received the concurrence of the Chambers. It was decided that the statement to the legislature would be accompanied by the demand for a credit of fifty million francs. Its adoption or rejection would give the Chambers an unambiguous means of expressing its will. Another credit of sixteen millions would be asked for the navy. New laws would also be presented: one to permit voluntary enlistments for the war; the other, to call the *garde mobile* to active duty.[49]

Ollivier read the statement to the Chamber of Deputies.

As the manner in which the country received our declaration

---

[47] See Lehautcourt, p. 527 and n. 3, and Eugénie's comments to Paléologue in *The Tragic Empress*, p. 124 (conversation on April 22, 1906).

[48] Lehautcourt, pp. 527–528. At about 10 o'clock the emperor received Vitzthum and implied that he would welcome the mediation of Austria and Italy or even the proposal of a congress. Vitzthum records that the emperor added, "Mais il ne faut pas que cela nous empêche de nous battre." Tg., Metternich to Beust, Paris, July 15, 1870, 3:30 P.M.; Vitzthum to Andrássy, Brussels, January 16, 1873, H. Oncken, vol. III, nos. 890, 891A.

[49] Lehautcourt, pp. 528–529.

of July 6 gave us the assurance that you would approve our policy and that we could count on your support, we began at once negotiations with the foreign powers to get their good offices to persuade Prussia to admit the legitimacy of our grievance.

In these negotiations, we have asked nothing of Spain, whose susceptibilities we did not want to arouse and whose independance we did want to offend; we did not negotiate with the prince of Hohenzollern whom we regarded as covered by the king; we have likewise refused to bring into our discussion any reproaches [about the past] nor to let it go beyond the subject within which we have limited it from the beginning.

Most of the powers have responded with alacrity, and they have, with more or less zeal, admitted the justice of our complaint.

The Prussian minister of foreign affairs has put us off, pretending that he was ignorant of the matter and that the Cabinet of Berlin had had nothing to do with it.

We then addressed ourselves to the king in person and we ordered our ambassador to go to His Majesty at Ems. While he acknowledged that he had authorized the prince of Hohenzollern to accept the candidacy that had been offered to him, the king of Prussia maintained that he had nothing to do with the negotiations carried on between the Spanish government and the prince of Hohenzollern, that he had intervened only as Head of the Family and never as Sovereign and that he had neither called together nor consulted his Council of Ministers. The king has admitted, however, that he had informed Count Bismarck of these various incidents.

We did not consider that these replies were satisfactory; we could not admit this subtle distinction between the Sovereign and the Head of the Family, and we insisted that the king advise and if necessary compel the prince to renounce his candidacy.

While we were carrying on our dispute with Prussia, the desistance of Prince Leopold came to us from a side from which we did not expect it and was delivered to us on July 12 by the Spanish ambassador.

The king having willed to remain apart from this, we demanded of him that he associate himself with it and to declare that if, by one of those sudden changes that are always possible in a country emerging from revolution, the crown were again offered to Prince

Leopold, he would not again authorize him to accept it, so that the debate could be regarded as definitely closed.

Our demand was moderate; the terms in which it was expressed were not less so — "Say to the king," we wrote to Count Benedetti at midnight, on July 12, "tell the king that we have no mental reservations, that we are not seeking a pretext for war and that all we want is to resolve honorably a difficulty that we ourselves have not created."

The king consented to approve the renunciation by Prince Leopold but he *refused* to declare that he would never in the future approve the renewal of this candidacy.

"I have asked of the king," Benedetti wrote to us at midnight on July 13, "to permit me to announce to you in his name that if the prince of Hohenzollern should come around again to this project, His Majesty would interpose his authority and block it. The king has *absolutely refused* to authorize me to transmit such a statement to you. I have energetically insisted but did not succeed in modifying the dispositions of His Majesty.

"The king ended our interview by saying to me that he could not and would not take such an engagement, and that for this eventuality as for every other, he must reserve the right to take account of the circumstances."

Although this refusal appeared unjustifiable to us, our desire to preserve for Europe the benefits of peace was so great that we did not break off the negotiations, and that in spite of your rightful impatience, we asked you to postpone our explanations until today lest a discussion hamper the negotiation.

Our surprise was then profound when, yesterday, we learned that the king of Prussia had notified our ambassador by an aide-de-camp that he would not receive him again and that, in order to leave no doubt as to the character of this refusal, his government had communicated it officially to all the Cabinets of Europe.

We learned at the same time that Werther had received orders to take leave of absence and that armaments were under way in Prussia.

In these circumstances, to make a further attempt at conciliation would have been neglectful of dignity and imprudent. We have neglected nothing to escape war; we are preparing to wage the war that is presented to us, leaving to each side the share of responsibility that falls upon it.

Yesterday we have called up our reserves and with your concurrence, we are going to take at once the measures necessary to safeguard the interests, the security, and the honor of France.[50]

In the Senate, Gramont's reading of the statement was received with enthusiastic and apparently unanimous applause. In the Chamber of Deputies, although the final result was a foregone conclusion, there was a sharp and bitter debate. Ollivier followed his reading of the statement with the request for a credit of fifty million francs and asked that it be acted on as a matter of urgency. Ernest Picard, of the left, tried to oppose the urgency but was shouted down, and it was voted by a rising vote. The handful of deputies on the left who remained seated were greeted with shouts of "Get up, get up! There are only sixteen of them! They are Prussians!" It was only with difficulty that Thiers obtained the floor. With the support of a small minority, chiefly on the left, and with constant interruptions, he challenged the expediency of the cabinet's decision. Other deputies joined him in the demand that the ministers communicate the dispatches on which the decision was based. The demand was rejected but it was agreed that they be given in confidence to a special commission. The report of the commission, which on the whole supported the cabinet statement, was followed by more impassioned debate. Thiers' insistence that France had obtained her essential demand, the withdrawal of the candidacy, and was going to war on a question of form and prestige, failed to affect the result. The credits were voted by 245 to 10.[51]

On July 15, while the French government was making its final decision for war, King William was traveling by special train from Ems to Berlin, greeted at every station with ovations from the crowds gathered to see him pass. The decision to

[50] Lehautcourt, pp. 531–534.
[51] Lehautcourt, pp. 531–592.

return to his capital could not have been an easy one. It meant Reichstag, mobilization, and war.[52] His conduct and his talk throughout the crisis show that he was reluctant, in his old age, to engage in another war. His remarks to Benedetti, as they parted at the railroad station about three o'clock on the afternoon of the fourteenth, that negotiations might be continued at Berlin,[53] suggest that even at that late hour he had not given up all hope. But the force of circumstances was pushing him on. As he had written to the queen on the thirteenth: "these incomprehensible proceedings" — Benedetti's request for another audience after the refusal of the guarantee and the suggestion of the letter to Napoleon — "lead to the conclusion that they are trying to provoke us at all costs." [54] On the morning of the fourteenth, it seems likely that before the promenade Abeken, as on the previous morning, reported to the king the chief telegrams that had arrived during the night: Werther's alarming reports from Paris, Bernstorff's assurances of how much the French attitude was condemned at London, Bismarck's reaction upon the suggested "letter of apology," and, above all, the joint telegram from Bismarck, Moltke, and Roon of the previous evening, proposing a kind of ultimatum to France. Presumably, all this was not without its effect, particularly the telegram last mentioned.

But the great surprise came in the course of the promenade, when the nine o'clock train brought the morning newspapers with Bismarck's edition of the Ems telegram. According to what seems to be a well-authenticated story, the king, on first seeing the text, read it over twice, and then, visibly affected by the tone of it, handed it to Eulenburg with the comment, "That is war." This news seems to have ended all hesitation. Returned to his quarters, the king conferred with Abeken and

[52] Lord, p. 108.
[53] See p. 205.
[54] William to Augusta, July 13, 1870 (late afternoon or early evening), Fester, *Briefe*, vol. II, no. 515.

announced his intention to set out for Berlin the next morning. The dispatch by which Abeken conveyed these welcome tidings to Bismarck contained no word of comment or protest about the manipulation of the Ems telegram, unless it may be found in the phrase, "His Majesty will not receive Count Benedetti again *here*." [55] About the same time orders were sent to Werther in exact accordance with Bismarck's suggestions. How completely William was coming around to his chancellor's standpoint is further indicated by his letter to Augusta of that morning, in which he rebuts the queen's arguments for peace as based on a situation that is "already behind us," has discovered that there had been no "negotiations" with Benedetti, only "conversations," admits that a formal interpellation will have to be addressed to Paris, and ends with the despondent cry: "All is vain if the *brouilleurs* [the French cabinet] demand war. It is clear enough!" [56] Yet even on the fifteenth, when Bismarck, Moltke, Roon, and the crown prince joined the train at Brandenburg with mobilization orders prepared for his signature, William seems to have stood out against immediate action, insisting that the decision be left to a ministerial council the next day.

When the train reached the station at Berlin, toward nine o'clock, Thile was waiting with the news from Paris. A telegram from Werther reported Gramont's statement to the Senate and Rouher's words in the name of the Senate that they placed their reliance "on the sword of France." A Wolff telegraph agency message stated that the session of the Chambers had ended with a declaration of war against Prussia. This was not literally true but on both sides of the Rhine, the vote of the French legislature to approve the credits for the armed forces was so understood. In the moment of confused excitement that followed, the king or the crown prince or Bis-

[55] My italics.
[56] Lord, pp. 109–110.

marck — each has claimed the honor — exclaimed that the only possible answer was immediate and total mobilization. The decision was shouted by the crown prince to the people outside. The king and his entourage then rode slowly through packed streets and wildly cheering crowds to the palace where the orders were signed.[57]

The formal declaration of war was sent from Paris on July 17 and was presented by Le Sourd to Bismarck at 1:30 P.M. on the nineteenth.[58]

SUPPLEMENTARY NOTE I

A European congress was a time-honored suggestion of Napoleon III whenever he needed to escape from a dilemma. In this case, the evidence for the suggestion is so confused and so contradictory that I have had to use the indefinite expression "Some one suggested a European congress . . ." Ollivier and Charles Louvet (minister of commerce) assert that the suggestion was made by Gramont (Ollivier, vol. XIV, p. 365; La Gorce, vol. VI, p. 292, citing an unpublished memoir of Louvet). On the other hand, Metternich, in a private letter to Beust (Paris, July 31, 1870, H. Oncken, vol. III, no. 934), reports that Gramont said to him, apparently on July 15: "C'est moi qui me suis opposé à l'idée du congrès. L'Empereur après Vous avoir vu est rentré au conseil et nous a lu la déclaration qu'il avait rédigée et qu'il Vous a montrée. Ce n'est pas sans peine que nous l'avons dissuadé de parler d'un congrès — mais lorqu'il a vu que je donnerais plutôt ma démission que d'en accepter la pensée, il a cedé." This statement refers primarily to the evening session of the Council. Gramont may have been protecting the emperor against Metternich's implication of bad faith or his own opinion may have changed between afternoon and evening. Vitzthum von Eckstädt, Austrian minister to Belgium and one of the principal go-betweens in the secret alliance negotiations, talked with Napoleon on July 15, at 10 A.M. In a letter to Count Andrássy, January 16, 1873 (*ibid.*, no. 891A), he reports that he said to Napoleon: "J'apprends que Vouz avez Vous-même, Sire,

[57] *Ibid.*, pp. 115–117.
[58] See *O.D.*, vol. XIX, nos. 8572, 8573.

au conseil d'hier émis l'idée d'un congrès . . ." and that the emperor appeared to like the idea of asking the Austrian emperor to propose one. That evening, Vitzthum, in company with Metternich, was received by Gramont. He tried to sound the minister on the idea of a congress but the word so exasperated Gramont that there was no point in continuing the conversation. In his memoir (*ibid.*, no. 891B), Vitzthum told substantially the same story and added a note: "Quaeritur: wie lässt sich die Sprache Napoleons am 15 Juli 1870 mit der Geschichtserzählung vereinen, die Gramont zwei Jahre später niederschrieb? Der Herzog behauptet, das sechsstündige Minister-conseil vom 14. habe eine 'Solution pacifique' zum Beschlusse erhoben, welche darin bestanden haben soll, einen Kongress der europäischen Mächte zu veranlassen. Wenn das wahr wäre, würde mich der Kaiser nicht sofort unterbrochen haben, als ich diese Idee anregte, um mir zu sagen, man habe tags zuvor den Kongress bereits beschlossen? Die Kongressidee war allerdings in dem conseil vom 14. von Napoleon selbst angeregt, dieser Anregung jedoch keine Folge gegeben worden. . . ." Ollivier, in a footnote to the statement "Gramont lance l'idée (vol. XIV, p. 365 and n. 1), wrote: "Nous déclarerions que dans le présent la question était suffisament résolue par l'approbation du Roi au désistement du prince de Hohenzollern et pour assurer l'avenir, nous nous addresserions à l'Europe, afin que, réunie en Congrès, elle confirmat solonnellement la jurisprudence internationale déjà tacitement admise, qui interdit, sans entente préalable, à tous les princes appartenant aux familles régnantes des grandes puissances, de monter sur un trône étranger." Gramont says nothing about initiative or authorship. He records (p. 212) as the outcome of the Council "le substance, sinon le texte, de la communication attendue au Sénat et au Corps Législatif: 'Nous croyons que le principe adopté tacitement par l'Europe a été d'empêcher, sans une entente préalable, aucune prince appartenant aux familles régnantes des grandes puissances de monter sur un trône étranger, et nous demandons que les grandes puissances européennes réunies en Congrès, confirment cette jurisprudence internationale.' " Although this version is very close to the summary given by Ollivier (vol. XIV, p. 365, n. 1), a note on the following page reads: "Gramont a presentè quelques lignes de l'Empereur comme étant ce projet; il se trompe. Les quelques lignes n'étaient qu'un canevas qui n'a pas servi. Mon projet avait une forme oratoire et pathetique; je ne l'ai pas retrouvé dans mes papiers." The emperor, on the other hand, told Metternich soon after the end of the Council (tg., Metternich to Beust, July 14, 1870, 7:50 p.m., H. Oncken, vol. III, no. 888) that the statement the government intended to make to the Chambers ("voici à peu près des paroles") was as follows: "Malgré un . . . [*sic*] refus de la Prusse sur notre demande légitime nous ne regardons pas le conflit comme imminent. Cependant nous sommes forcés d'appeler le contingent. Nous sommes prêts à accepter un Congrès dans lequel toutes les questions en litige recevraient une solution définitive en vue d'une paix durable."

SUPPLEMENTARY NOTE II

It has sometimes been claimed that the decision of the French Council of Ministers to ask for war credits was influenced and justified by their knowledge of Bismarck's menacing language to Lord Loftus in their conversation on the afternoon of July 13.

Ollivier includes among the telegrams and dispatches that Gramont brought to the Council on the evening of July 14, the report of Le Sourd on the attitude of Bismarck: "Le Sourd nous exposait que, depuis la nouvelle de la renonciation on s'était départi du calme qu'il avait constaté depuis une semaine et que l'irritation avait tout à coup succédé au sang-froid; il nous racontait les impressions pessimistes que Loftus avait rapportées de son entretien avec Bismarck." (vol. XIV, pp. 373–374). A few lines of the dispatch were given by Ollivier (vol. XIV, p. 319), and the full text is in *O.D.*, vol. XXVIII, no. 8453. Le Sourd did not report the most menacing parts of Bismarck's conversation with Loftus (cf. p. 176 above) — and read calmly, the report is not particularly alarming except in the suggestion that Bismarck might not be able to control events if public opinion continued to be stirred up by threatening language in Paris. Le Sourd warned his government that if they wanted peace they should speak in conciliatory terms; otherwise war would be unavoidable. Gramont (p. 223), claimed that he had received through indirect channels "un compte rendu très-exact du langage tenu par M. de Bismarck, la veille, à l'ambassadeur d'Angleterre, et de l'attitude prise, à partir du 13, par le cabinet de Berlin." In a note, he added that this confidential report reproduced almost word for word the conversation as published in Loftus' report of July 13 and was even more complete. As we know, Loftus' report was originally published in extract. The question of how Gramont obtained this information has attracted considerable attention. (See, for example, Temperly, "Lord Acton on the Origins of the War of 1870," *Cambridge Historical Journal*, vol. II, pp. 74–75. Gramont's story is consistent with his refusal to reveal documents not already known from other sources. I do not believe that, at the time, he learned of Bismarck's conversation with Loftus except from Le Sourd's dispatch. This may have been written in time to leave Berlin at 7:45 P.M. on July 13 and to arrive at Paris at 9:05 P.M. on July 14. See p. 204 above and Fester, *Briefe*, vol. II, p. 131, n. 1.) It is not certain that it was received in time to be considered by the Council.

Bourgeois and Clermont (*Rome et Napoléon III*, p. 250) quote a telegram, Cazaux to Gramont, Vienna, July 14, 1870, 5 P.M.: "J'ai communiqué au Comte de Beust votre télégramme du 13. Il m'a communiqué à son tour l'entretien de Lord Loftus avec M. de Bismarck. En présence de ces nouvelles arrivées de Berlin . . ." As published from the decipher in the French archives (*O.D.*, vol. XXVIII, no. 8512), the telegram, filed at 5 P.M., received July 15 at 9 A.M., reads, "Je viens de communiquer au Comte de Beust votre télégramme d'hier soir. En présence des nouvelles arrivées in Berlin . . ." The telegram nowhere mentions Bismarck's conversation with Loftus and in any case could not have been presented to the Council on July 14.

-❰ VII ❱-

Conclusion and Reflections

The idea that war between France and the North German Confederation was inevitable had been a commonplace of newspaper and political discussion from the end of the Austro-Prussian War in 1866 until the war actually occurred in 1870. That two great military powers were watching each other with suspicion was in itself cause for alarm.[1] In both countries there were some who wanted a preventive war and some who felt that the outbreak of war would be better than continued and tense uncertainty.[2] At the end of the crisis there were statesmen on both sides willing to take the responsibility. Ollivier, in the debate in the Chamber of Deputies, declared that he and his colleagues in the ministry accepted the burden "with a light heart." [3] Bismarck, on July 13, undertook to goad the French to war and for the rest of his life he boasted of his success. Yet this does not necessarily mean that they or their

[1] See, for example, Loftus to Clarendon, April 17, 1869, Valentin, *Bismarcks Reichsgründung im Urteil englischer Diplomaten*, p. 540.

[2] Bismarck told Keudell early in December 1869 that the banker Gerson Bleichröder had begged him to try to bring on a war to clear the situation. Keudell, *Fürst und Fürstin Bismarck*, p. 419.

[3] The French words "le coeur léger" do not convey quite the same frivolous connotation as the English; "a clear conscience" might be a better translation. Ollivier, vol. XIV, appendix 12. It was recognized at the time that the expression was unfortunate. Mme. Jules Baroche, *Second Empire, notes et souvenirs*, p. 639.

associates created the crisis in order to have a war or that, until quite late, they saw war as the only acceptable solution. The Franco-German War of 1870 was not the product of reasoned long-term policy.[4]

The decision to take up arms was made by the French government. The constitution left to the emperor the right to declare war and, in this case, Napoleon acted with the advice and consent of his cabinet and with the endorsement of an overwhelming majority in both houses of the legislature. These facts are not disputed. Nearly everything else about the decision and its background has been passionately discussed and the debate has raised questions, some of which can be answered with only approximate certainty.

A parliamentary commission was set up soon after the end of the war to investigate its origins. Many witnesses were heard and their testimony filled hundreds of pages of the official record. The commission was dominated by leaders of the Republic and the questioning had strong political overtones. The hearings were supplemented by a war of pamphlets, newspaper articles, and books. Of the books by participants, the most convincing was Benedetti's account of his mission in Prussia; the least revealing, Gramont's, for he held steadfastly to the position that a man of honor must not reveal state secrets, even those of a fallen regime; the fullest, Ollivier's multivolume history of the "Liberal Empire," which was not completed until the opening years of the twentieth century. Historians, French and foreign, have continued to analyze the evidence and to argue the issues raised.

As often happens after a lost war, the French leaders tried to put the blame on anyone and everyone but themselves. Gramont and Ollivier, for example, charged Benedetti with bungling his mission to Ems; Benedetti pointed out that the

[4] Classic examples of planned wars are the war of France and Sardinia against Austria in 1859 and the Austro-Prussian War of 1866.

government had disregarded his warnings and that Gramont's rigid instructions had spoiled a substantial success. Public opinion made Napoleon III the principal scapegoat. Many of his political opponents, however, denounced him as weak and vacillating and attributed great influence over his decisions to Empress Eugénie, who was said to have boasted "this is my war." [5] In general, those who held office under the emperor have tended to shift the basic responsibility for war to the influence of an aroused public opinion which forced the government's hand; while those who had been in opposition to the empire and had come to power after its fall continued to blame the fallen government. In each case, the motives and bias are obvious.[6]

In the 1890's, a series of revelations, beginning with the memoirs of Leopold's brother, King Charles of Rumania, showed that Bismarck had had more to do with the Hohenzollern candidacy than he was ever willing to admit. Since then, historical comment has tended to stress that he, Bismarck, more than anyone else wanted war and found the occasion for it. The charges that Napoleon and his ministers had deliberately used the opportunity for a war which they had long desired were generally dropped and their policy was presented as a response to Prussian provocation.[7]

After the crisis provoked by the Hohenzollern Candidacy for the throne of Spain had arisen, an influential and noisy section of the French public and of the Parisian press adopted an attitude of reckless bellicosity and did their utmost to render war inevitable.

[5] "Cette parole ['c'est ma guerre'], je ne l'ai jamais entendue textuellement, mais ce que j'ai vu, c'est l'excitation enthousiaste dans laquelle elle vivait au moment de la déclaration de guerre, enthousiasme qu'elle communiquait et qui gagnait autour d'elle toute la jeunesse" Comtesse des Garets, *Souvenirs*, p. 186).

[6] E. M. Carroll, "French Public Opinion on War with Prussia in 1870," *American Historical Review*, vol. XXXI, p. 679.

[7] One of the consequences of this in practical politics was the frequent insertion in treaties of alliance of the phrase "in case of unprovoked attack."

. . . It is now commonly held that the Emperor, although vacillating and inclined at times to defer too much to the clamors of the war party, would, on the whole, very much have preferred to keep the peace. Much the same may be said of Emile Ollivier, the head of the cabinet, and of the French Foreign Minister, the Duc de Gramont. Nevertheless, although the intentions of the French government of that time have been vindicated, the wisdom of their policy has not been. Except for Gramont and Ollivier, in their not too convincing *apologiae*, nearly all French historians have denounced that policy with a vigor that should leave nothing to be desired east of the Rhine. Indeed, it can scarcely be denied that the French ministers, by premature threats of war, notably in their public declaration of July 6, by their unnecessary and imprudent demands on July 12, and in general by their too persistent efforts to achieve a complete and spectacular diplomatic victory, did much to bring on the conflict and to drag their country into [war].[8]

The fact remains that it was France which declared war and that a war is not inevitable until it is begun formally by declaration or informally by attack. In the words of one of the ablest French students of the problem, "one does not make war by oneself alone and, notwithstanding the ambitions of Germany, that of 1870 would not have taken place if the French had not lent themselves to it." [9]

The attitude of the French people toward Germany and German unification on the eve of the war cannot be summarized in a neat formula. It was changing under the impact of the accomplished facts. The image of Germany as a nation of philosophers and dreamers was fading fast. The achievements of the Germans in philosophy, history, and science were still highly regarded and, to many French intellectuals, were models for their own countrymen to follow. In the case of some, Taine and Renan, for example, the interest in German culture led to sympathy for German aspirations for national unity. In general, however, a new image had taken

[8] Lord, *The Origins of The War of 1870*, pp. 3–4.
[9] Salomon, *L'Incident Hohenzollern*, p. 130.

shape, of a nationalistic and militaristic Prussia, moving relentlessly to reach its goals by force. Taine himself wrote at the end of 1869 that the character of Germany was changing. "It is becoming arrogant, contemptuous, unfair to foreigners. It is losing entirely the breadth of cosmopolitan spirit, the tolerance, the sympathy for other people that it had in Goethe's day. . . . Germany used to dream . . . now it acts." [10] Bismarck was taking the place in public opinion once held by Napoleon III as the trouble-maker in Europe and the world.

The most bellicose expressions came from the Bonapartist and ultranationalistic camps. German visitors to France reported conversations with army officers and civilians who were not only ready to block by military intervention any extension of German unity but seemed eager for a test of strength for its own sake. In other circles, even in some not especially friendly to Prussia, there is evidence of readiness to accept the union of South Germany with the North and the expectation that it might happen soon. It has been said that if peace could have been preserved for a few years longer, the French people would probably have made up their minds to accept the inevitable.[11]

The picture of French public opinion toward Germany is further confused by its attitude towards the imperial government. A secret agent of European reputation described this in a report to the Austrian chancellor. "France is irritated at Prussia and alarmed at her increases in territory. Louis Napoleon is not, himself, too eager for war. He is not a military commander, as he willingly admits himself, and, besides, his state of health could hardly stand the fatigues of a campaign. The country has ceased to be a simple spectator of events

[10] Dec. 28, 1869, quoted by Albertini, "Frankreichs Stellungnahme zur deutschen Einigung während des zweiten Kaiserreichs," *Schweizerische Zeitschrift für Geschichte*, vol. V, p. 354.
[11] Lord, p. 3.

from outside, and passes a severe judgment on them. It insists on the policy being national and absolutely French." [12] France demanded that the emperor be infallible but no longer believed that he was. The government was attacked for its military and political weakness. Yet the country seemed unwilling to grant the resources of men and money necessary for the strong and successful policy it wanted. The strong opposition to the army reform of 1868, despite a widespread belief that war with Prussia was something that France would have to put up with, has been interpreted by some as evidence of the pacific mood of the French people. It is more valid as evidence of the ingrained dislike of the French, of the peasants above all, for the burdens of peacetime military service. [13]

In the first months of 1870, the tension in the relations of France and Germany was slightly relaxed. The "Liberal Empire" had just been established, and the attention of the French public was concerned primarily with internal problems and politics. The cabinet, led by Emile Ollivier, had agreed to accept the *status quo* in Germany and apparently even agreed that France must not intervene if the south German states entered the North German Confederation of their own free wills. The minister of foreign affairs, Count Napoleon Daru, continued to stress the importance of respect for the *status quo* in his instructions and in his conversations with German and other ambassadors. The effect of his admonitions was weakened a little by Ollivier. In an interview "with a leading French statesman," published in the *Kölnische Zeitung*, the source of which soon became public, he too warned Prussia against forcing the south German states into the Confederation, but he added that if a popular movement, "which does not

[12] Klindworth to Beust, quoted by Robert Sencourt, *Napoleon III: the Modern Emperor*, pp. 298–299.
[13] Albertini, vol. V, p. 355; Case, *French Opinion on War and Diplomacy*, pp. 234–240.

exist at the present," should move the South to seek this union, it would be "unjust and ridiculous" to oppose it.[14]

At the same time, Napoleon and his advisers were still smarting from the diplomatic failures of the past few years. The attempt of the French Eastern Railway Company to buy some of the Belgian lines had been blocked, as many Frenchmen believed, at the instigation of Bismarck. France had not been able to induce Prussia to execute that part of Article V of the Treaty of Prague which provided for the return of the northern districts of Schleswig to Denmark. At the turn of the year 1869–1870, Count Maurice de Fleury, the newly appointed ambassador to St. Petersburg, was trying to persuade Tsar Alexander to intervene on behalf of Denmark, the fatherland of his daughter-in-law. Fleury's urgency was held in check by the new French cabinet, but his activity was known at Berlin. Nothing came of his efforts, but it was believed in many circles that this question was more dangerous to peace than it actually turned out to be.[15] Early in 1870, a proposal to Prussia through British mediation for partial disarmament was received unfavorably at Berlin. The negotiations for a triple alliance of France, Austria, and Italy — of which the cabinet had not been informed — were at a standstill, but a number of secret conversations took place between top-level officers of France and Austria to discuss an eventual war against Prussia. The French government, even after the appointment of the Duke of Gramont to the Foreign Office, continued to resist the pressure from the right in Parliament to adopt a

[14] Salomon, *L'Incident Hohenzollern*, pp. 148–150, 153–157; Daru to Benedetti and Daru to Tiby, March 8, 1870, Rothan to Daru, Hamburg, March 14, 1870, and annex, *O.D.*, vol. XXVII, nos. 7997, 7998, 8013.

[15] See, for example, Holborn, *Aufzeichnungen und Erinnerungen aus dem Leben des Botschafters Joseph Maria von Radowitz*, vol I, p. 203; Schweinitz, *Briefwechsel*, pp. 62–63. *Denkwürdigkeiten*, vol. I, pp. 249, 256; draft memorandum, Dec. 11, 1872, and Bernstorff to Bismarck, Dec. 30, 1872, in German archives, I. A. A. b. 53, Bd. I (Acta betr. die politische Umtriebe des Freiherrn späteren Grafen von Beust).

more outspoken anti-Prussian policy, but even the peaceful Ollivier felt that another open rebuff from Prussia would be fatal. " 'Un echec,' " he told the British ambassador soon after he took office, " 'c'est la guerre.' Those who had to render an account to Parliament and the country were less able than the former Government to put up with any wound to the national pride. Their main object was peace, but they must show firmness, or they would not be able to cope with Revolution and Socialism at home." [16]

When the report was confirmed that a Prussian prince had accepted the offer of the Spanish crown, the French government did show firmness, threatening war if the candidacy were maintained. Gramont's vigorous statements, especially that of July 6, were criticized then and later as needless provocation of Prussia and as evidence of his incapacity for his post. He should, in the opinion of many, have addressed his complaints to Spain, which had chosen the candidate, rather than to Prussia, which had supplied him. It can be argued that pressure on Spain would have led the worried Spanish statesmen to withdraw their offer. It is equally possible, and there was important contemporary opinion to this effect, that language hostile to Spain would have stirred up the national pride of the Spaniards and would have made it easy to obtain the majority needed for the election in the Cortes. It might have led step by step to French military intervention in Spain, whose bitter resistance to the armies of the first Napoleon was a more vivid memory than the lack of resistance to French troops in 1823. With French forces engaged in Spain as they had been in Mexico at the time of the Austro-Prussian War of 1866, it was taken for granted that Prussia would be free to disregard French interests in Germany.

[16] Lyons to Clarendon, Paris, Jan. 30, 1870, Lord Newton, *Lord Lyons*, vol. I, p. 249. See also Ollivier's interview, published originally in the *Daily News*, London, July 20, 1870, in *The War Correspondence of the Daily News*, vol. I, p. 8.

It had, moreover, become the practice, if not necessarily the obligation, of the powers to direct the protests to the government which supplied the candidate rather to the one which called him. In theory, of course, every sovereign state had an absolute right to choose its own form of government and its own monarch. France had maintained this right in 1851 and 1852 when Napoleon seized power first as prince president and then as emperor, even though formal international treaties barred the Bonaparte family from the rule of France. In practice, at least in the case of lesser powers, it was recognized that the choice of a monarch from abroad or even a foreign marriage in a ruling family was a matter of concern to the European community. It could affect the balance of power. A *de facto* veto had come into existence which was exercised by the great powers as a group or by individual powers in accordance with their interests and was sometimes backed up by threat of war. One of the rare exceptions to the enforcement of the veto was on the accession of Leopold's brother Charles to the principality of Rumania, an accomplished fact that was tolerated because the major powers were divided for and against. International practice, as well as regard for Spanish sovereignty, justified the direction of Gramont's threats.

The vigor of his language has been criticized even more than the direction of the protest. Pierre Magne, a former minister and strong adherent of Napoleon III, described Gramont's speech as "this categorical demonstration, filled with arrogance and threats, which cut off all further negotiation and prevented any attempt at conciliation." [17] What Magne and the public did not know was that the German Foreign Office had already cut off all negotiation. Hazardous as they may have been, Gramont's tactics were successful; the candidacy was withdrawn by Karl Anton on behalf of his son and the danger of war was a major element in the decision.

[17] J. Durieux, *Le Ministre Pierre Magne*, vol. II, p. 179.

It was the form rather than the substance to which Magne objected. "Certainly," he added, "no one would have admitted that France could abase herself to the point of tolerating this affront and of standing patiently by while Prussia, without having given us any notice, established her position on the other side of the Pyrenees." [18] It would be difficult to sum up more concisely and more accurately the core of the broadest sampling of French public opinion in the first half of July 1870. On July 7, the day after Gramont's declaration, the minister of the interior sent telegrams to the prefects of all departments outside of Paris asking for special reports on the reaction of the public to the candidacy for the Spanish throne. By July 12, the date on which the renunciation was announced, more than eighty replies had been received. Lynn M. Case, who has made the most thorough analysis of these reports, concludes that a majority of at least sixty-three to seventeen show a public ready to go to war to keep a Prussian prince out of Spain. "Indeed," he writes, "the tone of the reports is so general and all-pervasive in demanding war unless a very favorable diplomatic victory were won that the government could not have gained any other conviction than that the people supported a firm policy backed by the threat of war." [19]

When Gramont advised the emperor to insist on additional guarantees from the king of Prussia, it is not known whether he had learned the results of the poll of public opinion. It is possible, but not certain, that he had been told that early in the afternoon of July 12, a deputy had moved an interpellation asking the cabinet about "the guarantees that it has stipulated or that it intends to stipulate to prevent the return of successive complications with Prussia." [20] Regardless, however, of the expediency or wisdom of the decision, it is clear that in

[18] Durieux, vol. II, p. 180.
[19] Case, p. 250. See supplementary note at end of chapter.
[20] Lehautcourt, *Les Origines de la guerre de 1870*, pp. 375–376.

making it, the minister of foreign affairs was in harmony with a substantial segment of the deputies, the press, and the public.

On the specific point, Gramont acted without knowledge of the public reaction to "Father Anthony's" telegram; he anticipated rather than followed public opinion. The evening newspapers gave the first significant comments. As usual, the editors were divided, but the general impression was that the renunciation was unsatisfactory, even derisory, and in many papers expressions of joy at the preservation of peace were coupled with scornful criticism of the government.[21]

Public opinion may influence decisions; it does not make them. The major responsibility for the demand for guarantees was Gramont's. His unwillingness to be satisfied with the informal renunciation — an unwillingness for which there was some justification but which was contrary to the first impressions of Napoleon and Ollivier [22] — and his determination to underscore the diplomatic victory led the French into a position from which they could not escape with peace *and* honor. Bismarck's counterstroke, the publication and distribution of the Ems telegram, was the open rebuff that Ollivier had dreaded. The "echec" meant war — a war that France confidently expected to win [23] but did not.

On the basis of the evidence available in 1924, Robert Lord could affirm Bismarck's share of responsibility for the war with substantial confidence.

It is now agreed [by French and German historians] that, from

[21] Case, pp. 254–256.

[22] See p. 155 above.

[23] "The French army was regarded by all Frenchmen, even by the enemies of the regime, as the foremost in the world. That we were bound to be victorious was never in doubt, never to anyone. But it was admitted that the struggle would be stern enough. Le Boeuf, Canrobert, Ducrot, Vaillant, Frossart, Bourbaki, Lebrun, Gallifet — they all vouched for our victory" (statement of Eugénie in 1906, in Paléologue, *The Tragic Empress*, p. 124). Some competent Prussian officers expected that the French would win the first engagements of the war. Kraft zu Hohenlohe-Ingelfingen, *Aus meinem Leben*, vol IV, p. 6.

1866 on, Bismarck, like most of those prominent in Prussian political and military circles, regarded a war with France as inevitable sooner or later, convinced as he was that France would not peaceably permit the union of South Germany with the North, which was at that time the great object of his policy. It is tolerably well agreed that he also regarded such a war as in itself desirable, believing that the South Germans were not likely to seek that union, at least for a long time to come, unless they were shaken out of their selfishness and apathy by a shock from outside, such as could best be furnished by a great common effort for a national cause, and by a great common victory over "that neighboring nation which was our age-long aggressor." [24]

Two years later, another "neutral" historian, Temperley, was less confident.

While, therefore, Bismarck's negotiations were not intended to be friendly to France, it is possible that he did not believe war would occur as a result. What he unquestionably did think was that, if a Hohenzollern reigned in Spain, France's prestige would be lowered in Europe and her actual military power reduced. But the evidence does not justify us in assuming with certainty, that Bernhardi's manoeuvres or the Hohenzollern candidature were engineered with the certainty that France would fall into the trap and declare war. It is at any rate interesting that Beust, who viewed the whole situation from a more detached standpoint than either France or Prussia, denied that it in any way justified, or implied, the possibility of war.[25]

Jochen Dittrich, who had more evidence than his predecessors, stresses the fatalistic forces in the situation.

One might perhaps ask why the French did not just admit the unification of Germany? They would say: we were anxious about our security, and with right, as the two world wars have shown. We could reply that it was the resistance of France to the solution of the German problem that began the tragic development. It was the conflict of 1870–71 that brought up the problem of

[24] Lord, p. 6.
[25] "Lord Acton on the Origins of the War of 1870," *Cambridge Historical Journal*, vol. II, pp. 71–72.

Alsace-Lorraine and increased the hatred which helped indirectly to kindle the two last wars. But the question is, after all, unpolitical. What state has ever freely renounced its dominant position if it thought it had a chance of defending it? And, on the other side, what nation would let another deprive it of the right to organize its life as it saw fit? It is the essence of power politics that there are some issues that transcend the individual and become fatality.

Dittrich concluded that there was no "will to war" on the part of either government and that war guilt should be charged against neither. "Above and beyond the human failings and the volition of the actors in the drama were the forces of fate." Against a background of historical memories, conflicting interpretations of vital interests, and a lively sense of national honor, the Hohenzollern candidacy was a diplomatic weapon, a move in the jockeying for position and advantage in the game of power politics. As war was the *ultima ratio* in the political methods of the time, Dittrich believed that Bismarck must have considered it as possible but that to unleash it was not his aim.[26]

For some time after the organization of the North German Confederation, Bismarck believed that the momentum of the national movement would bring the south German states into union with the North. If, as he instructed his diplomatic representatives at the southern courts, Prussia and the North scrupulously refrained from pressure, the strength of the unionist elements would overcome the particularism of the governments. The Parliament of the *Zollverein* would join representatives of the South with those of the North on a national basis. He showed no enthusiasm for the proposed South German Confederation but he insisted that Prussian diplomacy must avoid all suspicion of opposition to it. He might even welcome it if it were organized with a popularly elected gen-

[26] "Bismarck, Frankreich und die Hohenzollernkandidatur," *Die Welt als Geschichte*, vol. XIII, pp. 43, 46, 56–57.

eral legislative assembly that could stimulate national feeling. He was determined to be patient in waiting for the South to make its own choice. But he did not intend to be patient forever. When General von Schweinitz, the king's military representative at St. Petersburg, reported that he had said to a Russian journalist that the erroneous commentaries on Prussian policy had their roots in the false opinion that Prussia was determined to cross the Main and that "we have no intention of weakening our healthy constitution by swallowing the republican and ultramontane elements of south Germany; we want to stay as we are and get rich in peace, something that is possible only in a general calm," Bismarck scrawled in the margin: "quite right, for the time being." [27]

At the beginning of 1870, Bismarck had not decided on a course of action, but there are signs that he was thinking of ways to reverse the trends that were becoming obvious in Württemberg and in Bavaria. In both countries, the particularist parties seemed to be gaining rather than losing strength. The elections to the Parliament of the *Zollverein* had been anything but favorable to Bismarck's ideal of a popularly elected assembly that would stimulate national feeling. The South sent forty-nine representatives who were hostile to Prussia and thirty-six who favored unity. In the elections to the Württemberg Diet in 1868 and to the Bavarian in 1869, the anti-Prussian democratic and clerical parties won. There was growing opposition in all the southern states, even in Baden, to the introduction of the Prussian military system. There were signs of revived enthusiasm for Austria.

To counter this, Bismarck toyed with the idea of persuading the king to take the imperial title. The diary of the crown prince for January 7, 1870, has the brief entry: "On the train with Count Bismarck, talked politics, he of his own accord came up with the suggestion of the Kaiser question, in

[27] *A.P.P.*, vol. X, p. 472.

connection with the change in designation of the 'Foreign Office' in place of 'Royal Prussian Ministry of Foreign Affairs.'" The crown prince told Sir Robert Morier, his friend in the British diplomatic service, that Bismarck had suddenly observed to him that "things were getting into a pass from which nothing but a decisive line of action will extricate them. It is time to take up the idea of the Empire." [28]

The elections to the Bavarian Landtag on November 29, 1869, had given a majority to the particularist-clerical party. In consequence, the cabinet of Prince Hohenlohe tendered its resignation, but it was not accepted by the king; he permitted only the ministers of the interior and of religious affairs to withdraw. Werthern, the Prussian minister at Munich, reported that the parties which favored closer ties with the North attributed their defeat to the lack of Prussian initiative in the German question. Prince Hohenlohe was said to see a close connection between the outcome of the election and the fact that there was a standstill at Berlin, and he expressed the hope that if Prussia should again take up a national policy, his probable successors, whether Count Bray or Baron von Schrenk, would be favorably influenced by it. Werthern, who favored these interpretations, quoted pro-Prussian Bavarians to the effect that if the German question were not revived very soon and very energetically, Bavaria would within three years be "completely in the hands of the priests." [29] In reply, Bismarck called attention to his circular of September 7, 1867, which had laid down the policy of avoiding even moral pressure on the decisions of the south German governments and to his special instructions of February 26, 1869, to Werthern. He drew a distinction between stagnation based on weakness or on indif-

[28] Unpublished diary of Crown Prince Frederick William, cited in *G.W.*, vol. VIb, p. 212; Wemyss, *Memoirs and Letters of Sir Robert Morier*, vol. II, p. 152. On the "Kaiserplan" see Becker, *Bismarcks Ringen um Deutschlands Gestaltung*, ch. xxii.

[29] *G.W.*, vol. VIb, no. 1459.

ference to higher national aims on the one hand, and well-considered reserve "which we oppose to the muddled officiousness of certain allies who feel moved to improve the condition of Germany but who neither know the means to do it nor have to bear the responsibility for it" on the other. How Prussian influence could have been brought to bear on the elections he could not see, but if it had been, he feared that the result would have been to drive many more voters into the arms of the ultramontanes. As a matter of fact, he suggested, if an ultramontane ministry were formed, it might even happen that an ultramontane "new era" would have the effect of furthering and strengthening the development that was desired more than the retention of office by Prince Hohenlohe in the present dubious circumstances.[30]

When the Bavarian Landtag opened its sessions in January 1870, vigorous attacks were made on the cabinet. On February 10, the first four paragraphs of an address to the king were passed. One of them stated that the treaties concluded with Prussia were subject to possible divergent interpretations. This, it was asserted, was a cause of alarm to the Bavarian people, and they desired to see a man in control of foreign affairs who enjoyed the confidence of the country. It was, in effect, a vote of censure against Hohenlohe personally. Although a few days before, Hohenlohe had received from the king assurances of unshaken confidence, he decided again to tender his resignation. Among the reasons for this which he gave to the Prussian minister was that if, in the spring, action occurred from abroad, for example, from France, it would be better that the particularistic, prussophobe party rather than the liberal be in control. For surely, under the impression of fear and of need for protection, the government would be overturned under the changed circumstances. A change in the opposite direction would bring incalculable consequences. He felt also that he

[30] *G.W.*, vol. VIb, no. 1459.

could not be absolutely sure that the king would back him up if he should undertake such far-reaching measures as dissolution of the Landtag and the creation of peers to secure a favorable majority in the Reichsrat.[31]

On receipt of Werthern's report of this conversation, Bismarck telegraphed, on February 13, that in his opinion, Hohenlohe's withdrawal would be a dangerous political blunder.[32] A dispatch followed, two days later, with a detailed explanation. "Up to the last few days," Bismarck wrote,

much was to be said for the opinion that Prince Hohenlohe had better step down. But the very reasons which at the time of my instructions of December 10 of last year argued for this are today on the other side. What made the situation at that time so ambiguous was not so much the uncertainty about the strength with which the ultramontane party . . . would appear in the new house, but doubt as to the king's power of decision. The advantage that we could expect from an ultramontane ministry was that it would demonstrate to the country and to the king that it was incapable of carrying on the government. The disadvantage that we feared in having Prince Hohenlohe stay in office was that he would wear himself out in skirmishes. The decisive intervention of the king on behalf of his minister has reversed all these presuppositions and arguments. The king has taken a decision and acted on it with unexpected energy against the members of the Reichsrat and of his own family. No experiment is any longer needed to convince him that he cannot get along with an ultramontane ministry. . . . I think it is asking too much that Prince Hohenlohe wants to know with certainty how far the king will go on the road he is taking. It seems to me that it lies largely in the hands of the prince himself to produce such certainty. As the king is standing up for him, he naturally counts on not being abandoned by him. The larger field of battle for which I wanted to see the prince spared has opened and I cannot think without serious anxiety of the consequences which his retirement at this moment would have. It could be that the king, in his disappointment, would experience an inward revulsion; it might be that he would abdicate to escape the

[31] *G.W.* vol. VIb, introductory note to no. 1502.
[32] *G.W.*, vol. VIb, no. 1502.

humiliation of reversing himself. Neither of these alternatives . . . can be regarded as out of the question if the young monarch, abandoned by the minister he trusts, were compelled to live with a ministry imposed upon him, of whose pernicious character he is convinced, and which at the same time he must think of as having won a victory over him. I would therefore definitely advise that Prince Hohenlohe remain in office. If the budget is denied him or . . . if payment of taxes is refused, I recommend another dissolution of the lower house and the creation of peers. Given the personal nature of the conflict between the king and the members of the Reichsrat, the latter measure has in any case become necessary.

Werthern was instructed to convey these views to Hohenlohe if the prince should discuss the question with him again. Bismarck went on:

I have to keep still another eventuality in mind: that disturbances might break out in Bavaria. I do not need to say how little we wish this and how dangerous it would be for the peace: our Romish-Guelph-Republican adversaries hope to bring about a war on the Bavarian question. If they could place King Ludwig in the position of needing to ask for our support under the Treaty of August 1866, their purpose would be close to success.[33]

During the year 1869, Bismarck's expressions of concern about ultramontanism were becoming more frequent. He described it as an anti-Prussian force in Hanover, in South Germany, and in Europe. In reference to Hanover, where opposition to Prussian rule was especially strong, he commented that "in any other nation, Guelph, infamy, ultramontanism, and treason would be synonymous terms."[34] To the Papal Chamberlain, Monsignor Wolanski, who gave the impression of being not unfriendly to Prussia, Bismarck complained of the hostile attitude of the Catholic clergy in South Germany and of their support for bitterly anti-Prussian journalists and

[33] *G.W.*, vol. VIb, no. 1503.
[34] *G.W.*, vol. VIa, p. 417.

newspapers.[35] In a long memorandum for King William, dated at Varzin on November 20, Bismarck referred to the overthrow of Prince Hohenlohe as the task in Germany that could — or apparently could — be accomplished. For Prussian policy in South Germany, it was essential, therefore, to maintain the *status quo* of the governments of Bavaria and Württemberg so that the cabinets of Munich and Stuttgart would not cooperate with either Paris or Vienna and would find no pretext to loosen or perhaps even to break the alliance concluded with Prussia.

The center of gravity rests at the moment in the person of the king of Bavaria, whose easily disturbed sense of sovereignty must be carefully respected if we do not want Munich and Bavaria, with five million inhabitants, to be a base for the Austrian-French-ultramontane efforts against us. That could easily come to pass if the king of Bavaria, irritated by concern about Prussia's intentions, should take in place of Prince Hohenlohe, a Catholic-Austrophil minister. . . . That would be a calamity for which no conceivable success of the present ministry in Baden could compensate.[36]

These quotations must be interpreted in relation to specific situations, yet they indicate that Bismarck was tending to think of ultramontanism as an obstacle to consolidation in Prussia, as a block to the national movement in South Germany, and as the possible catalyst of an anti-Prussian coalition in Europe.

It is impossible to say how much Bismarck knew about the secret negotiations between France, Austria, and Italy, but that he had some substantially accurate knowledge is proved by what he wrote to Reuss at St. Petersburg in March 1869.[37] For some time, however, he took the reports, especially those

---

[35] *G.W.*, vol. VIb, no. 1353.
[36] *G.W.*, vol. VIb, no. 1449.
[37] See p. 10 above.

about the adhesion of Italy, rather lightly.[38] He felt reasonably secure in the support of Russia and continued to devote special attention to keeping warm the Russian government's suspicions of Austria. On the other hand, before the end of 1869, there are indications of increasing concern on his part. His frequent remarks about "Austrian-French-ultramontane" activities suggest that the "nightmare of coalitions" was already haunting him.

The hypothesis put forward by Hans Delbrück in the 1890's that two offensives met in 1870 — Napoleon's laying a mine for Bismarck through his plans for the alliance and Bismarck's laying a countermine through the Hohenzollern candidacy to provoke the war before his adversaries had completed their preparations to strike — has been rejected by two of the best-informed students of the problem.[39] Yet given the nature and traditions of international relations in the middle of the nineteenth century, the possibility that Napoleon and Beust might be successful cannot be dismissed offhand,[40] Bismarck did not create the Hohenzollern candidacy as a countermine to explode the projected triple alliance, but the fear of such an alliance was a major factor, perhaps the major factor, in his decision to urge the acceptance of the Spanish offer. The thought that an "ultramontane" candidate, Bavarian or Austrian or Spanish, would be the link that would complete the chain stands out in the discussions from the receipt of Prim's letters at the end of February 1870 to the final acceptance by Leopold and his father at the end of June. In the diplomatic maneuvers to maintain or to modify the balance of power, small factors cannot be disregarded. An "ultramontane" king of Spain could add an increment of strength to the French forces, as Isabella II was said to have been planning before her fall, by replacing the French troops at Rome with

[38] See, for example, *G.W.*, vol. VIb, no. 1339 and note 5; no. 1340.
[39] Lord, p. 8; Dittrich, *Die Welt als Geschichte*, vol. XIII, p. 43.
[40] Artom, *Iniziative neutralistiche*, pp. 60–61.

Spanish. By doing so, he would also remove one of the obstacles to the participation of Italy in the alliance.

Bismarck's expressions of confidence in the maintenance of peace varied with the circumstances and especially with his estimate of the internal situation in France. In the fall of 1869, for example, he told the Saxon minister of state, Richard von Friesen, that he foresaw a war with France in the near future as an unavoidable necessity. "The Emperor Napoleon," whom Bismarck usually described as reluctant to undertake a war,

is becoming more and more insecure in his position at home; he has lost his power of clear decision and is making all kinds of mistakes in his domestic policy. Disaffection is spreading among the French people and the influence of his opponents growing more dangerous to him day by day. Soon he will have nothing left but to distract the attention of the nation from its internal affairs by a foreign war and to try by a victorious campaign to satisfy the vanity of the French who have not yet been able to forget his inglorious and weak attitude in 1866. Thereby he can consolidate anew his own position and that of his dynasty. For the North German Confederation too, a war with France is not only unavoidable but also needed, for, so long as the present unstable situation continues in France, a viable and secure development of our own affairs is unthinkable.

He did not, however, suggest provoking a preventive war. The Confederation must be prepared for every contingency, but it could afford to wait with calm and could only profit from the postponement for its military strength was steadily increasing.[41] On the other hand, early in February 1870, he told Count Waldersee, who was about to leave for his new post as military attaché at Paris, that the political situation at the moment was idyllically peaceful. "How long it will last, no one can know. At any rate, the French have so much to do at home that they are not contemplating external complications. Napoleon depends primarily upon the army and so long

[41] *G.W.*, vol. VII, no. 224.

as it remains sure, he can permit himself experiments at home. If it begins to waver, the chances of his domestic opponents rise and he might then try to divert them by trouble abroad. That seems to me the only thing that at the moment might create the prospect of war." At the end of the conversation, in which Bismarck could not afford to be insincere, he warned Waldersee against hasty judgments based on what he would hear in legitimist and Orleanist circles in Paris.[42]

Three weeks later, on the evening of the very day that Bismarck received Prim's letter from the hands of Salazar, he gave Moritz Busch instructions for the press to pay special attention to the situation in France

so that nothing should be done which might endanger the constitutional evolution of that country, an evolution hitherto promoted in every way from Berlin, as it signifies peace for us. The French Arcadians are watching the course of events in Germany, and waiting their opportunity. Napoleon is now well disposed to us, but he is changeable. We could now fight France and beat her too, but that war would give rise to five or six others; and while we can gain our ends by peaceful means, it would be foolish, if not criminal, to take such a course. Events in France may take a warlike or revolutionary turn, which would render the present brittle metal there more malleable.[43]

On February 24, 1870, Edward Lasker, as spokesman for a group of National Liberal members, introduced into the Reichstag a resolution for the speedy admission of Baden into the North German Confederation. Bismarck opposed this with vigor. In the debate, he emphasized his agreement with the objectives of the proponents, the completion of German unity. He insisted, however, that the time for this had not yet come. The admission of Baden would, in his opinion, hamper rather than accelerate progress to their goal. It would remove from South Germany the state whose ruler and people were most

[42] Waldersee, *Denkwürdigkeiten*, vol. I, p. 49.
[43] Busch, *Bismarck: Some Secret Pages from His History*, vol. I, p. 8.

ready for union with the North and which, if independent, could continue to exert a useful influence as mediator between the northern and southern points of view. It would remove one of the incentives of the other southern governments for closer union by extending the protective barrier of the Confederation as a shield for Württemberg and the main body of Bavaria against danger from France. It would — and this was most important — produce an unfavorable reaction on the kings of those states.[44]

In his instructions to Count Flemming, the Prussian minister at Karlsruhe, Bismarck described his policy more fully and more frankly than he could in his speeches to the Reichstag. About Bavaria, he repeated what he had written time and again. Nothing must be done which would offend the susceptibilities of the king of Bavaria. If, under the leadership of the crown, which up to this time had been opposed to it, the "ultramontane–pro-French–particularistic" party succeeded in consolidating its control of the government, there was no reason to suppose that it could not, "with support from abroad," develop a powerful and lasting regime. The disadvantage of that could not be outweighed by the early admission of Baden to the Confederation. About France, he still regarded it as possible that public opinion might be reconciled to the idea that union of one or all of the south German states was not prohibited by the Treaty of Prague. For the time being, he wanted to avoid anything that would hamper the consolidation of the new constitutional order in France. If the situation changed, if the new order in France were not consolidated, and if it became possible to form a more definite judgment about the future of Bavaria, he might have to reconsider and, without regard to what he had said in the debate, take up the question of admitting Baden. But, he added, even

[44] Kohl, *Die politischen Reden des Fürsten Bismarck*, vol. IV, pp. 305–325.

if the admission of Baden and South Hesse were opportune in other respects, the addition of their votes to the Bundesrat would not be expedient before the consolidation of the federal relationships which must take place sooner or later and might well bring a conflict with the crown of Saxony. If, to be sure, a European crisis occurred, other conclusions might be reached, for then it might no longer be necessary to nurse along the conditions for favorable development to which he must now have regard. He was not making the decisions that he did out of fear of war. He was confident of victory if war was forced upon them but held even a successful war as the means to bring about results which could undoubtedly be achieved without it as unworthy of a conscientious government.[45]

It is probably impossible to know *unquestionably* what Bismarck thought when he made up his mind to accept the Hohenzollern candidacy. He had, it is true, included relations with Spain as one of the means by which France could be provoked to attack or, at least, to threaten Germany,[46] but he had done nothing to follow up this suggestion. When he received Prim's letter, he had to decide one way or the other and, as his memorandum for the king tried to demonstrate, acceptance would offer advantages and avert disadvantages of various degrees of probability and importance.[47] There is no reason to believe that in making his decision he had any specific single result in mind. "It is to misconstrue the essence of politics," he told the Austrian historian Heinrich Friedjung in 1890, "to assume that a statesman can draft a far-reaching plan and prescribe as law what he wants to carry out in one, two, or three years. . . . The statesman is like a wanderer in the forest. He knows the direction of his route but not the point at which he will emerge from the woods."[48] This was

[45] *G.W.*, vol. VIb, nos. 1516, 1517.
[46] See p. 10 above.
[47] See p. 56 above.
[48] *G.W.*, vol. IX, p. 49.

said with special reference to the background of the Austro-Prussian War, but it is an apt description of Bismarck's position in the months before the war of 1870. The situation was complex and fluid. Such a situation is not easy to summarize, for it is possible to find statements in Bismarck's writings and conversations that can be used to support different interpretations of his policy. The contradictions suggest that he had not made up his mind but was exploring many possibilities and facing the contingencies day by day as they appeared.

The offer of the Spanish crown to a prince of the House of Hohenzollern provided Bismarck with the means to create a European crisis. What form it would take could not be predicted with certainty. In Spain and in Germany, it was believed by those in the secret that France would use both influence and gold to block the election and, if necessary, would stir up civil war in Spain. The Spanish civil war of the 1830's had touched the interests of the Great Powers and established a precedent for intervention. There were also precedents in Belgium and Greece where candidates had been opposed by protests to the government with whose dynasty they were related. In the case of the Sigmaringen Hohenzollerns, the blood relationship was closer to Napoleon III than to King William, but officially they were members of the Prussian royal family. A protest to Prussia would be in accordance with international practice and comity, but Bismarck planned to meet it by the fiction that Leopold was independent in his decisions and by insisting that the Prussian government as government and King William as king must have nothing to do with the business. Prim hoped that he might be able to persuade Napoleon that Leopold was the last hope for stability in Spain and more to the interest of the French empire than Montpensier or a republic. Bismarck may have shared this hope but there is no convincing evidence that he did. In any case, given his views of the general situation, he would not have rejected the offer regardless of the danger involved. The disadvantage in his opinion of an "ultramontane" king in Spain was reason enough. If a crisis did come, it could be turned to some advantage.

There is evidence, though from an unfriendly source, that soon after the Spanish offer Bismarck was looking for a crisis. He was quoted as saying that things couldn't go on as they were; it was necessary to make some advance and he was prepared to face not only one war but four.[49] An equally informed and equally unfriendly source states that he was pursuing his great objective, the unification of Germany, and would like to do it without war.[50]

Until Leopold accepted the Spanish offer late in June, the time and the nature of the crisis were academic questions. Bismarck continued to wait and watch. The appointment of Gramont to the Foreign Office at Paris was an alarming symptom,[51] but his conciliatory reply to attacks in the Chamber of Deputies on Bismarck's support of the St. Gotthard railway tunnel project contributed to reducing the tension. As late as June 7, Bismarck reiterated his confidence in the desire of Napoleon and of the French people for peace. "I know," he wrote to Bernstorff, the ambassador at London,

that Napoleon regards a foreign war as a great danger and the internal conflict with the revolution as a lesser one. . . . According to my knowledge of conditions in France and the dominating need of the people for quiet and the maintenance of the *status quo*, as well as from my knowledge of the emperor, I myself cannot share the anxieties for the near future nor indeed for as far as political calculation can take us — though of course I take into full account the uncertainties of European politics. . . . That such eventualities are nearer today than at any time since 1866 is a conclusion that I cannot draw from the present state of affairs in France.[52]

[49] Franz von Roggenbach, quoted by Hohenlohe, *Denkwürdigkeiten*, vol. II, p. 5.
[50] Stosch to Freytag, April 5, 1870, Stosch, *Denkwürdigkeiten*, p. 181.
[51] *G.W.*, vol. VIb, p. 321.
[52] *G.W.*, vol. VIb, no. 1560.

At the time Bismarck expressed his confidence to Bernstorff, Leopold had agreed only that if conditions remained substantially the same, he would accept the Spanish offer in the fall. Some time in June, however, Bismarck began to show greater interest in a crisis. Versen recorded in his diary that while the Hohenzollern princes were preparing the final decision, "Then came various scruples on Karl Anton's part. What would France say about it? Would it not give rise to complications? I said: 'Bismarck says that is just what he is looking for.' " [53] "Complications" ("Verwickelungen") may have been a euphemism for "war"; it could also mean merely a diplomatic crisis like that of 1867 over Luxemburg, which had inflamed national feeling in Germany and could do so again. But whatever impression Bismarck intended to convey, it was obvious that complications meant crisis and crisis meant risk of war.

In 1867 Bismarck had contributed to find a compromise with France; in 1870, he did not do anything to avert the crisis or to guide it to a peaceful solution. In 1867 he had argued against Moltke that "Only for the honor of the country — not to be confused with so-called prestige — only for its most vital interests, may we engage in war. No statesman has the right to commence it merely because in his own subjective judgment he regards it as unavoidable in any given time." [54] In 1870, the withdrawal of the candidacy in the face of threats from the French ministers and the French press seemed a "second Olmütz," a humiliation that wiped out his distinction between honor and prestige. Prestige was an element of national power and as Bismarck had said soon after he took office, "it is not to Prussia's liberalism that Germany looks but to her power." [55]

---

[53] "Bismarck sagt, die seien ihm gefunden." Versen diary, translation, Bonnin, p. 278. Bucher added the reassurance that Bismarck had often told him that if in the last two years Napoleon had wanted war, he could have found plenty of grounds for it.

[54] *G.W.*, vol. VII, no. 156. See also Jeismann, *Das Problem des Präventivkrieges*, ch. iii.

[55] Kohl, *Die politischen Reden des Fürsten Bismarck*, vol. II, p. 30.

In his opinion as in that of the French cabinet, diplomatic defeat must be wiped out by war but he was skillful enough and patient enough to put the onus of declaring it on the enemy.

SUPPLEMENTARY NOTE

These are a few examples of the reports on public opinion in the departments outside of Paris. (L. M. Case, *French Opinion on War and Diplomacy during the Second Empire*, pp. 248–250; Case's translations.)

"There is no warlike enthusiasm; there is something better than that because enthusiasm dies down easily. There is a sentiment of reasoned and reflective patriotism boldly asserting itself and expressing itself thus: Prussian policy is tending towards a state of things that France must not allow to be constituted in Europe; only force can turn Prussia from her objective, so war with her is fatally inevitable; the occasion is good, the moment propitious, better now than later." (Eure-et-Loire.)

"Commercial affairs are not going well right now, and the merchants, whose opinion is ordinarily for peace, appear to believe that an event like war, whether with Prussia or with Spain, would bring a change in the situation. Yesterday they had a festival in the public park in Bordeaux, and this opinion I consign in this report, however strange it may appear, was frequently expressed to me. May I add that the central commissioner, whom I consulted this morning, reported to me the same tendencies among the people with whom he has contacts. I believe that at heart they dread war." (Gironde.)

"If the question could be decided by a congress, that is, without war, they would be particularly satisfied. But they do not want things to remain as they are today. They are tired and humiliated by being exposed to the consequences of Prussia's activities. They hope that the government will take advantage of a dispute which it certainly has not provoked, to redeem the situation. And, if war alone must bring an end to a state of things considered compromising to our national dignity and our interests, I affirm that they will frankly and resolutely accept war. I may add that even those that dread it or pretend to dread it at present would be the first to denounce the government if it did not persist in the firm and resolute attitude it has adopted." (Rhone.)

"I summarize public opinion in these words: No one wants a Prussian prince in Spain; they hail war patriotically; they prefer peace with a moral victory; they would not forgive the government if it showed weakness or even timidity." (Charente.)

"The idea of a war with Prussia is very popular. People do not go so far as to desire it, but they would be very sorry to see it avoided at the price of any sacrifice which would hurt or compromise our dignity and patriotism." (Haute-Loire.)

Appendices
Bibliography
Index

-❧[Appendix A]❧-

Genealogical Tables

I. *Hohenzollern (younger or royal line)*

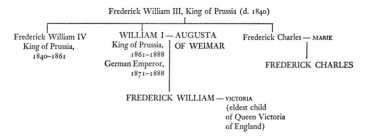

Frederick William III, King of Prussia (d. 1840)

Frederick William IV
King of Prussia,
1840–1861

WILLIAM I — AUGUSTA
King of Prussia, | OF WEIMAR
1861–1888
German Emperor,
1871–1888

Frederick Charles — MARIE

FREDERICK CHARLES

FREDERICK WILLIAM — VICTORIA
(eldest child
of Queen Victoria
of England)

II. *Hohenzollern (elder or Swabian line, Hohenzollern-Sigmaringen)*

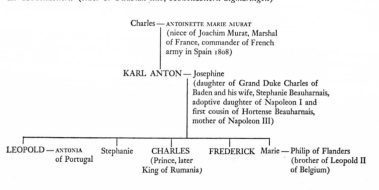

Charles — ANTOINETTE MARIE MURAT
(niece of Joachim Murat, Marshal
of France, commander of French
army in Spain 1808)

KARL ANTON — Josephine
(daughter of Grand Duke Charles of
Baden and his wife, Stephanie Beauharnais,
adoptive daughter of Napoleon I and
first cousin of Hortense Beauharnais,
mother of Napoleon III)

LEOPOLD — ANTONIA
of Portugal

Stephanie

CHARLES
(Prince, later
King of Rumania)

FREDERICK

Marie — Philip of Flanders
(brother of Leopold II
of Belgium)

III. *Italy*

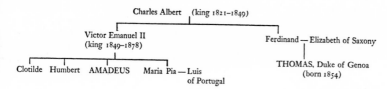

Charles Albert (king 1821–1849)

Victor Emanuel II
(king 1849–1878)

Ferdinand — Elizabeth of Saxony

Clotilde Humbert AMADEUS Maria Pia — Luis
of Portugal

THOMAS, Duke of Genoa
(born 1854)

IV. *Portugal*

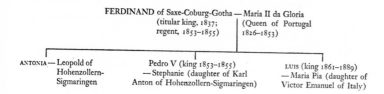

FERDINAND of Saxe-Coburg-Gotha — Maria II da Gloria
(titular king, 1837;   (Queen of Portugal
regent, 1853–1855)   1826–1853)

ANTONIA — Leopold of
Hohenzollern-
Sigmaringen

Pedro V (king 1853–1855)
— Stephanie (daughter of Karl
Anton of Hohenzollern-Sigmaringen)

LUIS (king 1861–1889)
— Maria Pia (daughter of
Victor Emanuel of Italy)

-⟦ Appendix B ⟧-

Bismarck's Letters to Prim

We know Bismarck's letters to Prim only from the secret file. The letter dated April 1, 1870, is a copy in Thile's hand,[1] the one dated June 1, 1870, is a draft in Bucher's hand with autograph revision in pencil by Bismarck. To avoid confusion in the printed texts, I have reconstructed the two versions. The file does not contain a fair copy. Bonnin has published a translation of the two letters, the latter only in the revised draft.[2] (The pointed brackets < > indicate crossed-out words.)

April 11, 1870

Le Maréchal Comte de Reus, Président du Conseil des Ministres, Madrid.

Mr. le Cᵗᵉ

V. E. aura sans doute appris par M. de Salazar que j'ai accueilli l'ouverture qu'Elle a bien voulu me faire avec l'empressement sympathique qui résulte de mes convictions personnelles et qui est tout en harmonie avec les dispositions de l'opinion publique en Allemagne. Je me suis sans hésitation loyalement associé à Vos projets Mr. le Cᵗᵉ; mais j'ai trouvé le terrain peu préparé. Le Prince Frédéric voyageait incognito en Italie et ce n'est que plus tard à Paris que la communication a été établie de manière à pouvoir le rappeler à Berlin.

Dans les familles souveraines des résolutions d'une grande

[1] *Marginal note in Thile's hand*: Das Original ist am 13. April Abends von [?] Versen mit nach Madrid genommen. Auch hat er zu seiner und zu Bucher's Orientierung Abschrift des Abschr. genommen. v. Th.

[2] Nos. 79 and 143.

importance ne se prennent pas avec plus de facilité au moins que parmi nous autres particuliers. On doit être préparé à rencontre des délais et des doutes, quand il s'agit de disposer un jeune prince à accepter la responsabilité d'une mission historique jusque là a été étrangère à ses pensées et dont les difficultés sont peut-être exagerées par les inquiétudes qu'inspire aux parents la perspective d'une séparation à vie et d'un avenir incertain. Le Prince est majeur il est vrai, mais moralement il reste tenu à respecter les decisions de ses parents, chez lesquels à l'heure qu'il est, je n'ai pas réussi encore à calmer toutes les appréhensions et à avoir raison de tous les scrupules qui se puisent dans le coeur maternel plutôt que dans le raisonnement politique. J'aurais voulu ne répondre à Votre lettre, Mr. le Cte, qu'en Vous annonçant que l'accomplissement de nos projets était assuré et je suis convaincu qu'avec un peu de patience encore nous verrons venir ce moment; mais il m'a paru urgent de Vous mettre au fait de la situation et de Vous faire savoir quelles sont les questions qui en première ligne pré-occupent les personnes interessés. J'en ai chargé Mr. Bucher qui connait toute ma pensée, et qui, si Vous voulez bien le permettre, vous les expliquait en toute franchise. Je n'ai pas pu profiter de son départ pour écrire à V. E. et pour La prier de bien vouloir excuser le retard qu'à la suite des circonstances ma réponse a du subir; j'ai souffert dans le tems [*sic*] d'un rheumatisme tellement violent que toute occupation m'a été interdite et ce n'est pas sans difficulté encore qu'aujourd'hui je puisse écrire ces lignes. Je m'en suis fait le devoir le plus pressant et le plus agréable de même tems [*sic*], des que mes forces me l'ont permis. Voulant éviter l'attention qu'attirerais l'envoi d'un de nos courriers officiels, j'ai prié un de mes amis personnels M. de Versen de se charger de cette lettre pour la remise de laquelle entre les mains de V. E. il va demander l'avis de M. de Salazar.

Agréez, Mr. le Cte, l'expression de la très-haute considération avec laquelle j'ai l'honneur d'être

de V. E.

le très humble et obéissant serviteur

Signé: v BISMARCK

June 1, 1870.
Bismarck to Prim. Draft in Bucher's hand, corrections in pencil
by Bismarck. Translation of the corrected draft in Bonnin, no. 143.

Son Excellence Mr. le Maréchal Comte de Reus, Président du
Conseil des Ministres, Madrid.

Durch Feldjäger.

Monsieur le Comte

Je saisis le premier moment de recueillement pour remercier
V. E. de la lettre que vous avez bien voulu m'écrire en date du
24. Avril. Je ne l'ai reçue qu'étant de retour de la campagne,
imparfaitement remis encore d'une sévère indisposition et as-
sailli sur le champs par une foule d'affaires dont l'expédition
devait précéder la clôture du Reichstag. Informé comme vous
êtes de l'accueil sympathique que j'avais fait, j'espère que,
malgré un si long delai, V. E. ne doutera pas de mon empressement de vous rendre compte des démarches que je fais pour
témoigner les sentiments qui m'animent à votre égard et pour
l'avenir de votre pays.

Je suis arrivé à la conviction que le Prince Frédéric ne ré-
unit pas toutes les qualités désirables pour le souverain d'Espagne. J'ai donc dirigé mes efforts, nonobstant le premier refus,
sur le Prince héréditaire; et il parait que lui ainsi que son père
se sont affranchis des préoccupations et les soucis spécifiques,
avec lesquels ils avaient d'abord envisagés le projet et l'état des
choses en Espagne. Mais la difficulté générale, que j'ai eu l'-
honneur d'indiquer à V. E. dans ma lettre du 11. Avril retard-
ent encore une détermination. Toutefois, je viens de recevoir
de la part de S. A. R. l'assurance que son fils ainé ne persiste
plus dans sa résolution negative, de même que la promesse que
ce dernier accepterait l'automne prochain le résultat des suffrages, pourvu qu'on ⟨entend⟩ parvint jusqu'à l'automne à
s'entendre sur les conditions et la position future du roi en tant
qu'elle n'est pas reglée par la Constitution. Si le Gouvernement
Espagnole peut (?) de même ou non d'accorder cet atermoiement, c'est une question qui échappe à mon appréciation. [Dans
la pensée que la présence de M. de Salazar pourrait accelerer le

denouement, je viens de le prier par le télégraphe de se rendre
à Berlin.] ³ Quelle que soit la tournure de cette affaire, je prie
V. E. de se tenir convaincue que j'ai fait tout mon possible et
que, si je n'arrive pas au résultat désiré également par nous
deux, c'est à cause de la difficulté de mettre d'accord des personnes dans la position dont il s'agit, sur des résolutions graves.
Je suis vivement touché des souhaits que vous faites pour ma
santé et je vous prie M. l. C. d'agréer l'expression de la plus
haute considération avec laquelle j'ai l'honneur d'être
de V. E.

Corrected draft

Je saisis le premier moment de recueillement pour remercier
V. E. de la lettre que vous avez bien voulu m'écrire en date du
24. Avril. Je ne l'ai reçue qu'étant de retour de la campagne,
imparfaitement remis encore d'une indisposition très grave et
de nature à m'interdire absolument toute participation aux affaires. J'espère que, malgré un si long delai, V. E. ne doutera pas
de mon empressement de vous rendre compte des démarches
que j'ai faites en vue de la réalisation des projets qui répondent
si bien aux sentiments qui m'animent à votre égard et pour
l'avenir de votre pays.

Ayant acquis la conviction qu'il fallait mettre tout à fait hors
de cause le Pᶜᵉ Frédéric, j'ai < repris > renoué les négocia-
tions avec le Pᶜᵉ Héréditaire, et aujourd'hui il me parait, que
malgré son premier refus, nous avons <réussi triompher>
réussi à <illegible word> prouver au Prince comme à Msgr
son père, que les préoccupations et spécifiques inquiétudes avec
lesquels ils avaient d'abord envisagé le projet et l'état des choses
en Espagne sont mal fondées. Mais toujours les difficultés géné-
rales, que j'ai eu l'honneur d'indiquer à V. E. dans ma lettre du
11. Avril, arrêtent encore une détermination définitive. Je viens
de recevoir de la part de S. A. R. le Pᶜᵉ Père l'assurance que son
fils ainé le Pᶜᵉ Héréditaire ne maintient plus son refus person-
nel. Le Pce à cette déclaration <y> ajoute la promesse que

³ Sentence in brackets added in margin by Bucher.

l'automne prochain < le Pce Héréd > son fils ainé accepterait le résultat des suffrages pourvu que jusqu'à là on parvint à s'entendre sur les conditions et la position future du Roi en tant qu'elle n'est pas reglée par la constitution. Si le Gouvernement Espagnol se trouve à même ou non d'agréer cet atermoiement, c'est une question qui échappe à mon appréciation. < Croyant > Espérant encore que la présence de M. de Salazar pourrait peut-être accelerer le denouement, je viens de le prier par le télégraphe de venir à Berlin. Quelle que soit la tournure de cette affaire, je prie V. E. de se tenir convaincue que j'ai fait et que je ferai tout ce qui dépend de moi et que, si je n'arrive pas en temps utile au résultat désiré également pars nous deux, il n'est qu'à cause de la difficulté de mettre d'accord aussi promptement qu'il le faudrait des personnes dans la position de celles dont il s'agit.

Je suis vivement touché des souhaits que vous faites pour ma santé et vous prie, de croire que je serai très-heureux de vous rendre service à vous personellement et à votre patrie.

Agréez, M. l. Cte l'expression de la plus haute considération avec laquelle j'ai l'honneur d'être,

de V. E.

-⦆Appendix C⦆-

The "Ems Telegram"

See Lord, nos. 163 and 187; E. Walder, *Die Emser Depesche*, pp. 13–16. The lefthand column is the telegram from Abeken to Bismarck, Ems, July 13, 1870, sent to telegraph station at 3:10 P.M., dispatched at 3:50 P.M., received at 6:09 P.M. The right-hand column is Bismarck's condensed version.

S. M. der König schreibt mir: "Graf Benedetti fing mich auf der Promenade ab, um auf zuletzt sehr zudringliche Art von mir zu verlangen, ich sollte ihn autorisieren, sofort zu telegraphiren, dass ich für alle Zukunft mich verpflichtete, niemals wieder meine Zustimmung zu geben, wenn die Hohenzollern auf ihre Candidatur zurückkämen. Ich wies ihn, zuletzt etwas ernst, zurück, da man à tout jamais dergleichen Engagements nicht nehmen dürfe noch könne. Natürlich sagte ich ihm, dass ich noch nichts erhalten hätte, und, da er

Nachdem die Nachrichten von der Entsagung des Prinzen von Hohenzollern der Kaiserlich französischen Regierung von der Königlich spanischen amtlich mitgetheilt worden sind, hat der französische Botschafter in Ems an Seine Majestät den König noch die Forderung gestellt, ihn zu autorisiren, dass er nach Paris telegraphire, dass Seine Majestät der König sich für alle Zukunft verpflichte, niemals wieder seine Zustimmung zu geben, wenn die Hohenzollern auf ihre Kandidatur zurückkommen sollten.

über Paris und Madrid früher
benachrichtigt sei als ich, er
wohl einsähe, dass mein Gouvernement wiederum ausser
Spiel sei."

Se. Majestät hat seitdem ein
Schreiben des Fürsten bekom-
men. Da Se. Majestät dem
Grafen Benedetti gesagt, dass
er Nachricht vom Fürsten er-
warte, hat Allerhöchstder-
selbe, mit Rücksicht auf die
obige Zumuthung, auf des
Grafen Eulenburg und mei-
nen Vortrag beschlossen, den
Grafen Benedetti nicht mehr
zu empfangen, sondern ihm
nur durch einen Adjutanten
sagen zu lassen, dass Se. Majestät jetzt vom Fürsten die
Bestätigung der Nachricht erhalten, die Benedetti aus Paris
schon gehabt, und dem Botschafter nichts weiter zu
sagen habe.

Se. Majestät stellt Eurer.
Excellenz anheim, ob nicht die
neue Forderung Benedettis
und ihre Zurückweisung
sogleich sowohl unseren Ge-
sandten als in der Presse mitgetheilt werden sollte.

Seine Majestät hat es darauf abgelehnt, den französischen Botschafter nochmals zu
empfangen, und demselben
durch den Adjutanten vom
Dienst sagen lassen, dass Seine
Majestät dem Botschafter
nichts weiter mitzutheilen
habe.

Bibliography

ARCHIVES AND MANUSCRIPTS

The German documents have been microfilmed; see The American Historical Association Committee for the Study of War Documents, *A Catalogue of Files and Microfilms of the German Foreign Ministry Archives, 1867–1920*, 1959. After the title of each file mentioned below I have given in parentheses the number of the column of the catalogue in which the file is listed.

I. A. B. o. (Spanien) 32 secreta. Acta secreta betr. die Berufung eines Prinzen von Hohenzollern auf den Spanischen Thron. (584)
In the references, I have designated this "secret file." Most of the documents have been published in English translation by Georges Bonnin in *Bismarck and the Hohenzollern Candidature for the Spanish Throne*.

I. A. (Deutschland) 158 secreta. Die Benutzung der politischen Akten des Auswärtigen Amtes zu publicistischen Zwecken. Bde. 1–5, 1890–1920. (123)
This contains the part of the diary of Major von Versen which records his activity on behalf of the Hohenzollern candidacy (translation in Bonnin, appendix A) and some unpublished items from the diary of Theodor von Bernhardi.

Asservat 36. Vorgänge betreffend die Hohenzollernsche Thronkandidatur in Spanien 1869–1870 und die Veröffentlichung darauf bezuglicher Geheimdokumente durch Prof. Hesselbarth, 1911–1925. Dabei Gutachten Platzhoff — Rheindorff, Berlin 14.III. 1924. (1175)

Bibliography

I. A. A. b. (Deutschland) 53. Bd. 1. 1853. 1854. 1864–1874. Acta betr. die politischen Umtriebe der früheren Freiherrn späteren Grafen von Beust. (34)

I. A. A. l. (Oesterreich) 57. Bde. 1–5. Acta betr. Schriftwechsel mit der Königlichen Gesandtschaft zu Wien sowie mit anderen königlich Missionen und fremden Kabinetten über die inneren Zustände und Verhältnisse Oesterreichs. (417)

I. A. A. l. (Oesterreich) 57 adh. Briefe des Frh. von Werther an den Unterstaatssekretär v. Thile. 1868–1869. (417)

I. A. A. l. (Oesterreich) 59. Acta betr. Schriftwechsel mit der Gesandtschaft zu Wien sowie mit anderen Missionen und fremden Kabinetten über die inneren Zustände und Verhältnisse Oesterreichs. Bde. 1–3. Jan. 1 to Oct. 31, 1870. (418)

I. A. B. c. (Frankreich) 68. Acta betr. die angeblichen Verhandlungen Frankreichs mit Italien und Oesterreich über eine gegen Preussen zu schliessende Tripel-Allianz. (305)

I. A. B. c. (Frankreich) 69. Bde. 1–2. Schriftwechsel mit der Botschaft zu Paris, sowie mit anderen Missionen und fremden Kabinetten über die inneren Zustände und Verhältnisse Frankreichs. Jan. 1 to Oct. 31, 1870. (305)

I. A. B. e. (Italien) 51. Acta betr. Schriftwechsel mit der Gesandtschaft zu Florenz sowie mit anderen Missionen und fremden Kabinetten über die inneren Zustände und Verhältnisse Italiens. 1870. (374)

I. A. B. i. (Russland) 46. Bd. 1. Acta betr. die politische Beziehungen Preussens zu Russland. 1868–1873. (490)

I. A. B. i. (Russland) 47, 48. Acta betr. Schriftwechsel mit der königlichen Gesandtschaft zu Petersburg sowie mit anderen Kabinetten über die inneren Zustände und Verhältnisse Russlands. (490)

I. A. B. o. (Spanien) 32. Acta betr. die Berufung eines Prinzen von Hohenzollern auf den Spanischen Thron. Bde. 1–7. (584) (Almost all of the documents in this file were published by Robert H. Lord, *The Origins of the War of 1870.*)

Public Record Office, London: F. O. 64/688. Prussia. Lord Loftus. June 16 to July 20, 1870.

I have also looked at the reports of the American minister, George Bancroft, from Berlin, and at the Bancroft papers in the Library of Congress, the Massachusetts Historical Society, and the New York Public Library.

Bibliography

BOOKS AND ARTICLES

Abeken, Heinrich. *Ein schlichtes Leben in bewegter Zeit, aus Briefen zusammenstellt.* 4th edition. Berlin, 1910.

[Abel, Karl.] *Letters on International Relations before and during the War of 1870.* By 'the Times' Correspondent at Berlin. 2 vols. London, 1871.

Acton, John Emerich Edward Dalberg-Acton, First Baron. "The Causes of the Franco-Prussian War," *Historical Essays and Studies,* London, 1908. First published separately in 1899.

Aegidi, L. K., and A. Klauhold. *Das Staatsarchiv: Sammlung der officiellen Aktenstücke zur Geschichte der Gegenwart.* Bde. 1–21. Hamburg, 1861–1871.

Albertini, Rudolf von. "Frankreichs Stellungnahme zur deutschen Einigung während des zweiten Kaiserreichs," *Schweizerische Zeitschrift für Geschichte,* vol. V, pp. 305–368.

Artom, Angelo, ed.; *Isacco and Ernesto Artom. Iniziative neutralistiche della diplomazia Italiana nel 1870 e nel 1915. Documenti inediti a cura di Angelo Artom.* n.p. 1954.

Auswärtige Politik Preussens, Die. See *Reichsinstitut.*

Ballesteros y Beretta, Antonio. *Historia de España y su influencia en la historia universal.* Vol. VIII. Barcelona, 1936.

[Bamberger, Ludwig.] *Bismarcks grosses Spiel. Die geheimen Tagebücher Ludwig Bambergers.* Edited with introduction by Dr. Ernst Feder. Frankfurt am Main, 1932.

Bapst, Germain. *Le Maréchal Canrobert. Souvenirs d'un siecle.* Vol. IV. Paris, 1909.

Baroche, Céleste Letellier (Mme. Jules Baroche). *Second empire, notes et souvenirs.* Preface by M. Frédéric Masson. Paris, 1921.

Barschak, Erna. *The Innocent Empress.* New York, 1943.

Bartlett, C. J. "Clarendon, the Foreign Office and the Hohenzollern Candidature, 1868–1870," *English Historical Review,* vol. LXXV (April 1960), pp. 276–284.

Becker, Otto. *Bismarcks Ringen um Deutschlands Gestaltung.* Edited and supplemented by Alexander Scharff. Heidelberg, © 1958.

Benedetti, Vincent. *Essais diplomatiques.* Paris, 1895.

——— *Ma Mission en Prusse.* 2nd edition. Paris, 1871.

Bermejo, Ildefonso Antonio. *Historia de la interinidad y guerra civil de España desde 1868.* Vol. I. Madrid, 1876.

Bernhardi, Theodor von. *Aus dem Leben Theodor von Bernhardis.* Achter Theil: *Zwischen zwei Kriegen. Tagebuchblätter aus den Jahren 1867 bis 1869.* Neunter Theil: *In Spanien und Portugal. Tagebuchblätter aus den Jahren 1869 bis 1871.* Leipzig, 1901, 1906.

Bernstein, Paul. "The Economic Aspects of Napoleon III's Rhine Policy," *French Historical Studies,* vol. II, no. 3 (Spring 1960), pp. 335–347.

Bertrand, R. Olivar. *El caballero Prim. (Vida política y revolucionaria.)* 2 vols. Barcelona, © 1952.

Beust, Friedrich Ferdinand Graf von. *Aus drei Viertel-Jahrhunderten.* 2 vols. Stuttgart, 1887.

Bismarck-Schönhausen, Otto Eduard Leopold von. *Die gesammelten Werke.* 15 vols. Berlin, © 1924–1932.

[Blumenthal, Leonhart Graf von.] *Tagebücher des Generalfeldmarschalls Graf von Blumenthal aus den Jahren 1866 und 1870/71.* Edited by Albrecht Graf von Blumenthal. Stuttgart and Berlin, 1902.

Bonnin, Georges. *Bismarck and the Hohenzollern Candidature for the Spanish Throne. The Documents in the German Diplomatic Archives.* Edited with an introduction by Georges Bonnin, translated by Isabella M. Massey, with a foreword by G. P. Gooch. London, 1957.

Bourgeois, Emile, and E. Clermont. *Rome et Napoléon III (1849–1870). Etude sur les origines et la chute du second empire.* Paris, 1907.

Brandt, Joseph A. *Toward the New Spain.* Chicago, © 1933.

Brase, Siegfried. *Emile Olliviers Memoiren und die Entstehung des Krieges von 1870.* Berlin, 1912.

Busch, Moritz. *Bismarck: Some Secret Pages from His History. Being a Diary Kept by Dr. Moritz Busch during Twenty-five Years' Official and Private Intercourse with the Great Chancellor.* 3 vols. London, 1898.

———— *Graf Bismarck und seine Leute während des Kriegs mit Frankreich. Nach Tagebuchsblättern.* 3rd edition. Leipzig, 1878.

Carnota, John Athelstane Smith. *Memoirs of the Field Marshal the Duke of Saldanha.* 2 vols. London, 1880.

Case, Lynn M. *French Opinion on War and Diplomacy during the Second Empire.* Philadelphia, 1954.

Clark, Chester A. "Bismarck, Russia, and the War of 1870," *Journal of Modern History,* vol. XIV (June 1942), pp. 195–208.

Corti, Egon Caesar. *The Reign of the House of Rothschild 1830–1871.* Translated from the German by Brian and Beatrix Lunn. New York, 1928.

Craig, Gordon A. "Great Britain and the Belgian Railways Dispute of 1869," *American Historical Review*, vol. L (July 1945), pp. 738–761.

Darimon, Alfred. *Histoire d'un jour. La journée du 12 juillet 1870.* Paris, 1888.

Deschanel, Paul. *Gambetta.* Paris, © 1919.

Diest, Gustav von. *Aus dem Leben eines Glucklichen. Erinnerungen eines alten Beamten.* Berlin, 1904.

Dittrich, Jochen. "Bismarck, Frankreich und die Hohenzollernkandidatur. Der Kriegsausbruch von 1870 und das deutschfranzösische Problem," *Die Welt als Geschichte*, vol. XIII (1953), pp. 42–57.

———— "Bismarck, Frankreich und die Hohenzollernkandidatur. Eine Untersuchung zur Frage von Schuld und Schicksal beim Kriegsausbruch von 1870 (mit einem Anhang von bisher unbekannten Briefen und Aktenstücken aus dem Fürstl. Hohenz. Familienarchiv.)." Dissertation, Freiburg, 1948. Microfilm copies in the University of Chicago and University of Minnesota libraries.

Dittrich, Z. R. *De Opkomst van het moderne Duitschland.* 2 vols. Groningen, 1956.

Dugué de la Fauconnerie. *Souvenirs d'un vieil homme (1866–1879).* 4th edition. Paris, 1912.

Dupuy, Aimé. *1870–1871. La Guerre, la Commune et la presse.* Paris, © 1959.

Durieux, Joseph. *Le Ministre Pierre Magne 1806–1879 d'après ses lettres et ses souvenirs.* 2 vols. Paris, 1929.

Eckhardt, Julius von. *Lebenserinnerungen.* Leipzig, 1910.

Eyck, Erich. *Bismarck.* 3 vols. Erlenbach-Zurich, © 1941, 1943, 1944.

Fernandez de los Rios, Angel. *Mi mision en Portugal; anales de ayer para enseñanza de mañana.* Paris, [1877].

Fester, Richard. *Briefe, Aktenstücke und Regesten zur Geschichte der Hohenzollernschen Thronkandidatur in Spanien.* 2 vols. Leipzig and Berlin, 1913.

———— *Die Genesis der Emser Depesche.* Berlin, 1915.

———— *Neue Beiträge zur Geschichte der Hohenzollernschen Thronkandidatur in Spanien.* Leipzig, 1913.

Fisher, Herbert Albert Laurens. "Ollivier's Memoirs," *Studies in History and Politics*, pp. 45–74. Oxford, 1920.

Fitzmaurice, Edmond George Petty-Fitzmaurice. *The Life of*

Granville George Leveson Gower, Second Earl Granville, K.G., *1815–1891.* 2 vols. London, 1905.

Fleury, Maurice Comte. *La France et la Russie en 1870. D'après les papiers du Général Comte Fleury.* Paris, 1902.

—— *Memoirs of the Empress Eugenie. Compiled from Statements, Private Documents and Personal Letters of the Empress Eugenie. From Conversations of the Emperor Napoleon III and from Family Letters and Papers of General Fleury, M. Franceschini Pietri, Prince Victor Napoleon and Other Members of the Court of the Second Empire.* 2 vols. New York and London, 1920.

[France, Ministère des Affaires Etrangères.] *Les Origines diplomatiques de la guerre de 1870–1871. Recueil de documents.* 29 vols. Paris, 1910–1932.

Friedrich III, Kaiser. *Das Kriegstagebuch von 1870/71.* Edited by Heinrich Otto Meisner. Leipzig, 1926.

Friis, Aage. "Spaniens Krone og dynastiske Skandinavisme," *Politiken* (Copenhagen), February 11, 12, 1937.

Fröbel, Julius. *Ein Lebenslauf. Aufzeichnungen, Erinnerungen und Bekenntnisse.* 2 vols. Stuttgart, 1890–1891.

Garets, Comtesse des (née Marie de Larminet). *Souvenirs d'une demoiselle d'honneur auprès de l'impératrice Eugénie.* Published by Marie-Louyse des Garets. Paris, 1928.

Gramont, Antoine Agénor, Duc de. *La France et la Prusse avant la guerre.* Paris, 1872.

Grunwald, Constantin de. *Le Duc de Gramont: gentilhomme et diplomate.* Paris, © 1950.

Hahn, Pauline. *Varzin: persönliche Erinnerungen an den Fürsten Otto von Bismarck.* Berlin, 1909.

Halperin, S. William. "Visconti-Venosta and the Diplomatic Crisis of July 1870," *Journal of Modern History*, vol. XXXI, no. 4 (December 1959), pp. 295–309.

—— "Bismarck and the Italian Envoy in Berlin on the Eve of the Franco-Prussian War," *Journal of Modern History*, vol. XXXIII, no. 1 (March 1961), pp. 33–39.

Hampe, Karl. *Wilhelm I: Kaiserfrage und Kölner Dom. Ein biographischer Beitrag zur Geschichte der deutschen Reichsgründung.* Stuttgart, 1936.

Hesselbarth, Hermann. *Drei psychologische Fragen zur Spanischen Thronkandidatur Leopolds von Hohenzollern. Mit Geheimdepeschen Bismarcks, Prims, usw.* Leipzig, 1913.

[Heyderhoff, Julius.] *Deutscher Liberalismus im Zeitalter Bis-*

marcks. Eine politische Briefsammlung. Vol. I. *Die Sturmjahre der preussisch-deutschen Einigung 1859–1870.* Bonn and Leipzig, 1925.

Hohenlohe-Ingelfingen, Kraft, Prinz zu. *Aus meinem Leben.* Vol. IV (7th ed.). Berlin, 1908.

Hohenlohe-Schillingsfürst, Alexander Prinz zu. *Denkwürdigkeiten des Fürsten Chlodwig zu Hohenlohe-Schillingsfürst.* 2 vols. Stuttgart and Leipzig, 1906

Holborn, Hajo. *Aufzeichnungen und Erinnerungen aus dem Leben des Botschafters Joseph Maria von Radowitz.* 2 vols. Stuttgart, 1925.

[Holstein, Friedrich von.] *Die geheimen Papiere Friedrich von Holsteins.* Band I. *Erinnerungen und politische Denkwürdigkeiten.* Göttingen, 1956.

Howe, Mark Antony deWolfe. *The Life and Letters of George Bancroft.* 2 vols. New York, 1908.

Jeismann, Karl-Ernst. *Das Problem des Präventivkrieges.* Freiburg-München, 1957.

[Karl I, King of Rumania.] *Aus dem Leben König Karls von Rumänien. Aufzeichnungen eines Augenzeugens.* 4 vols. Stuttgart, 1894–1900.

Keudell, Robert von. *Fürst und Fürstin Bismarck. Erinnerungen aus den Jahren 1846 bis 1872.* Berlin and Stuttgart, 1901.

Kohl, Horst. *Fürst Bismarck. Regesten zu einer Wissenschaftlichen Biographie des ersten deutschen Reichskanzlers.* 2 vols. Leipzig, 1891–1892.

———— *Die politischen Reden des Fürsten Bismarck. Historisch-kritische Gesammtausgabe.* 14 vols. Stuttgart, 1892–1905.

La Gorce, Pierre François Gustave de. *Histoire du second empire.* 7 vols. Paris, 1904–1906.

Langer, William Leonard. "Bismarck as a Dramatist," *Studies in Diplomatic History and Historiography in Honour of G. P. Gooch, C.H.,* ch. xi. Planned and edited by A. O. Sarkissian. London, 1961.

Lehautcourt, Pierre (General Palat). *Les Origines de la guerre de 1870: la candidature Hohenzollern 1868–1870.* Paris and Nancy, 1912.

Lema, Salvador Bermudez de Castro y O'Lawlor, Marqués de. *De la revolucion á la restauracion.* Madrid, 1927.

Leonardon, Henri. *Prim.* Paris, 1901.

Loftus, Lord Augustus. *Diplomatic Reminiscences, 1862–1879.* 2d series, 2 vols. London, 1894.

Bibliography

Lord, Robert Howard. *The Origins of the War of 1870. New Documents from the German Archives.* Harvard Historical Studies XXVIII. Cambridge, Mass., 1924.

Lorenz, Ottokar. *Kaiser Wilhelm und die Begründung des Reichs. Nach Schriften und Mittheilungen beteiligter Fürsten und Staatsmänner.* Jena, 1902.

Luz, Pierre de. *Los Españoles en busca de un Rey (1868-1871).* Barcelona, 1948. (Translated from *Les Espagnoles en quête d'un Roi.*)

────── *Isabella II Reine d'Espagne.* Paris, © 1934.

Malmesbury, Earl of. *Memoirs of an Ex-minister. An Autobiography.* New edition (2 vols. in 1). London, 1885.

Meyer, Arnold Oskar. *Bismarck: der Mensch und der Staatsmann.* Stuttgart, © 1949.

────── *Bismarcks Glaube. Nach neuen Quellen aus dem Familienarchiv.* 4th edition. Munich, © 1933.

Michael, Horst. *Bismarck, England und Europa (1866-1870).* Munich, 1930.

Miguel i Vergés, J. M. *El General Prim en España y en Mexico.* Mexico, n.d. [1949?]

[Moltke, Helmuth von.] *Moltkes militärische Korrespondenz. Aus den Dienstschriften des Krieges 1870/71.* Edited by Grossen Generalstabe, Abtheilung für Kriegsgeschichte. Erste Abtheilung, *Der Krieg bis zur Schlacht von Sedan.* Berlin, 1896.

Morier. See Wemyss.

Morley, John. *The Life of William Ewart Gladstone.* 3 vols. New York, 1903.

Mosse, W. E. *The European Powers and the German Question 1848-71. With Special Reference to England and Russia.* Cambridge, 1958.

Muralt, Leonhard von. *Bismarcks Verantwortlichkeit. Göttinger Bausteine zur Geschichtswissenschaft,* Vol. XX. Göttingen, © 1955.

Muret, Pierre. "Emile Ollivier et le Duc de Gramont les 12 et 13 juillet 1870," *Revue d'histoire moderne et contemporaine,* vol. XIII (1909-1910), pp. 305-328; vol. XIV (1910), pp. 178-213.

Newton, Thomas Baron. *Lord Lyons. A Record of British Diplomacy.* 2 vols. London, 1913.

Nigra, Costantino. "Souvenirs diplomatiques 1870," *Bibliothèque universelle et revue suisse.* Centième année, troisième periode, tome LXV (1895), pp. 449-474.

Nye, Russel B. *George Bancroft, Brahmin Rebel.* New York, 1945.

Bibliography

O.D. See [France]

Ollivier, Emile. *L'Empire libéral: études, récits, souvenirs.* 17 vols. Paris, 1895–1915.

Ollivier, Jocelyn-Emile. *La Dépêche d'Ems.* Paris, 1935.

Ollivier, Marie-Thérèse. "L'Epouse de l'empereur. Souvenirs personnels," *Revue de Genève* (February 1921), pp. 163–182; (March 1921), pp. 356–374.

Oncken, Hermann. *Die Rheinpolitik Kaiser Napoleons III. von 1863 bis 1870 und der Ursprung des Krieges von 1870/71.* 3 vols. Stuttgart, 1926.

Oncken, Wilhelm. *Unser Heldenkaiser. Festschrift zum hundertjährigen Geburtstage Kaiser Wilhelm des Grossen.* Berlin, n.d. [1897?]

Pahncke, Robert. *Die Parallel-Erzählungen Bismarcks zu seinen Gedanken und Erinnerungen.* Halle a/S., 1914.

Paléologue, Maurice. *The Tragic Empress: A Record of Intimate Talks with the Empress Eugenie, 1901–1919.* New York and London, 1928.

Pirala y Criada, Antonio. *Historia contemporanea. Segunda parte de la guerra civil. Anales desde 1843 hasta el fallecimento de Don Alfonso XII.* Vol. II. Madrid, 1895.

Ponsonby, Sir Frederick. *Letters of the Empress Frederick.* London, 1928.

Radowitz. *See* Holborn.

[Rangabé.] "Aus den ungedruckten Memoiren Rangabés," *Deutsche Revue,* vol. XXXVII (1912), pp. 197–207.

Reichsinstitut für Geschichte des neuen Deutschlands. *Die auswärtige Politik Preussens.* 8 vols. published. Oldenburg i/O, 1932–1939.

Renouvin, Pierre. *Histoire des relations internationales.* Vol. V, *Le XIXe siècle, I. De 1815 à 1871. L'Europe des nationalités et l'éveil de nouveaux mondes.* Paris, © 1954.

Rheindorf, Kurt. *England und der Deutsch-Französische Krieg 1870/71.* Bonn and Leipzig, 1923.

Ritter, Gerhard. *Staatskunst und Kriegshandwerk. Das Problem des "Militarismus" in Deutschland.* Erster Band, *Die altpreussische Tradition (1740–1890).* Munich, 1954.

Romanones, Alvaro de Figueroa y Torres, Conde de. *Amadeo de Saboya. El rey efímero. España y los origenes de la guerra franco-prusiano de 1870.* Madrid, 1935.

——— *Sagasta o el político.* Madrid, 1930.

[Roon.] *Denkwürdigkeiten aus dem Leben des Generalfeldmar-*

schalls Kriegsministers Grafen von Roon. Sammlung von Briefen, Schriftstücken und Erinnerungen. 5th edition. 3 vols. Berlin, 1905.

Rothan, Gustave. *Souvenirs diplomatiques. L'Allemagne et l'Italie 1870–1871.* 2 vols. Paris, 1884–1885.

Saint Marc, Pierre. *Emile Ollivier (1825–1913).* Paris, © 1950.

Salomon, Henry. *L'Incident Hohenzollern. L'Evénement, les hommes, les responsabilités.* Paris, 1922.

Sass, Johann. "Hermann von Thile und Bismarck. Mit unveröffentlichten Briefen Thiles," *Preussische Jahrbücher,* vol. CCXVII (1929), pp. 257–279.

Schulz, Eduard. *Bismarcks Einfluss auf die deutsche Presse (Juli 1870).* Halle a/S., 1910.

[Schweinitz, Hans Lothar von.] *Briefwechsel des Botschafters General v. Schweinitz.* Berlin, © 1928.

——— *Denkwürdigkeiten des Botschafters General v. Schweinitz.* 2 vols. Berlin, © 1927.

Smith, Willard A. "The Background of the Spanish Revolution of 1868," *American Historical Review,* vol. LV (July 1950), pp. 787–810.

——— "The Diplomatic Background of the Spanish Revolution of 1868," *The Historian,* vol. XIII (Spring 1951), pp. 130–153.

——— "Napoleon III and the Spanish Revolution of 1868," *Journal of Modern History,* vol. XXV (September 1953), pp. 211–233.

Steefel, Lawrence D. "Bismarck and Bucher. The Letter of Instructions, June 1870," *Studies in Diplomatic History and Historiography in Honour of G. P. Gooch, C.H.,* ch. xii. Planned and edited by A. O. Sarkissian. London, 1961.

Stengers, Jean. "Aux origines de la guerre de 1870: Gouvernement et opinion publique," *Revue Belge de Philologie et d'Histoire,* 1956, pp. 701–747.

Stern, Alfred. *Geschichte Europas seit den Verträgen von 1815.* 10 vols. Berlin, 1894–1924.

Stolberg-Wernigerode, Otto Graf zu. *Deutschland und die Vereinigten Staaten von Amerika im Zeitalter Bismarcks.* Berlin and Leipzig, 1933.

Taylor, A. J. P. *Bismarck, the Man and the Statesman.* New York, 1955.

Tallichet, E. "La Guerre franco-prussienne, ses causes et ses consequences," *Bibliothèque universelle et revue suisse,* June 1871.

Temperley, Harold. "Lord Acton on the Origins of the War of 1870, with Some Unpublished Letters from the British and

Bibliography

Viennese Archives," *Cambridge Historical Journal*, vol. II (1926), pp. 68–82.

——— "Lord A. Loftus and Count Beust on Russian Influences at Berlin, July-August, 1870," *Cambridge Historical Journal*, vol. IV (1932), pp. 100–102.

Valentin, Veit. *Bismarcks Reichsgründung im Urteil englischer Diplomaten.* Amsterdam, 1937.

[Victoria, Queen of Great Britain.] *The Letters of Queen Victoria.* Second series, 3 vols. London, 1926–1928. Third series, 2 vols. London, 1930–1931.

Walder, Ernest. *Die Emser Depesche.* Bern, 1959.

[Waldersee.] *Denkwürdigkeiten des General-Feldmarschalls Alfred Grafen von Waldersee.* Erster Band, 1832–1888. Stuttgart and Berlin, 1922.

War Correspondence of the Daily News 1870, The. Edited with notes and comments forming a continuous history of the war between Germany and France. 3rd edition. 2 vols. London and New York, 1871.

Weibull, Curt. *Bismarck och Krigsutbrottet 1870.* Stockholm, © 1944.

Welschinger, Henri. *La Guerre de 1870. Causes et responsabilités.* 2 vols. Paris, 1910.

Wemyss, Mrs. Rosslyn. *Memoirs and Letters of the Right Hon. Sir Robert Morier, G.C.B. from 1826 to 1876.* 2 vols. London, 1911.

Wertheimer, Eduard von. "Kronprinz Friedrich Wilhelm und die spanische Hohenzollern Thronkandidatur," *Preussische Jahrbücher*, vol. CCV (1926), pp. 273–307.

——— "Zur Vorgeschichte des Krieges von 1870. Nach neuen Quellen," *Deutsche Rundschau* (October 1920 to January 1921), vol. CLXXXV, pp. 1–26, 220–241, 342–356; vol. CLXXXVI, pp. 35–76.

[Wilhelm I, King of Prussia, German Emperor.] *Kaiser Wilhelms I. Briefe an seine Schwester Alexandrine und deren Sohn Grossherzog Friedrich Franz II, Bearbeitet von Johannes Schultze.* Berlin and Leipzig, 1927.

Windell, George G. *The Catholics and German Unity 1866–71.* Minneapolis, © 1954.

Zingeler, Karl Theodor. "Briefe des Fürsten Karl Anton von Hohenzollern an den Grossherzog Friedrich I. von Baden," *Deutsche Revue*, vol. XXXVII (1912).

——— "Briefe des Fürsten Karl Anton von Hohenzollern an seine

Gemahlin Josephine," *Deutsche Revue,* vol. XXXIX (1914), part 2, pp. 338–346; part 4, pp. 112–120.

────── "Das Fürstliche Haus Hohenzollern und die spanische Thronkandidatur," *Deutsche Revue,* vol. XXXVII (1912), pp. 59–68.

────── *Karl Anton Fürst von Hohenzollern; ein Lebensbild.* Stuttgart, 1911.

Index

Index

and South German States, 10, 232ff, 234ff, 238, 241ff, 245; and projected anti-Prussian alliance, 10, 238ff; and ultramontanism, 55, 76, 233, 235–239, 242, 245
Bleichröder, Gerson, 220
Bonaparte family, 228
Bourbaki, General, 156
Bourbon dynasty, Spanish line, 51, 59, 65, 120
Bourqueney, Baron, French courier, 150
Braganza, House of, 28
Brandenburg, 215
Braun, code name for Bucher, 87
Bravo, Gonzales, Spanish minister of foreign affairs, 12
Bray-Steinburg, Otto, Count, 234
British government, 122, 172
Briviesca, 30
Bruchsal, 142
Brunnenpromenade, Ems, meeting of Benedetti and William, 183
Brussels, 78, 173
Bucharest, 81, 139, 158f, 164
Bucher, Lothar, counselor of legation, 83ff, 87, 94ff, 106; missions to Spain, 17, 67f, 70f, 73f, 76, 82, 88, 91ff; and King William, 96ff
Budapest, 7
Bülow, 166
Bundesrat, North German Confederation, 243
Burgos, 35
Busch, Moritz, official of North German Foreign Office for press relations, 118, 172, 174, 241
Bylandt, C. M., Count van, Dutch minister at Berlin, 192

Cadiz, 35, 51
Canitz und Dallwitz, Julius, Baron, North German envoy at Madrid, 14f, 23, 42, 72, 84–89, 91f
Canovas de Castillo, Spanish politician, 93
Carlists, 48, 59, 90, 96, 102, 139

Carlos, Don, of Bourbon, claimant to Spanish throne, 24, 102
Case, Lynn M., American historian, 229, 247f
Cassagnac, Paul de, French editor, 161
Catholic clergy in south Germany, 237
Chamber of Deputies, France, 111, 114ff, 118, 128f, 132, 134, 145, 162, 179, 195, 210, 213, 220, 245
Charles V, Emperor (1519–1556), 25, 58, 65, 105, 114, 118
Charles of Hohenzollern-Sigmaringen, prince of Rumania, 25, 41ff, 76, 81, 104, 138, 140, 158f, 222, 228
Charles Theodore, prince of Bavaria, 49
Chevandier de Valdrôme, Jean, French minister of the interior, 151, 209
Cintra, 29
Civita Vecchia, 133
Coblentz, 193, 202
Coburgs, 27, 29
Cochèry, Adolphe, French deputy, 112, 116, 118
Constitutionnel, newspaper, 104, 160f, 208
Corps Législatif, French, 179, 201, 215, 221
Cortes, Spanish, 16, 18, 35, 37, 39f, 48, 50f, 59, 62, 67, 69, 71, 84, 89, 93–96, 99, 102f, 105f, 111, 117, 123f, 128, 138, 172, 204, 227
Council of Ministers, France, 47, 52, 106, 116, 134, 144f, 149, 161f, 191, 198f, 201ff, 207ff, 218, 226, 247
Council of Ministers, Prussia, 211
Council of Ministers, Spain, 204
Crown Prince. *See* Frederick William

Daru, Napoleon, Count, French minister of foreign affairs, January to May 1870, 150, 225

Index

Index

Index

of, abandoned, 140–143, 145, 156, 166f, 169f, 174, 176, 180, 184, 211f
Leopold Maximilian, prince of Bavaria, 49
Le Monde, newspaper, 27
Le Sourd, Georges, French chargé d'affaires at Berlin, 105ff, 109, 198, 216, 218f
"Letter of apology," 154, 184, 192, 214.
Liberal Empire, 221, 225
Liberal Union (Spain), 22, 28, 35
Liberté, La, newspaper, 161
Limburg, 4
Lindau, 42
Lisbon, 27, 32f, 37, 69, 98, 102; *coup d'état* at, 74
Loftus, Lord Augustus, British ambassador at Berlin, 55, 176, 185, 187, 218f
London, 116, 173, 178, 186f, 191, 214
Lord, Robert Howard, American historian, 20, 111, 117, 119, 154f, 166n, 167n, 188, 192, 230, 239
Louis XIV, king of France (1643–1715), 51
Louis Leopold, prince of Bavaria, 49
Louise, princess of Bourbon, sister of Isabella II and wife of the Duke of Montpensier, 28
Louvet, Charles, French minister, 146, 206, 216
Ludwig II, king of Bavaria, 237
Luis I, king of Portugal, 24, 28, 30f, 34, 74f
Luxemburg, Grand Duchy of, 4ff, 13, 177, 188, 246
Lyons, Richard, Earl, British, ambassador at Paris (1867–1887), 111, 121, 135f, 146, 155, 163f, 178, 187, 227

MacMahon, Marshal, 132
Madrid, 14, 29, 32, 45, 47, 68, 72, 74, 77, 83, 85, 88f, 98–101, 103ff, 107f, 111, 122ff, 131, 135f, 138, 148, 158, 179. *See also* Spain

Magne, Pierre, 228f
Magyars, 6
Main, river, 2, 8f, 233
Mainz, 4
Malaga, 35
Malet, Sir Edward, 9
Maria de la Gloria, reigning queen of Portugal (1834–1853), 31
Marie, princess of Baden, 102
Marie, princess of Prussia, 24
Maximilian, late emperor of Mexico, 27, 110
Mengen, telegraph station, 96
Mercier de l'Ostende, Baron, French ambassador at Madrid, 69, 89f, 102, 104f, 123ff, 204
Metternich-Winneburg, Prince Richard, Austrian ambassador at Paris (1859–1871), 121, 135ff, 146, 203, 207, 216f
Mexico, 2, 227
Military preparations, French, 177, 191, 193, 213; Prussian, 199, 212
Ministry of the Interior, French, 145, 162
Ministry of State, Prussian, 130
Mitchell, Robert, editor of the *Constitutionnel*, 160f, 208
Moldavia, 159
Moltke, Helmuth von, Count, Prussian field marshal and chief of the general staff, 2, 5, 61, 67, 78–81, 214f, 246; and Bernhardi, 16–19; favors Hohenzollern candidacy, 64; and Bismarck, July 12, 171; supper with Bismarck and Roon, July 13, 186ff
Montemar, Francesco, Spanish envoy at Florence, 29, 32f, 41
Montpensier, Antoine of Orleans, Duke of, youngest son of Louis Philippe, king of the French (1830–1848), candidate for the Spanish throne, 11f, 19, 28, 30, 34, 37f, 60, 84, 89–92, 94, 102, 108, 139, 244
Morier, Sir Robert, British diplomat, 234
Mulert, pastor of Wussow, 165